EXTRAORDINARY PRAISE FOR SEAN PARNELL AND
Outlaw Platoon

"*Outlaw Platoon* is an exceptional look into the mind of a US Army platoon leader in Afghanistan; Captain Parnell shares his experiences of leadership, loss, and aggressive military tactics on the battlefield. It's a unique look at the inner workings of a combat platoon in Afghanistan and the forging of a cohesive fighting force out of a wildly diverse group of men under an exceptional leader. You can really feel the bonds forged between these brothers in arms as the battle plays out in the Hindu Kush."
—Marcus Luttrell, author of *Lone Survivor* and *Service*

"The range of emotions that Sean Parnell summons in *Outlaw Platoon* [is] stunning. A nuanced, compelling memoir. . . . Parnell shows he's a gifted, brave storyteller." —*Pittsburgh Tribune*

"Sean Parnell is one of the few who knows the honor and courage that is the legacy of the battlefield. *Outlaw Platoon* is expertly told by a man who braved the heat of battle time and time again. An epic story as exacting as it is suspenseful, it reveals the bravery and dedication of our armed service men and women around the world." —Clive Cussler

"Reading *Outlaw Platoon* is like hunkering down with a few old foxhole buddies from bygone battleground literature. Echoes of war stories of yore reverberate in this gritty account of one of the most decorated Army platoons to come out of the ongoing war in Afghanistan. . . . After riding with Parnell and the Outlaws for 374 colorful and sometimes brutal pages, readers may share the soldiers' disheartening outlook as it erodes from spirited determination to simply enduring. . . . But read further, and you might find some reassurance that hope can still rise from horror."

—*Plain Dealer* (Cleveland)

"Sean Parnell and John Bruning's *Outlaw Platoon* is a soulful story of men at war, but more importantly, it shows us that the love and brotherhood forged in the fires of combat are the most formidable qualities a unit can possess. And that the maturation of a natural leader—Sean's own story—is one that we will never grow tired of reading."

—Steven Pressfield, author of *The Warrior Ethos*

"Two of the grittiest, most intense tales of courage and camaraderie under fire I own are *Black Hawk Down* and *Lone Survivor*. I now have a third, *Outlaw Platoon*. It's *Black Hawk Down* for the twenty-first century. And an absolutely gripping, edge-of-your-seat ride. . . . An absolute must read!"

—Brad Thor, author of *Black List*

"May well be the most searing and unforgettable portrait of war and the bond between soldiers to come out of the conflict in the mountains of Afghanistan. . . . A vivid, action-packed, and highly emotional true story." —*Military Press*

"*Outlaw Platoon* is a detailed and utterly gripping account of what our soldiers endure on the front lines of America's war in Afghanistan—the frustrations, the fear, the loneliness, the nastiness, the occasional rage, the difficulties of finding and identifying an elusive enemy. Here, in these pages, are the on-the-ground realities of a war we so rarely witness on news broadcasts."

—Tim O'Brien, author of *The Things They Carried*

"Parnell vividly captures the sounds, sights, and smells of combat, and proves most eloquent when describing the bond that developed among his men. . . . [He] balances sentimentality with sincerity and crisp prose to produce one of the Afghan war's most moving combat narratives."　　　　　—*Publishers Weekly*

"*Outlaw Platoon* put me back on the battlefield again. It's a heartfelt story that shows how very different people can be thrown together in combat and find a way to make it work. Parnell and the soldiers who fought beside him are all courageous heroes—real badasses."　　　　　—Chris Kyle, author of *American Sniper*

"I just finished *Outlaw Platoon* and I'm filled with different emotions—confusion, sadness, wonderment, respect, a sense of having survived something harrowing. At times, I forgot I was reading about a war as I was drawn up in the drama the same way you [are] when reading Krakauer's *Into Thin Air*. . . . This is a book of probing honesty, wrenching drama and courage."

—Doug Stanton, author of *Horse Soldiers*

"This is the story of a brotherhood of soldiers whose bond was forged in the fire of battle during an intense year of fighting. . . . [Parnell] relives specific battles, and his retelling of the stories reads at times like an adventure novel, full of adrenaline. . . . A stark reminder of war's toll on honorable women and men."

—*Library Journal*

"This book is more than just a rip-roaring combat narrative: it is a profoundly moving exploration into the nature and evolution of the warrior bond forged in desperate, against-all-odds battles. A significant book, not to be missed."

—Jack Coughlin, author of *Shooter: The Autobiography of the Top-Ranked Marine Sniper*

OUTLAW PLATOON

★ ★ ★

Heroes, Renegades, Infidels, and the Brotherhood of War in Afghanistan

★ ★ ★

SEAN PARNELL
WITH JOHN R. BRUNING

WILLIAM MORROW
An Imprint of HarperCollinsPublishers

HarperCollins books may be purchased for educational, business, or sales promotional use. For information please write: Special Markets Department, HarperCollins Publishers, 10 East 53rd Street, New York, NY 10022.

A hardcover edition of this book was published in 2012 by William Morrow, an imprint of HarperCollins Publishers.

FIRST WILLIAM MORROW PAPERBACK PUBLISHED 2013.

Designed by Jamie Lynn Kerner
Interior map by Lum Pennington

Library of Congress Cataloging-in-Publication Data has been applied for.

ISBN 978-0-06-206640-4

13 14 15 16 17 OV/RRD 10 9 8 7 6 5 4 3 2 1

To the men of Third Platoon, Bravo Company, 2nd Battalion, 87th Infantry Regiment, "The Outlaws," whose extraordinary courage in the face of great adversity inspired me to write this book

Many heroes lived . . . but all are unknown and unwept, extinguished in everlasting night, because they have no spirited chronicler.
—QUINTUS HORATIUS FLACCUS (HORACE)

AUTHOR'S NOTE

★ ★ ★

ONE IMPORTANT PURPOSE OF THIS BOOK HAS BEEN TO CHRONI-
cle my soldiers' incredible journey in one of the most dangerous
places on the face of the planet. These remarkable men spent six-
teen months on a small Forward Operating Base in the Bermel
Valley, roughly twelve kilometers from Pakistan. Throughout the
course of their deployment, these soldiers endured continuous
close, direct-fire contact with a combat-hardened, tactically profi-
cient enemy on its home terrain. I was both blessed and cursed to
have led one of the most valorously decorated conventional combat
units in the history of Operation Enduring Freedom. When the
haze of combat dissipated, the Outlaws were awarded seven Bronze
Stars, including five for Valor, twelve Army Commendations for
Valor, and thirty-two Purple Hearts. I am writing this book to tell
the world of their amazing accomplishments and to secure their
place in American military history.

It's also worth noting that this book displays no political agenda
nor is it a review of U.S. foreign policy in Afghanistan. This story is
not intended to hurt anyone's feelings but rather to provide an honest
assessment of what combat was like for these young warriors.

Regrettably, it was impossible to mention every member of the platoon in this book. The men portrayed herein are representative of the unit as a whole. My goal was to show the world their sacrifices and, in doing so, provide readers with a much-needed window into the heart of American infantry soldiers everywhere. Also, I have no desire to expose any soldiers who did not live up to this standard, so I have changed the names and identifying characteristics of some soldiers.

Finally, this book is a work of nonfiction. Every event in this book took place. Actions and experiences have been retold using both my own memory and interviews with my men. Dialogue is presented here from my own recollection and is not intended to be a word-for-word documentation; rather, it is intended to capture the essence of the moment. Any errors made in the story were not intentional and likely can be attributed to the intense pace and chaotic nature of combat.

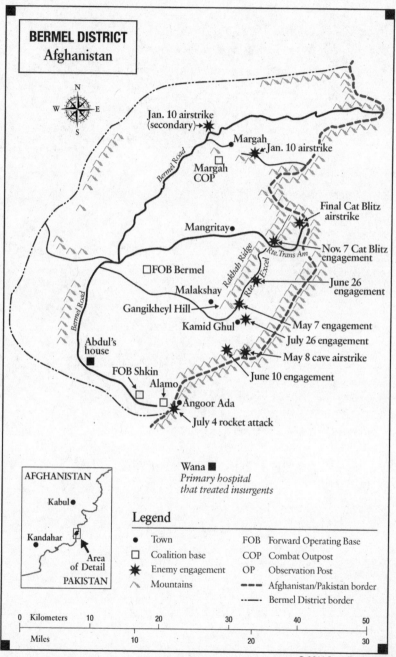

BERMEL DISTRICT
Afghanistan

N
W E
S

Jan. 10 airstrike
(secondary)→

Margah

Jan. 10 airstrike

Bermel Road

Margah
COP

Final Cat Blitz
airstrike

Mangritay•

Nov. 7 Cat Blitz
engagement

Rte. Trans Am

□FOB Bermel

Rakhah Ridge

June 26
engagement

Malakshay•

Rte. Excel

Gangikheyl Hill

May 7 engagement

Kamid Ghul•

July 26 engagement

May 8 cave airstrike

Bermel Road

Abdul's
house

FOB Shkin

June 10 engagement

Alamo

Angoor Ada

July 4 rocket attack

AFGHANISTAN

Wana ■
*Primary hospital
that treated insurgents*

Kabul•

Kandahar
•

Area
of Detail

PAKISTAN

Legend

• Town

□ Coalition base

✳ Enemy engagement

⋏ Mountains

FOB Forward Operating Base

COP Combat Outpost

OP Observation Post

▬ ▬ Afghanistan/Pakistan border

·—·— Bermel District border

| 0 | Kilometers | 10 | | 20 | | 30 | | 40 | | 50 |

| | Miles | | 10 | | 20 | | 30 |

© 2011 Lum Pennington

PROLOGUE

★ ★ ★

February 5, 2006
Eastern Afghanistan

THE SNOWCAPPED RIDGES STRETCHED FROM HORIZON TO horizon, a vast dragon's back of peaks and valleys. An hour before, as we had left Bagram Air Force Base, the landscape had been salted with villages and walled qalats interspersed with the ruins of ancient fortresses constructed during Alexander the Great's time. As we choppered eastward, such signs of civilization began to vanish. The qalats and farms grew sparse. Finally, even the Kuchi nomads and their tent camps disappeared.

Towering mountains, their rocky cliffs wrinkled like an old man's face, flanked the red-brown flatlands where not a road could be seen. Here the earth was untransformed by human endeavor. I found beauty in its pristine hostility. It was perhaps the last place on the planet that had defied the efforts of man.

I found it lonely too. I wished my men were with me in this helicopter. Our battalion commander, Lieutenant Colonel Chris Toner, had ordered us platoon leaders to fly out a few days ahead of our men to our assigned base on the Pakistani border. We were to be briefed by the unit we were replacing, learn the area, and prepare the way for our platoon's arrival. After the orientation, we would begin combat operations. In the meantime, a hollow sense of loneliness remained ever present.

I was sitting in the back of a Boeing CH-47 Chinook, the venerable "Flying Banana" that harkened back to the Vietnam War. The airframe of that bird was older than I was. Eighty feet long and powered by two jet engines mounted on the back pylon, the Chinook looked about as aerodynamic as a metropolitan transit bus with rotors. We entered and exited via an aluminum ramp in the back of the cargo bay.

The Chinook crews were a breed apart. They usually flew with the ramp down and the flight engineer sitting on the end of it like a kid fishing off an old dock. Except instead of a pole and Zebco reel, he wielded an M240 machine gun capable of spewing out up to 950 bullets a minute. In an age of Mach 2 jets and satellite-guided munitions, going to war at about ninety miles an hour with your feet dangling in space seemed old-school hard core.

Beyond the flight engineer, the ranks of ridges marched out behind us. Two months before, I had been home in Pittsburgh enjoying Christmas with my family. My six-year-old cousin, Freddie, was hovering close. He had been in a strange mood all morning, alternating between excitement over gifts and anxiety over my pending departure. Finally, in the midst of present opening, he asked, "Sean, are you gonna die over there?" Leave it to a kid to voice what everyone was thinking. The hubbub drained away, replaced by a shocked, uneasy silence. I had pulled Freddie close, "No, no. I'll see you next Christmas. I'll be fine."

My Italian grandfather, Frederick Sciulli, whose fingerless right hand (the result of a childhood fireworks accident) had never ceased to fascinate me as a kid, observed the moment with somber eyes. He'd never missed a day of work in fifty years, but after retiring, his health had finally started to fail, and he had spent much of the fall in the local ICU. Only a few days before Christmas, he'd been released from the hospital, and we were all in the mood to celebrate that.

"Sean," he said softly, "you just be careful."

How does an infantry platoon leader respond to that? It is our job to set the example in combat, and that meant I would have to take risks, expose myself, and place myself in the center of any fight we found ourselves in. My grandfather was not a man to bullshit. Freddie had squirmed out of my arms and pounced on a gift. I remember watching him send strips of wrapping paper flying and smiling at his innocent enthusiasm.

"Sean," my grandfather said again, "you be careful."

I turned to look at him. He was the greatest man I'd ever known. Medically disqualified during World War II, he had spent his entire adult life working a printing press. On nights and weekends, he had earned extra money as an usher at Steelers and Pirates games. He'd hung out with a bunch of blue-collar throwback Italians with nicknames like Vinnie the Creep and Fast Eddie. The nicknames were deceptive. They were the men upon whose backs this country was built—hardworking, principled, and devoted to family and company. I never saw him lose his temper or even heard him raise his voice. He loved his wife with singular passion, and my grandmother returned it with an intensity I'd not seen in any other relationship.

Be careful? Going to war in Afghanistan, how do you do that? I met his eyes and saw the old spark, the flint and grit of a man who had forged a life of simple nobility with his hands and heart. "Grandpap, I love you."

His face registered surprise. It dawned on me that I had never said that to him before.

"I love you too, Sean."

The Chinook banked and slipped between two sawtooth ridges. We were getting close to Forward Operating Base Bermel, the patch of real estate my platoon would call home for the next year. The air inside the cargo bay grew ever colder, and I was grateful to have put my gloves on before we climbed aboard. Winter in Afghanistan is no joke, and with the icy slipstream pouring through the door gunners' windows, the feeble heaters under our seats had no prayer of keeping us warm.

I'd come into the company late, a branch transfer from, of all things, the air defense artillery. I'd spent the first part of my career in the army learning how to shoot down planes when all I really wanted was to be a straight-legged infantry officer. The bond I'd seen shared by riflemen in such movies as *Saving Private Ryan* appealed to me. I wanted to experience that. In the first weeks with my platoon, I'd learned that Stephen Ambrose had perpetuated a myth. The *Band of Brothers* thing? That was based on fading and selective memories of the Greatest Generation. Like all myths, there was truth wrapped up within it, but the reality, I discovered, was far more nuanced and complex.

Our company's weeks in training divided the men into cliques, and that created tension. Within each platoon of about forty men, personalities clashed, and some men didn't give their full measure to the platoon. The weeks we spent practicing for war sifted my platoon. Those who appeared to measure up earned respect. Those who didn't were regarded with distrust and became outsiders. An inner circle formed around the men who demonstrated they could handle anything thrown at them. They were men of character, and they became the core of the platoon. I was lucky; when a platoon coalesces around alpha males who lack character, bad things happen.

The Chinook's nose dropped, and we dived low into a narrow valley; our pilots kept us close to one side of it so the enemy could not catch us in cross fire. It worked well tactically, but for a nonaviator like myself, seeing these desolate mountains flash past only a few dozen meters from the porthole window in the fuselage was not for the faint of heart. If the pilots sneezed, we'd be a flaming smear on one of these rocky cliffs.

Unconsciously, my right hand went to my throat. My fingers dug under my body armor until they found the St. Christopher medal I'd worn since my last leave. Its flat silver surface slipped across my gloved fingers as I rubbed it gently. The feel of it was a comfort.

Across the aisle from me, Second Platoon's leader, Lieutenant Dave Taylor, sat lost in thought, his eyes tracking the countryside through one of the Chinook's Plexiglas bubbles. Even though our platoons did not get along well, Dave was my closest friend among my officer peers. We had spent many nights playing Halo together on our Xbox. At work, Dave shared his training plans with me, and I learned much of how to serve as an infantry officer by following his lead.

Just before we left Bagram, we had stood on the flight line near the rotary wing terminal, rows of Black Hawks lined up behind us. The mountains around Bagram were dusted with snow; the sky was a flawless ice blue. It was hard not to be captivated by the raw beauty of Afghanistan.

While we had waited for our ride, I'd asked Dave for two favors: "If I die, just make sure to wipe all the porn off my computer."

He'd gotten a laugh out of that one.

Turning serious, I added, "Make sure my St. Christopher medal gets back to my mother."

Dave nodded, then asked me for a favor: "If I get killed, I want you to carve a postage-stamp square of skin off the back of my neck and send it to my brothers."

"What?"

"You heard me. Send a piece of my skin back to my brothers."

I couldn't tell if he was kidding. The other officers laughed uneasily.

"Dude, you're a fucking nut!" I exclaimed.

"Why?" Dave looked puzzled.

"I'm not cutting off a piece of your skin and mailing it back to your family."

Dave seemed disappointed. "Whatever, man. Whatever."

I didn't know what to make of Dave's peculiar request. He'd also given serious thought to the stagecraft of his potential final moments. "If I know the end is coming—like if I see an RPG fired at me or I know a sniper is about to shoot me—I want my last word to be 'Rats.'"

Our Chinook pitched nose high. The flight engineer stood and raised the ramp to the halfway-closed position to deflect some of the dust that was sure to blow into the cargo bay when our rotor wash reached the ground. We swung over FOB Bermel's landing zone. The Chinook's six rotor blades generate Katrina-force winds. Dust and rocks are churned up by the whipping power of the wash, often creating a total brownout that obscures vision and fills the aircraft with flying debris. At such moments, the gunners lean out their windows, scan for signs of Mother Earth, and talk the pilots down. It takes trust and coordination, a leap of faith similar to trusting someone in the backseat of your car who is talking you into a parking spot while you're blindfolded.

Though everyone hates browning out, the pilots sometimes use the rotor wash offensively. If an animal wandered into the landing zone and wouldn't get out of the way, the poor beast would surely get blasted. More than one unfortunate goat had been blown clear of landing zones like the cows in the movie *Twister*. Little kids who threw rocks or made gestures at the Chinooks sometimes paid for their sins with the mother of all dirt baths.

With a final turn, the Chinook settled into a hover and touched down. The flight engineer dropped the ramp, and we hurried out of the aircraft. Chinooks are at their most vulnerable while on the ground like this. The insurgents know this and try to target them, so we are trained to transition as quickly as possible.

We all cleared the ramp in seconds and the Chinook's pilots poured on the torque, lifted off, and raced away to their next assignment. As it departed, the rotor wash pelted us with debris and dirt. We shielded ourselves by putting our backs to the bird, yet within seconds every piece of exposed skin was coated in brownish dust, even the postage-stamp-sized bit of Taylor's neck that he wanted me to send to his family in case of his demise.

"Welcome to Forward Operating Base Bermel," came a voice somewhere ahead of us in the brownout. It was smooth and measured and deep. A voice of authority.

A captain from the 173rd Airborne Brigade materialized out of the dust. Taller than my six foot one, he wore an old-style desert combat uniform that had recently been replaced army-wide by our digital-gray-and-green ACUs (Army Combat Uniforms).

"I'm Ryan Canady," the captain said. Our group of newbies took turns shaking hands. He walked us over to the FOB's rear gate and told us to drop our gear off on the concrete pad next to the tactical operations center. Captain Canady gave us a tour of our new home. Bermel was a small FOB, fit only for a reinforced company on the U.S. side, plus a battalion of troops on the Afghan National Army (ANA) side. Near the operations center, three flags fluttered in the breeze—one American, one Afghan, and one that looked like the French tricolor but turned out to be the 173rd Airborne's unit flag. The base stretched about two kilometers east–west and about a kilometer north–south. It was formed by a curving wall of sand-filled Hesco bags that enclosed some weatherized tents, about a dozen wooden structures, and four guard towers. The Hesco bags were double stacked and more than ten feet high, but behind them an enormous ridge dominated the eastern skyline. It looked like the back hump of a sleeping dinosaur. "That's Rakhah

Ridge," Canady told us. "On the other side is the Pakistani border. When we take incoming fire, it usually originates from behind that ridge."

The base seemed almost deserted. Canady's company of airborne troops had already started to leave. Only a platoon remained on the base. A couple of dogs followed us at a distance. We later learned that the 173rd had turned them into pets after its medics had vaccinated them and given them clean bills of health. By general order, keeping pets on the FOBs was not allowed, but out here on the edge of civilization nobody seemed to care.

We walked past a line of beat-up, dirt-encrusted Humvees. Some of them were unarmored, and when I noticed that my heart sank. "Those belong to the marines," Canady explained. "They have an embedded training team here working with the Afghan National Army unit on the other side of the FOB.

"Make no mistake, the enemy is very capable. They are cunning, well led, and well equipped. Do not underestimate them. You won't be fighting goat herders. You're going to be up against their first team."

We returned to the concrete pad and our duffel bags. Our room assignments were handed out; then Canady continued his orientation. "The enemy leader is a legend in this part of Afghanistan. He's elusive. He rarely talks on the radio, but we hear references to him all the time. Whenever he's mentioned, it is with awe, almost reverence. He fought the Soviets for years. He knows what he's doing."

After a quick brief on the facilities available at Bermel, Canady turned to an important topic: interpreters. Every company received at least a couple of " 'terps" so the platoons could patrol with somebody who spoke the language. Out here on the border, many different languages were spoken. A good 'terp could make a huge difference in daily operations.

"We have a couple of interpreters here. We inherited Abdul and Yusef. They both worked for the Special Forces teams that were here before us. Abdul's the head 'terp. He's quite good. Yusef—I can't put my finger on it, but something about him bothers me. Keep an eye on him."

I filed that away in the back of my mind. *Watch Yusef.*

An hour later found us just outside the Hesco bag walls on a rifle range, where we busied ourselves with resighting our weapons. Even though FOB Bermel sat in a narrow valley, it was still seven thousand feet above sea level. At that altitude, the thin air changes a bullet's trajectory. Had we gotten into a fight before we'd had a chance to do this, we wouldn't have been able to hit anything.

I was next to Lieutenant Taylor on the range when another Chinook overflew us. It had been buzzing in and out throughout the afternoon, dropping off supplies and taking more of Canady's people out to Bagram. I watched this one touch down, kicking up another massive cloud of brown dust. Overhead, the Chinook's wingman circled protectively.

As the Chinook lifted off to join its wingman, I heard a distant shriek. It grew in intensity, like an onrushing freight train. Whatever created the noise went right overhead. The shriek faded. A moment later, we heard a dull thud. The ground trembled. A small pall of smoke rose in the distance.

"What was that?" I asked Lieutenant Taylor.

"No clue," he replied.

Another shriek grew in the distance. I could pinpoint it this time, coming from the east.

Rakhah Ridge. Whatever it was, it was coming from Rakhah Ridge.

The shriek grew to a wail, like a harpy screaming in agony. A moment later, the ground shook again.

"Are we under attack?" I asked. Logically, a greenhorn knows this can happen, but the reality of it creates shock and confusion the first time. We were new lieutenants just off the bird, and we stood in the open, unable to grasp the truth of the moment.

The Chinooks formed up and sped away; the sky was their refuge.

Taylor and I looked around, puzzled. Another distant whine began to the east. As it rose to a crescendo, several NCOs on the range began running for the FOB's rear gate. Staff Sergeant Greg Greeson, Lieutenant Taylor's weapons squad leader, shouted at us, "Incoming! Get inside the wire now!"

His words acted like ice water to the face. Lieutenant Taylor and I sprinted after our sergeants and back into the FOB. With our new home at seven thousand feet, it took only a few seconds before my lungs started to burn from lack of oxygen. I stopped at the concrete pad next to my gear and watched Greeson and the other sergeants dash off toward the battalion aide station. Taylor bolted into the operations center.

What the hell do I do?

I felt rooted in place, observing the action around me yet with no purpose of my own.

Captain Canady ran into view. "Some kids got hit with those rounds. They're at the front gate."

My legs started to move. I felt myself run after Canady, wanting to go faster but feeling an impenetrable wall between will and action.

We rounded a corner, and perhaps fifty yards away, I could see some of the 173rd Airborne soldiers opening the front gate. Crying, distraught Afghan civilians poured into the base. I kept running.

Then I saw the kids; I heard their screams. A few thrashed in agony; others lay still in their parents' arms. I dropped my rifle, pulled my helmet off and dumped my body armor in the dirt, and sprinted the last stretch to the scene.

One of the interpreters was shouting at an angry father. Two more Afghan dads ganged up on him, yelling insistently. Finally, a soldier demanded, "Abdul—what the hell are they saying?"

Abdul, his face a mask of rage, replied, "They're telling me to make sure the boys get treated before the girls."

"Get them all to the battalion aid station."

Abdul turned to the fathers and passed that order to them. They shook their heads and shouted again at him.

Abdul announced, "They refuse. They want the boys treated first."

"Grab them all!" the soldier roared again.

The other men at the gate picked up some of the wounded kids. Perhaps seven were still alive. I scooped up the nearest child and turned to follow the other soldiers as they dashed for the aid station.

I'd taken a half-dozen steps before I realized I had a little girl in my arms. I looked down at her. She wore a tan dress that felt like burlap in my hands. The collar was ornate, red and green with little designs that converged in a V-neck. She felt so light.

"It's okay. It's okay," I said to her. Her eyes were bright emerald green, deep and filled with pain. Her raven hair was splayed across her face and plastered to her skin by her tears.

She keened hysterically, pain-racked and panicked. Her pitch hurt my ears.

I kept running, her head and shoulders cradled in my left hand, her slight body pressed tight against my ribs, hip, and thigh by my right forearm. Her left hand flailed. She gasped, then screamed again. It seemed to never end.

"It's okay, it's okay." I began to wonder who I was talking to, the girl or myself.

My cousin Freddie, his eyes wide and full of anxiety, asked me, "Are you going to die over there?"

Freddie's this girl's age. Maybe a little older.

Keep running.

Her breathing grew ragged, her screams choppy. I glanced down at her. Her eyes were growing dull. She stared up at me, this stranger in uniform, and I could see the terror in those fading eyes.

With my right hand, I tried to brush her hair off her face. Instead, my fingers smeared blood across her cheek.

I sensed warmth on my thigh. What was that? I wanted to look down, but something stopped me. My legs carried us forward in autopilot mode as my eyes stayed fixed on hers.

She screamed again, hoarse and weak this time. The warmth spread to my hip and trickled past my knee.

I couldn't bear not to look. When I did, my brain didn't register what my eyes saw.

One bare foot, tiny, delicate toes, covered in brown dust. Crimson dots splattered her khaki dress, which now rode high above her knees. Tendrils of torn, burnt flesh tapered below the other knee to a bleeding stump. A white stripe of bone projected through the ruined skin and muscle.

I lost my stride and looked up to regain my balance. The little girl uttered a deep, guttural cry. One step. A second. Perhaps a third before I realized she wasn't screaming anymore.

Aid station. We have to make it to the aid station.

"Itsokayitsokayitsokay."

Her hand fell away. Her neck grew slack in my cradling hand.

This is not happening.

How long did it take me to look down at her again? Her breaths grew shallow. The warmth continued to spread.

I looked down. Her fear was gone, the spark in her eyes snuffed out.

The world around me went on. Soldiers ran. Parents cried. Abdul argued. Canady barked orders. I held a dead child in my arms.

I sleepwalked back to her parents. Her mother, clad in a black burka that covered her face, sobbed into her hands. Her father regarded me stoically. I realized that his little girl had inherited his green eyes. I handed him his daughter's body. He turned and walked through the gate, her bare foot—those sculpted, tiny toes—dangled limply by his side. I watched them go, stripped of words.

SOMETIME LATER—HOW MUCH LATER I HAVE NO IDEA—I FOUND myself inside a hooch, staring at the bloodstains on my uniform.

How do you even process something like this?

I felt numb. Slowly, I began to take off my ruined uniform. I'd worn it since leaving the States. By now it felt almost like another layer of skin. I shed the pants, shucked off the shirt, and dropped them in a heap on the floor. I found a towel and forced myself to walk to the showers.

The water felt slick and warm, and my stomach turned.

Back at the hooch, I dressed slowly. New uniform. New skin. Combat leaders do not show weakness. They set the example for their men. And if the whole year was going to be anything like this first day, they were going to need me to be strong for them.

I walked across the hall and found Lieutenant Taylor in his room.

"Hey," I said.

"So, you think we earned our CIBs today?" he asked in a flat voice.

The CIB is the coveted Combat Infantryman Badge, awarded to men who come under enemy fire. It is one of the most respected decorations an infantryman can wear.

"Don't know. I guess so."

"Check it out," Taylor said, pointing into his room. "I'm going to put the TV right there on that desk."

"Awesome."

"We'll be able to play Halo in our off-hours."

I leaned against the doorjamb and nonchalantly said, "That'll be cool."

Inside, I was screaming.

He reached over and grabbed a pen. I watched him write something on the back of his door. When he was done, he backed up, and I peered around to see what it said.

There is no try. Only do, or do not.

"Yoda," I said.

"The Master."

I was a *Star Wars* fan. I knew the line well. It was from *The Empire Strikes Back*, but Taylor had quoted it wrong. I was debating whether to tell him when he asked, "Wanna grab dinner?"

I nodded.

We walked to the chow hall. Canady saw me and asked, "How you doing?"

I shrugged.

He understood. After a year here, how could he not? "Look, Bro, this is Afghanistan," he said. "This kinda shit happens. These people . . . their goats mean more to them than their kids— especially their girls." He paused, waiting for a response. When I didn't reply, he added, "They can always have more kids."

Inside the chow hall, Abdul sat alone at one table. The 'terp's eyes were soft, and he was clearly absorbed in thought. A few tables over, Staff Sergeant Greeson, our company first sergeant, and a few other of our NCOs who had come out early with us were clustered together. I grabbed a tray and got in line with Taylor.

It was spaghetti night. I looked down at the noodles covered in red sauce, and all I could think of was the little girl's face and how

I had smeared it with blood while trying to brush the hair away from her eyes.

We sat down with a few other officers. Soon the conversation turned to the CIB again. I sat quietly and tried not to listen.

I overheard our company's first sergeant say, "Well, this attack should get the locals moving after the insurgents, you know?"

My weapons squad leader, Staff Sergeant Jason Sabatke, said, "Yeah, I hope they whack all them fuckers."

Sergeant Greeson grunted his agreement.

First Sergeant Christopher added, "Bet we don't take another indirect-fire attack for a month."

Somebody said, "This is a victory for us. Sucks to be Taliban right now after killing all those kids."

Did these guys check their humanity at the door?

I stirred my plate with a plastic fork. Hunger eluded me. I sat as long as I could, then fled back to the silence of my hooch.

The bloody uniform still lay on the floor. I stepped around it as I entered my room.

I sat on the edge of my bed and forced myself to calm down. The girl's face came back to me, and I saw those emerald eyes shining through her tears.

I reached under the neckline of my shirt and pulled free my St. Christopher medal. In my palm, it became a comfort. I held it tight and closed my eyes.

I feel like part of me is dying.

How could those men be so matter of fact after what we experienced today? Then the realization hit me. Everyone at the sergeants' table had already seen combat. They'd already experienced a moment similar to this one. It had made them hard long ago, and now they wore their calluses like armor.

Is this the kind of man I am destined to become?

I regarded the bloody uniform at my feet. I'd never get the blood out. My stateside ACUs were a lost cause now. I didn't want to even touch them.

Survival. That's what they had already learned. Greeson, Sabatke, First Sergeant Christopher—they'd all learned how to navigate these psychological waters. This was my test.

I closed my eyes and forced the pain down into a deep and remote place.

I bent down, collected my bloody former skin, and walked into the cold Afghan night. The stars shone overhead, undimmed by the lights of civilization. Out here in this desolate place, the velvet beauty of the universe had no peer.

I made my way to the black scar of earth that served as our refuse dump. Salt-and-pepper-colored ashes coated its bottom. Charred bits of trash studded its walls. I stood beside the pit and let go of my bloodstained uniform.

Tomorrow my men would arrive, and I would be ready for them.

PART I

OUTLAW COUNTRY

★ ★ ★

ONE

GAME FACES

★ ★ ★

SPEEDOMETER NEEDLES TOUCHING FIFTY, OUTLAW PLA-toon's six armored Humvees blasted down the Afghan road, trailing plumes of dust that could be seen for miles. In an area that lacked even a single asphalt highway, this was the best dirt road we'd yet encountered. Smoothed and tempered by generations of passing travelers, it had no cart tracks to give our shock absorbers a workout, no drifts of desert dust to bog us down. After weeks of cross-country patrols so jarring they knocked fillings loose, our run south through the district of Gamal seemed as effortless as taking a lap at Daytona Speedway.

In Afghanistan, we Americans have to adjust our transportation expectations. We are used to traveling fast. The men of my platoon favored muscle cars such as GTOs and Mustangs, or suspension-lifted pickup trucks. Out here, the terrain rarely allowed us to go more than fifteen or twenty miles per hour. It was like being stuck in a perpetual school crossing zone.

Today, when we turned onto this unusual stretch of road, our drivers capitalized on the opportunity. They grew lead feet and poured on the coals. The speed felt glorious.

The road bisected a broad valley six hours' drive south of our base at Bermel. In this flat, treeless area, the only sign of life we'd seen for miles was patches of rugged plants that had somehow thrived in an environment of extremes: heat and cold, drought and floods. To our left, a wadi veined through the ancient landscape. Earlier, we had tried to use it to traverse the valley in the hope of avoiding roadside bombs. As our rigs splashed through the trickle of water at the bottom, Staff Sergeant Phil Baldwin's Humvee sank to its doors in quicksand. So much for that idea.

Steep ridges defined the valley's boundaries. Even without a tree or a bush to give color to their slopes, these spines of the Hindu Kush still gave refuge to our enemy. They ceded us the low ground while they hid out in well-stocked caves that had been in use since the Soviet war of the 1980s.

The signs of that war lingered. During this drive south, we'd seen the skeletal remains of villages cratered by Russian bombs. In the surviving towns, the locals told us horror stories of the Soviet occupation. One farmer spoke of watching his son be thrown to the ground and stomped to death by laughing Red Army troops. After that, his entire village had braved the harsh mountains to escape on foot to a refugee camp in Pakistan.

This was our area of operations, a harsh and barren land whose people had known nothing but violence for decades.

I glanced over at my driver and radioman, Specialist Robert Pinholt. We'd been on the road since dawn, and his face was striped with dirt and sweat. His helmet rode low over his brow, his uniform and body armor powdered with Afghan dust. The only time we were ever truly clean was in the shower. When he sensed my gaze, he tore his eyes from the road to steal a quick look at me.

"What, sir?" he asked. His piercing blue eyes stood in contrast to the dull grime on his face. He was a broad-chested twenty-year-old with earnest good looks and an engaging smile. If he'd been in overalls instead of ACUs, he'd have looked like an extra on the set of *Green Acres*.

He'd been railing about the U.S. Postal Service again, and I couldn't help but laugh at his passionate hatred for this small section of our federal government.

"Pinholt," I said, "I don't understand where all this hostility comes from."

"What do you mean, sir? Isn't it obvious? The government's violating the Sherman Antitrust Act of 1890. It has a captive monopoly and can cross subsidize to expand into other business areas, undercutting the private corporations that compete in those areas."

Government waste was one of Pinholt's biggest pet peeves. So far, he'd managed almost an hour's rant on the post office. I was impressed.

"Sir, look: not privatizing the post office is just bad fiscal policy. They've got seventy billion in unfunded liabilities, they're running billions in the red every year in a business where everyone else is in the black, and they compete unfairly against UPS and FedEx."

"They deliver the fucking mail, Pinholt. My shit gets from point A to point B quickly, and that's all I care about. What more do you want?"

He ignored me. "The post office is tax-exempt. That's one advantage. It is free of SEC reporting requirements. Its accounting procedures would trigger an IRS investigation in any other American corporation. The postmaster can go to the U.S. Treasury and borrow money whenever he wants, at rates no private company could ever get."

"So?" I asked, goading him. Pinholt had the heart of a warrior but the mind of an economist. I loved to provoke him, as he usually had very well thought out opinions. Plus, the more I got to know him, the more I realized he was a case study in contrasts, and that intrigued me. He was a Texas native who spoke without an accent. Dallas born and raised, he hated the Cowboys and loved the Don Shula–era Dolphins. He was a buttoned-down conservative who didn't touch liquor, didn't smoke or even drink caffeine, but in his spare time I'd catch him listening to hippie rock like Phish. He had a thing for opera, too.

"So?" he said in surprise. "Even with all those advantages the post office is a huge drain on the taxpayers! Even the European Union's privatizing their mail delivery. Think about that. All those socialist countries are going that route, while we let the federal government mismanage a business that would otherwise make billions. And those billions would be taxable. Instead of a drain on the budget, mail delivery could be a revenue enhancer."

With nothing else to do but talk or debate, those long vehicular patrols were like college road trips with heavy weapons.

We came to a slight bend in the road. "Hey, watch out, Pinholt." I warned. He was drifting a bit again, distracted by our conversation. This happened a lot. "Don't try to kill us twice in one day."

That annoyed him, "Come on, sir. That's getting old already."

"Hey, you almost drove us off a cliff. You're never going to live that down."

Earlier that day, we'd had to negotiate a treacherous mountain trail to get into this valley. It wound down a cliff in a series of switchbacks so sharp that our Humvees couldn't take them without our drivers executing three-point turns. On one, Pinholt had edged the nose of our rig over the cliff, shifted into reverse, and gunned the gas. Unfortunately, our rigs had been beaten up by months of hard use. The transmissions, which had not been designed for all the weight our armored Humvees now carried, sometimes stuck or jammed. In this case, ours didn't move out of drive. We lurched forward and almost went over the edge. The rig teetered on the brink as we all started to scream at Pinholt. I grabbed my gunner,

Chris Brown, and yanked him inside the rig out of fear he'd be thrown clear if we did go over. Not that it would have mattered. The valley floor was at least five hundred feet below us.

Truth was, I was impressed by how Pinholt came through in the clutch. He stayed calm, shifted gears again, and waited to hit the gas until he was absolutely certain the transmission was functioning properly. When he heard a soft thunk as it finally shifted into reverse, he eased off the brake and backed us away from the brink.

We'd been harassing him unmercifully ever since.

"Gettin' old, sir," he said again.

"Tell you what, I'll lay off when you give me my MREs back." Pinholt knew I was a picky eater. Before leaving on patrols, he made a point to purloin my favorite MREs—meals, ready to eat—and hide them, just to get a rise out of me. We'd had a running battle for weeks over this.

"I'll think about it, sir."

"You're a hell of a radioman, Pinholt. But I swear to God, you drive like a blind old lady."

"Awww, sir, cheap!"

The late-afternoon sun perched atop the ridgelines, spilling red-gold light across the valley. We sped along, each Humvee topped by an armored turret with a heavy weapon mounted inside. Our five machine guns and one automatic grenade launcher gave our gunners ready access to more firepower than any other platoon from any other war. Our dads in Vietnam could have used this much heat. When combined with the thirty men and six vehicles we had, Outlaw Platoon possessed muscle, mobility, and numbers to handle almost any challenge. Even if we got in over our heads, we had my radios. With them, I could call in artillery, unleash helicopter gunships, or target satellite-guided bombs on our enemy.

In the month since we'd arrived in country, the enemy had remained elusive and we had yet to encounter them in a stand-up fight. Yet the hills had eyes. I had a nagging sense that we were always being watched. Studied, really. We were the new kids in town, and they knew enough about the U.S. Army to know that units, like people, have their own quirks. Some are disciplined; some are lax. Some are aggressive; some are timid. Until they figured us out, they were content to observe. But sooner or later, I knew they would pick a time and place to give us our first test.

The road curved slightly as it followed the lip of the wadi. As we came around the bend, I could see our destination rising out of the valley floor along the horizon. A hundred and fifty years ago, the British had constructed a redoubt atop a sheer walled mesa that dominated the entire southern half of the valley. From the base of the mesa, the slate-colored cliffs rose almost straight up for a full kilometer before flattening to a narrow plateau. The mud walls of the old British fort ran along the edge of the plateau. Medieval-style towers abutted the walls at regular intervals.

This was Bandar, the most important coalition base in the area. It towered over the valley road, affording the soldiers atop it a clear view of the traffic moving below. Because of that, it was a natural choke point, one that was virtually impregnable to attack thanks to its thousand-meter cliffs. No insurgent force could ever scale them—hell, not even the Rangers who'd taken Pointe du Hoc on D-Day could have climbed them under fire.

We drew close, and our drivers eased off the gas. We reached an intersection and turned toward the mesa. The road narrowed and entered the northern cliff face. We could see how long-dead British engineers had blasted through the sheer rock to build the track up to the fort. It would be an impressive feat today, let alone in the 1850s.

"Pinholt," I said as we stared at the steep road ahead.

Before I could continue he interrupted me. "Sir, I know. I know."

We stopped, and one of my men jumped out to guide us forward. As we inched along, the clearance between the cliff on one side and the sheer drop on the other diminished until we barely had a meter on either side of us. I would not have even been able to open my door if I had wanted to. Pinholt stayed on the ball and did a good job.

The track snaked up the mesa, making regular forty-five-degree turns, until we reached the fort's front gate. The original entrance had been destroyed long before and had been replaced by strands of concertina wire stretched across a metal-framed gate. A rusted conex box had been placed nearby to give the guards cover from the elements. I saw no fighting positions nearby, but in the distance a Soviet-era ZU-23 double-barreled antiaircraft cannon stood silhouetted against the twilight sky.

A teenage Afghan Border Policeman (ABP) wearing a green camouflage jacket, khaki pants, and a Chicago Bulls 1990 National Championship cap stepped out of the conex to greet us. His AK-47 dangled carelessly at his side. Flecks of rust marred its receiver; the magazine was dinged and scuffed. Ancient gear, poorly kept. I made a note of that.

Our 'terp, Abdul, spoke a few words to the guard, and he waved us through the entrance, pulling the gate open as he eyed us with interest.

We rolled into the fort. As we passed the ZU-23, I could see it was but a rusted hulk. There was no way it could be returned to firing condition. Hell, it had probably been there since the Reagan era.

Here and there, Afghan Border Policemen stood with their weapons slung haphazardly. Some smoked home-rolled cigarettes. All of them looked stupefied with boredom. They stared at us as we passed as if we'd come from a different planet.

Neglect and age had combined to leave the fort in a state of near ruin, something we could not detect as we made our approach along the valley's floor. Now we slid by crumbled guard towers, their wooden frames jutting out of the hardened mud like ancient bones. A few old buildings still had enough walls and roof left to be used to store equipment and supplies in. The rest of them were of little use to anyone except, perhaps, military archaeologists. The outer wall had many gaps, which had been haphazardly screened with strands of concertina wire. If it hadn't been for the thousand-meter cliffs, the place would have been a catastrophe waiting to happen.

We parked outside the only modern structure within the fort, a single-story, double-cubed concrete building with a few undersized windows. A pair of exhaust vents stuck out on either side of the door, and a smear of black soot streamed up from them along the concrete wall.

This would be our home for the next few days. Our battalion had deployed to this part of Afghanistan for one purpose: to control the border with Pakistan. The mountain caves around here were the insurgents' equivalent of forward operating bases. Pakistan was their safety zone, where they would resupply, rearm, and train between missions into Afghanistan. After sneaking across the frontier, they'd reoccupy their cave complexes and use them as springboards to launch attacks against coalition bases or units. Then they'd escape across the border to start the cycle all over again.

Recently, the insurgents in Pakistan had grown more ambitious. Instead of being content with attacking local forces here along the frontier, they were now trying to infiltrate deeper into central Afghanistan. They had established "ratlines" consisting of caves, safe houses, friendly villages, and secondary trails that now stretched all the way to Kabul. After years of relative peace in the Afghan heartland, the violence that flowed from the ratlines was threatening to destabilize the government and posed a significant threat to all we'd accomplished in country since 2001.

Our job was to stanch the flow of enemy troops and supplies into Afghanistan, and Bandar was one of the key bases to support that intent. From there, coalition troops could patrol the surrounding area and establish checkpoints on the road leading into Pakistan. Controlling the enemy and securing the populace are the aggressive keystones of any successful counterinsurgency operation. By getting out there and actively patrolling, we could disrupt the ratlines and force them to react to us.

Clearly, none of that was happening here at Bandar, manned by a battalion of Afghan Border Police. Everything we'd seen here suggested that the men were stagnating behind their dilapidated walls. No doubt Lieutenant Colonel Toner had known that, which is why he'd sent us down here. Perhaps, he thought, a U.S. platoon could instill a fighting spirit in the ABP.

I dismounted from my Humvee into a chilly evening wind that made me grateful I had my neck gaiter and gloves on. The sour stench of human filth lingered in the breeze. Up and down our platoon line, my men climbed out and went straight to work. I stood and watched them, marveling at the fact that they'd been on the road all day without a break or decent chow. Now, at a moment where they could let their hair down and relax, their sense of professionalism kept them focused. Team leaders barked orders. Some men stood guard while the gunners began cleaning their weapons. Pinholt and the other drivers went about checking the oil, transmission fluid, and coolant levels of their respective vehicles. Other men poked their heads under the vehicles to see if anything had been damaged by the rough terrain we'd encountered earlier in the day. Nobody stood around, smoking and joking. For a young leader like myself, it was a beautiful thing to see.

All of twenty-four years old, I had been Outlaw Platoon's leader for about eight months now since joining the 10th Mountain Division's 2nd Battalion, 87th Infantry Regiment (2-87). Our battalion was famous in the army and known as the Catamounts since it fought the Germans in Italy at the end of World War II. Outlaw Platoon was part of 2-87's Blackhawk Company, an easily identifiable nickname over the radio.

I'd learned a lot in a short amount of time, but that had given me just enough knowledge to know that I didn't know anything. As a leader responsible for every American in the platoon, plus Abdul our interpreter, I had to project confidence around my men at all times. Truth was, half the time that was the last thing I was feeling inside. I had come to know my men and their families. I knew that their wives and parents, children and friends had entrusted with me the safety and well-being of their loved ones. A year before, I had been a partying college student, obsessed with *The Lord of the Rings* and the Harry Potter books. Getting to class and writing papers had been pretty much the limit of my responsibilities. Now I was a leader in a combat zone, entrusted with the role after the army had invested millions of dollars in my training. Any decision I made could have unseen consequences. I second-guessed myself constantly, concealed it from the men, and did my best to absorb every lesson thrown my way.

At full strength, an infantry platoon consists of four squads of nine men each. On top of those thirty-six soldiers, we had a medic, two forward observers (FOs), a two-man 60mm mortar team (casually attached), our platoon sergeant, and the platoon leader. So by the book we should have had forty-three men. But that was almost never the case. For the past six years the army had been strapped for men because of the constant deployment cycles. We usually patrolled with about thirty men, which amounted to roughly four undermanned squads loaded into six Humvees.

The squad is the heart of a U.S. infantry platoon. Divided into two fire teams and usually commanded by a staff sergeant, the squad balances firepower with flexibility. When moving in combat, for example, a squad's fire teams can bound forward one at a time while the other one provides covering fire for them. Each fire team carries three M4 carbines, a grenade launcher, and an M249 squad automatic weapon (SAW) light machine gun that can carry two hundred rounds and blow through them all in a matter of seconds. Usually, a squad also has a designated marksman, a sharpshooter armed with the venerable wooden-stocked M14 rifle from the Vietnam War era. The M14 used a larger bullet, the 7.62mm, and had greater hitting power at longer ranges than our M4s.

The first three squads were what we called maneuver or line squads. Number four, our weapons squad, included our platoon's heavy weapons, such as the mortar, the machine guns, and the Mark 19 grenade launcher. In any platoon, the most important leaders are the sergeants who lead each squad. They are usually experienced, dedicated noncommissioned officers who have spent their entire careers in the infantry. For a young lieutenant still trying to find his way, such leaders are pure gold. A good platoon leader is one who will let his sergeants mentor him. I was lucky to have three outstanding squad leaders and several top-notch young team leaders.

"Lieutenant Parnell?" I turned around to see Abdul walking toward me. He wore ACUs, body armor, and a green Russian-made chest rig for his extra AK magazines on his slight frame. He held his rifle with deft professionalism. Earlier, I'd seen him helping check out our lead Humvee, his mop of black hair bobbing under the rig's hood. Unlike the other 'terps at Bermel, Abdul shared the workload.

"Yeah, Abdul?"

"Would you like me to go find the base commander?" he asked, his eyes dark and expressive. He offered an easy grin that never failed to set me at ease.

"Thank you. That'd be great."

An Afghan Border Policeman strolled by, regarding us curiously. I nodded at him, and he returned my cautious greeting. He took a few more steps, then stopped and dropped his trousers. Right there in the open, he squatted and relieved himself.

The men of my platoon paused in their work and took notice. A few lost their composure and gaped. The rest put on their game face, turned away, and returned to the tasks at hand. The border cop finished his business, wiped himself with his left hand, and continued on his way.

That was an unexpected cultural moment.

I watched the Afghan depart and could not help being proud of my men for their reaction. Though we had been in country for only a few weeks, it had already become very apparent that we had to be very careful with our reactions to some of the things our Afghan allies did.

Staff Sergeant Phil Baldwin, my second squad leader, approached. Six foot four and built like a fullback, Baldwin cut an imposing figure in the growing darkness. At thirty-four, he was the second oldest member of our platoon. He had joined the army in 2001 after watching the towers fall on 9/11 on TV in his house in small-town Illinois. It had been no small sacrifice for his family; Baldwin had been a dispatcher for a railroad company, earning a formidable salary. He had enlisted as a private, which had cut his income by about 80 percent. Had he been a single man, such a reduction might not have seemed so significant. But Baldwin had married his high school sweetheart, Regina Sechrest, some years before, and they'd had two children together. When Baldwin was assigned to our parent unit, the 10th Mountain Division, Regina had given up her career so they could move to Fort Drum, New York. To survive on his meager income, the family had auctioned off most of their possessions, including Regina's childhood bedroom set.

The first time I met Baldwin, I didn't know what to think of him. The men had caught me at the end of our last major field exercise before we left for Afghanistan. I was fresh from Army Ranger School and had become their platoon leader only three days before the start of the exercise. They had pinned me down, tied me to a stretcher, and scrawled "CHERRY" on my forehead with a Sharpie. In triumph, they had carried me to the colonel's outhouse and left me propped against it.

Later that night, after they'd untied me, I had left the chow hall alone. Baldwin had been lingering in the shadows, clearly waiting for me. He had stepped up to me. "Lieutenant Parnell, you are a member of this platoon now. Don't fuck it up."

As I got to know and understand him, I realized that Baldwin was the platoon's voice of wisdom. He possessed more life experience than the rest of us, and he had a measured, analytical mind that I had come to rely on. He had also already deployed to Afghanistan once before and had seen combat, which made his tactical knowledge indispensable.

My other squad leaders, Staff Sergeants Campbell, Sabatke, and Waites joined us to discuss our course of action for the night. The three men could not have been more different. Tall and athletic, Campbell stayed within himself and was hard to get to know. Sabatke was a human tempest who blew through life fueled by a raging inner passion. While serving in a mechanized unit, he'd had "SABO" tattooed in a half circle over his belly button. A sabot is a type of antiarmor round Bradley Fighting Vehicles carry that uses kinetic energy to destroy its target. After dropping the "t," it had become his nickname, and few were ever as apt.

Waites was a leadership challenge. He was never quite in sync with the other leaders in the platoon, and his negativity tended to cause issues in training exercises. During his first deployment here, his unit had not fired a shot. As a result, he considered any preparation or training for that sort of eventuality to be a waste of time. He seemed unable to process the fact that perhaps the war had changed since his last deployment. Since we'd started patrolling, I'd had to watch him carefully.

Waites stood off a bit from our group and stared off in the

distance. Campbell moved next to me. Sabatke stood alongside Baldwin. They made an unusual pair. Baldwin's face was round, Sabatke's narrow. Baldwin stood half a head taller than Sabo and had at least forty pounds on him. Sabo was all muscle and sinew barely containing his pent-up energy. Baldwin looked like the neighbor everyone loved to barbecue with.

Some men are born warriors. Their spirit and their character are forged for the fight. That was Sabo. Others pick up arms because they see no other solution. They wield their swords to protect those they love, spurred by their sense of purpose and idealism but taking no pleasure in it. When the threat is defeated, they return to their homes, shed their uniforms, and return to their lives. That was Baldwin. Together, they formed the yin and yang of my platoon: the born soldier and the born citizen soldier.

Usually, in such moments, the banter between us would fly fast and furious. Right now, with the men nearby and Afghan Border Policemen lurking all around us, my squad leaders kept their game faces on. When alone together, they were irreverent, sometimes vile and always funny. But in situations like this, I knew I could trust them to be consummate professionals.

We quickly discussed plans for the evening. The men were tired and hungry. They'd spent the entire day on the road, and some hot chow would have done wonders for their morale. But before we could eat and clean up, we needed to establish a security plan for the platoon.

While the men kept about their tasks, the squad leaders and I decided to walk the fort's perimeter. We'd get a sense of its true defensive capabilities and figure out how best to add our firepower to the mix.

"Watch your step, sir," Campbell warned me as he pointed to the ground. "Shit mines everywhere." Sure enough, piles of human crap dotted the area. We had to zigzag around them as we scouted the terrain. We soon realized that the fort lacked even a single outhouse. The border police had been using some of the ruined buildings as latrines, but now they'd reverted to a more primal state and went wherever they pleased. Beyond the smell, the filth created significant health risks for our men. As we walked, I thought about how we could mitigate them without offending the Afghans.

We climbed onto the fort's ramparts to get a good look around. Baldwin used his tactical expertise to point out weak spots in the defenses, and we put together a plan to strengthen them. Each Humvee would be driven to a specific firing position around the fort in such a way that their heavy weapons could cover one another should we be attacked.

Truth was, the Salvation Army could have defended this mesa top even if no fort existed. Our biggest concern was the Afghan Border Police. How loyal were they? After some of the things Captain Canady had told me about them before we'd left Bermel on this mission, I knew enough to be on guard.

When we regrouped back at my Humvee, darkness had fallen and the men had finished their work. Some were eating MREs, others were playing cards next to their rigs. Pinholt sat in his driver's seat, eating beef stew while reading John Steinbeck's *East of Eden*. I was pleased to see that all the men assigned to pull security were alert and eyeballing the border cops carefully.

Our platoon sniper, blue-eyed, blond-haired Sergeant Wheat, was waiting for us at my rig, a piece of straw dangling out of his mouth. From southern Louisiana, Wheat had spent most of his life hunting, fishing, and camping. His natural outdoorsman skills had helped earn him the highest score in his sniper school class, an exceptional achievement. It was one of the army's toughest courses. He had told me once that when his enlistment was up, he planned to go home to Louisiana and become a horse farrier.

Before I could say hello to Wheat, a hulking figure materialized out of the darkness. The sudden arrival startled me, and when I turned to meet the person, I found myself facing the tallest Afghan I'd ever encountered. At least six foot five with powerful shoulders, he wore a tan headdress and khaki man jams, which look like a knee-length nightshirt with baggy pants. He sported a pair of Ray-Ban sunglasses tucked into the collar under his chin. I guessed he was around forty years old. We stared at each other, my surprise at his presence evident on my face. His was expressionless.

Abdul stepped up next to the Afghan and said, "Lieutenant Parnell, this is Major Alam Ghul. He is the commander of the border police here. The major would like to meet with you."

Part of my job as a platoon leader included working with local Afghan leaders. The nature of the war here required us lieutenants to be warrior-diplomats, a challenging task for somebody like me who had been eating Christmas cookies in Pittsburgh four months before and had never left North America. The army counted on us to be emissaries and power brokers in moments like these.

"Where and when would he like to meet?" I asked Abdul. Abdul looked at the major and, to my surprise, spoke to him in Farsi. Here on the border, the people spoke a diverse array of languages, including Pashtun, Dari, and Wazari. Abdul spoke them all, plus a little Arabic, which made him invaluable when we tried to connect with the locals. I hadn't known he spoke Farsi as well.

"The major would like to meet you now in that building," Abdul replied after listening to Ghul's answer. Our 'terp gestured to the concrete cube I had noticed earlier.

I turned to my squad leaders, "Okay, what's the play, guys?"

"Might as well do it now. Everything's under control here, sir," said Sabatke.

"Okay. Who wants to go with me?"

Baldwin waved his hand. "I will, sir."

Wheat, who was leaning against my Humvee whittling a horse out of a piece of wood with a Gerber knife, asked, "Sir, y'all gonna need some extra guns with ya?"

I thought that over. The Afghan police were notoriously corrupt and easily compromised. Al Qaida and the Taliban routinely infiltrated their ranks. More than once, an operative within an Afghan police unit had launched a surprise attack against U.S. troops.

It would have been good to have Wheat and a few others inside with us. Wheat was a lanky character, skinny and unassuming. But he was a rock in a crisis. I never saw him lose his cool, and he had a thoughtful way about him. Taking him would have been the safe thing to do. Yet the major would have probably seen that as a sign of distrust, and that would not have helped get our relationship off to a good start. We would be in the area for the next year. I had to set the tone right away.

"No, thanks, Sergeant Wheat. I appreciate the offer, though."

"Roger that, sir! Just holler if ya need me." He patted his rifle. "I'll be raght here."

Major Ghul put his hand on Abdul's shoulder and spoke to him. Our 'terp nodded and said to me, "Lieutenant Parnell, the major hopes that you will eat dinner with him tonight."

"Please tell him I look forward to that," I replied. A local meal was customary during these types of leader meetings. They were also famous for getting young lieutenants dreadfully sick. I was going to need Cipro and lots of it. I'd found out right after my arrival in Afghanistan that Cipro was the antibiotic of choice for dealing with the parasites in the local food our American stomachs have a hard time dealing with.

Abdul and Major Ghul walked ahead of Baldwin and me as we made our way toward the concrete building. I kept my head down to negotiate around the shit mines. As I did, I noticed that the major was wearing Birkenstocks.

An odd choice of footwear out here in the middle of nowhere.

Abdul opened the main door to the concrete building and let the major step inside. We followed close behind. Before Abdul had even shut the door, the smell assailed us—a combination of BO, rotting hay, feces, and mildew that overpowered our noses. I had to tamp down my first impulse, which was to bolt back outside. But that would have been a bad diplomatic move, especially considering how many eyes were now riveted on us.

We'd entered the fort's main barracks. Border cops lived here in rickety cots stacked four high against the walls with hardly any space between their rows. There was no concrete or wood floor, just hay-covered dirt mixed with what looked like goat shit. At least I hoped it was from goats.

Most of the cots were occupied. Some of the Afghans were huddled under burlap blankets, trying to sleep. A few were drinking tea. In one corner, the cots had been pushed closer together to make enough room that a group of police could play a dice game on the ground.

When we entered, the game stopped, and the Afghans regarded us with dark eyes freighted with suspicion as we picked our way to a Hobbit-hole sort of door in the left-hand wall. We walked by a couple of cops sitting next to a woodstove. One had a home-rolled cigarette in his mouth, and as Baldwin and I approached, he exhaled a wide plume of smoke in our path.

We reached the door. It was narrow and only about five feet high. After Abdul opened it, Baldwin had to duck low to get through it. The door opened onto a set of rotting wooden stairs that led down into pitch darkness. Baldwin and I exchanged nervous expressions, and I sensed we were thinking the same thing.

Are we gonna get beheaded on Al Jazeera tonight?

We couldn't refuse to go down. Despite my limited experience, I had enough cultural sensitivity to realize to do that would have been insulting to Major Ghul. *Mission first. Men always. The infantry's unofficial creed.*

Cautiously, I put one boot on the stairs and started down into the blackness after Baldwin.

TWO

PRISONER OF THE DIVIDE

★ ★ ★

THE STEPS CREAKED LIKE SOMETHING OUT OF A BAD HORROR film. Silence took hold of our little party as Baldwin's bent frame melted into the darkness. I put a gloved hand against the concrete wall, using it as a frame of reference. After a few more feet, the concrete gave way to rough-hewn rock. We were descending into the mesa itself.

At the base of the stairs, a dim corona of light appeared at the edge of the wall to our left. A few more steps, and we reached a dirt-and-rock floor perhaps ten or fifteen feet under the main barracks. Major Ghul waited for us to gather. Satisfied, he led us into a narrow chamber dominated by a small fire pit in its center. Flames crackled beneath a black cauldron that hung from a metal rack. Two motionless figures sat Indian style on the far side of it. Both had shiny AK-47s in their laps, hands on their pistol and fore grips as if ready to spring into action. Behind them, next to crates of rocket-propelled grenades, an RPK light machine gun leaned against the wall. A belt of ammunition was coiled around its barrel.

I second-guessed my decision to leave Sergeant Wheat with the vehicles.

Small carpets and sleeping mats covered portions of the floor. A single lightbulb dangled overhead, attached to an electrical line that disappeared into the ceiling next to the vent for the cooking fire.

We moved deeper into the room. Major Ghul gestured for us to take a seat. I picked out the least filthy carpet in sight. Baldwin picked one next to mine as Major Ghul walked around the cooking pit and settled down between the two motionless figures.

I found myself seated directly across from one of the Buddhas. Baldwin sat opposite the other one. Abdul took a position on a mat between us and the Afghans. Our bridge. Without him, we'd be dead in the water right now.

There was a chill in the air, thanks to the wind whistling through some ventilation slits cut into the top of the outer walls. Each gust made the lightbulb overhead sway back and forth, causing the shadows around us to dance.

I shucked off my helmet and body armor, grateful that I had put on my winter boots. At least my feet would be warm. Next to my gear, I propped my rifle on its bipod—within easy reach, of course.

Major Ghul spoke to us. When he finished, he offered a sad smile. He had white teeth, something that was almost unheard of around here.

Abdul translated for us: "Sir, the major wishes to apologize for having to meet in this basement. He said his house is much nicer than this place, but it is too risky for him there right now, so he sleeps here at Bandar."

"Why too risky?" I asked.

"Sir, he says he has received night letters for many weeks now."

Night letters. Death threats from the local enemy forces.

"Abdul, tell him I understand and appreciate his circumstances."

"Yes, sir," Abdul replied. Before he could speak to the major, I added, "And ask him who these other guys are."

Abdul and Ghul spoke for several minutes. As we watched them, Baldwin whispered to me, "Those guys look hard core."

The one across from me appeared to be about fifty years old. Granite face, cold eyes; he stared at me with intensity. These were different men from the other border police. They carried themselves with more pride and possessed an air of professionalism I hadn't seen here.

"He says these two men are his bodyguards. He keeps them with him at all times since he began receiving the night letters."

Major Ghul said something else. Abdul listened, then translated. "Both men fought with the Mujahadeen against the Russians in the 1980s."

They were survivors, lifelong warriors who had been fighting in these mountains since before I had even been born.

Abdul continued, "They were also in the civil war in the nineties, after the Soviets left."

I thought about that. It was so far out of the realm of my own experience. Back home, friends came and went. A few from my childhood remained, but none of them was in close contact with me anymore. I felt a bond with the soldiers of my platoon, but I'd been with them only eight months. Here, decades of violence had forged lifelong ties that defined much of Afghanistan's social fabric. Looking at the men across from me, their faces bathed in firelight, I felt out of my depth.

Both men rose to their feet. Baldwin and I did the same and shook their outstretched hands after taking our gloves off. Though their palms felt like sandpaper, there was a warmth in their greeting that I had not detected when we first arrived. The one directly in front of me even attempted a smile. It made him look like a piranha.

As we sat back down, Major Ghul motioned to the cauldron between us. One of his bodyguards leaned forward to stir its contents. The sight flashed me back to high school English class in Pittsburgh when we read *Macbeth*. I could almost see the passage about the witches in their cave, huddled around their pot. *"Double, double, toil and trouble . . ."*

Something was cooking. The brew inside the cauldron simmered, filling the chamber with the smell of meat that at least partially concealed the more unpleasant aromas lingering in this man-made cave.

At least, I hoped it was meat. I was going to need a triple dose of Cipro after this.

Captain Canady had done his best to prepare me for this moment. Before we had left Bermel, he had taken me aside and explained the basics of interacting with our Afghan allies. There was a subtle dance at play with every interaction between our cultures. As Americans, we're blunt and get straight to the point. The Afghans are more nuanced. Small talk here is an art form. It can go on for hours before anything of substance is brought up. But within the small talk, the Afghans often drop hints as to what they're really after.

"Lying is a part of their culture," Canady had told me. "There's no stigma to it; it is expected. Don't trust Ghul, and be careful what you give him. But remember, he's the power broker around Gamal. Maybe even more than the mayor. We need him on our side."

Before reaching the old fort this evening, we had stopped at the Gamal district center—a collection of about a dozen buildings thirty minutes north of Bandar—and met the mayor. He was an ancient man, stooped and sedate. We had spent the morning with him making small talk until we finally got around to discussing the school project the 173rd had started in the area. I had promised that we would see it through to completion, and the mayor had appeared very grateful to us. The playbook Captain Canady had given me had worked perfectly.

Major Ghul studied Baldwin and me in silence. Apparently he was waiting for us to start the dance. I noticed he held a two-way radio in one hand, and I asked Abdul what it was for. That opened a torrent of conversation between him and Abdul. As we waited for the translation, Baldwin produced a notebook and drew a pen from his sleeve pouch. He scribbled something at the top of one page.

At length, Abdul explained, "Sir, Major Ghul says that he uses the radio to stay in constant contact with his men. They have been attacked many times recently. He must stay alert so he can lead them in battle."

"What sort of attacks? Where?" I asked.

Major Ghul went on to tell us of Taliban ambushes on his checkpoints in the valley. Other times, they launched hit-and-run raids on his men stationed at Gamal. Several times, he said, they had even tried to overrun Bandar. He had lost men, and his personal vehicle had been shot to ribbons.

I remembered a bullet-scarred Toyota pickup parked out front of the barracks. That must have been his.

So much for small talk. The major got straight to business. In Gamal that morning, I'd spent at least twenty minutes getting a lecture from the mayor on the weather around here. The blunt talk threw me off my game, and I leaned on Abdul for advice.

"What do you think? Is this all true?" I asked.

Abdul covered his reply with a smile. "No. He's lying. He wants something."

The major took Abdul's grin as a cue to continue. He spoke for several minutes, all smiles and hand gestures, getting more animated by the minute. Finally he paused to let Abdul explain.

"Sir, he says that his men fought bravely, but they were taken by surprise. The enemy stole their best weapons."

Keeping my tone measured, I said, "That sounds like utter bullshit." Baldwin, who was head down over his notebook, nodded.

"Yes, sir, it is," Abdul agreed. "When I was with the 173rd, we came down here many times after the major called us and said he was under attack. Several times, he had his own men shoot up his trucks and checkpoints to get better equipment from us."

Captain Canady had mentioned that to me. He'd also said that the 173rd had started watching Bandar and the surrounding area with drones and had never seen an enemy attack.

Baldwin made a show of writing all this down, which seemed to please Major Ghul.

Major Canady had told me about a big ceremony the 173rd had hosted for Major Ghul a few months back to honor his police battalion and give his men factory-fresh uniforms, weapons, and ammunition. Aside from the two AK's the bodyguards held, nothing here looked new.

"Where is all their new equipment now?" I asked, thinking about the rusty AKs the border cops were carrying. As if to underscore the point, a young Afghan policeman appeared at the base of the stairs wearing half a uniform and a stained Nike ball cap. His AK looked as though it had been unearthed in a trash dump.

He and Major Ghul shared a short conversation before the cop, who couldn't have been more than seventeen, walked behind our circle by the fire to retrieve a box. Hefting it to his shoulder, he carried it upstairs.

After the interruption, Abdul said, "We suspected that Major Ghul sold the new weapons on the black market."

"Why?" I asked.

"To make money for himself," Abdul replied.

"Where do weapons sold on the black market end up?"

"All over. With the enemy, mainly."

How do I work with such a man, let alone fight beside him?

A year before, my nights had been carefree, drinking and studying, playing bass in a band—those had been my evenings. Once my friends and I had stolen construction barricades and scattered them around campus. Now I was expected to be a representative of my country in a place I had yet to understand. I felt a surge of appreciation for Abdul. The other 'terps would never have been so patient with me or offered me this council. Without him, there was no hope that I could breach the cultural divide. He had become more than a 'terp. He was my guide.

Canady trusted Abdul implicitly as a result of the firefights they'd been through together. On our earliest patrols, we'd discovered that he was known among the locals as a courageous fighter and compassionate man who had done great work in bringing Afghans together with the Americans at Bermel.

The other 'terps rarely left the wire without covering their faces. Though they were from different provinces, they were paranoid that their identities would be discovered by the enemy. That had happened far too many times in the past and usually resulted in the nocturnal murder of the 'terps' families.

Abdul was different. He had grown up in Shkin, a village about an hour's drive south from Bermel. As he was a local, I had assumed he'd be even more concerned about covering his face. But he never bothered with it, even though he had a younger brother and mom still living in his hometown.

As I watched Abdul and thought about his importance to our platoon, Major Ghul launched into another long explanation of something. This time he didn't pause for Abdul to give us the gist. Outside, the wind died down. The lightbulb ceased to sway; the shadows grew still. The cooking fire soon grew almost oppressively hot. Even without my body armor, I started to sweat. My winter boots heated my feet, and I could feel my socks grow damp with perspiration.

Major Ghul rattled on. Baldwin and I sweltered in silence. My rear grew sore; the carpet offered no cushion to the hard ground. I began to fidget, trying to get comfortable. Baldwin peered up from his notebook, and I got the hint. I tried to stay still, but I just couldn't for long. I wasn't used to sitting without a chair. Or a couch.

Finally, the major allowed Abdul to translate his monologue. "Sir, he's spinning a big story for you. He says his men have little supplies, almost no ammunition, and he fears the enemy will try to overrun Bandar again. He says that if they try, they will succeed unless he gets new weapons. His men need MREs. They need new uniforms, AKs, machine guns. He wants mortars and RPGs [rocket-propelled grenades] too."

When we had walked the perimeter, we had seen no damage from enemy attack, just ample evidence of neglect. The only bullet holes we had seen were the ones in Major Ghul's Toyota pickup. I wondered if he had ordered one of his men to empty an AK magazine into it so he could get a sweeter ride.

Major Ghul checked the cauldron. "Our food is ready," he told Abdul. From a nearby pouch, he produced six oval-shaped pieces of flatbread, which he handed out to us. I tried to smile as I thanked him. Sweat dripped off my brow. My back itched from all the perspiration. My feet felt like Virginia in August.

He ladled out a spoonful of what looked like greasy stew and poured it over my flatbread. I held it carefully and sat back down.

"What is this, Abdul?" I asked.

"Goat and vegetables."

Baldwin took a bite. While he chewed, I saw a light go on in his head. He turned to me and asked in a low voice, "Sir, wasn't this guy at the meeting with us this morning at the Gamal district center?"

With a start, I realized that Baldwin was right. There had been so many elders and leaders at the meeting that I hadn't placed his face until Baldwin mentioned it. Major Ghul had been in the background the entire time and hadn't said a word. He had been so low-key that if Baldwin hadn't said something, I never would have recalled seeing him there.

"Yeah. You're right. He sure as hell was."

Baldwin considered this. After another bite of goat stew and flatbread, he asked, "Well, why didn't he discuss all these attacks then?"

"Good question. Abdul, why don't you ask him that?"

Our 'terp nodded and fired off a few sentences in Farsi. Major Ghul grew serious and lowered his voice. It sounded conspiratorial.

"Sir, the major says the mayor asked him to discuss these events with you in private. He is not sure who to trust and was being careful around the other elders."

This smelled to me. "Abdul, what do you think? Is he telling the truth?"

"No, sir, he's lying."

I agreed. But what to do about it? "Should I press him?"

"No, sir. This is just how business is conducted here," replied Abdul.

"No point," Baldwin echoed.

Major Ghul went to work on his food and motioned to us to do the same. I have always been a picky eater, and goat was never on my approved dietary list. Still, I could not spurn the offering. I tore off a piece of flatbread, wrapped it into a funnel, and scooped some of the stew up and into my mouth. It did not taste like chicken.

"Okay, we don't push him. What's the play here then?"

We talked over what to do next. There was probably a power struggle going on between Major Ghul and the mayor, and that's why he'd wanted this backdoor conversation with us. Also, if the attacks were all fabrications, the mayor would probably not have supported his line of bullshit. Unless, of course, doing so would have lined his pockets as well. But I got the sense that Major Ghul did not like to share.

"I'd just move on, sir," Abdul suggested.

Okay. I thought it over and realized that Major Ghul's tale of woe had given me the perfect entry to bring up something I wanted from him. "Ask him where the enemy is around here. Where are they hiding?"

Ghul shrugged and smiled like a Cheshire cat. "No idea." After a pause, he added through Abdul, "But if I find out, I promise I will tell you."

"Ask him if he knows how many enemy in the area."

Major Ghul shrugged again and said he did not know.

"Are there foreign fighters here? Arabs?" I asked.

Major Ghul shrugged a third time. "Who knows where they come from?" he replied.

Before he left, Captain Canady had told us about a cagey enemy leader operating in our area. Through the first month of our time at Bermel, we'd received more intelligence suggesting that Canady was right. We had a signals team listening to all the enemy radio frequencies. The leader's name was spoken only occasionally and with great awe. Our men listening in reported his name to be "Galang." Once or twice, he had come onto their net. As soon as he did, all chatter stopped cold, something that was very unusual and telegraphed respect for him. He would utter a few cryptic commands, then sign off.

I wanted to know more about him, but trying to open that door with Major Ghul only got it slammed in my face. I tried a few more questions, only to get the same nonanswer.

Major Ghul might not have been on the enemy's side, but he sure wasn't on ours either. Perhaps he was on his own, operating from pure self-interest. The war, for him, was the Afghan version of a get-rich-quick scheme. I had no idea how we were going to work with him in the year ahead. I'd have to sort that out with Abdul and Baldwin later.

As we finished dinner, the spicy goat meat burning my stomach, Major Ghul returned to the desperate plight of his command. Once again, he told Abdul that without more guns and ammo, Bandar stood no chance against an enemy assault. He had intelligence that the Taliban was planning to hit his base again. He needed weapons, and fast. He also needed a new personal vehicle, since his had been turned into a redneck lawn ornament during the last attack.

I wanted to ask about his intelligence. If he knew an attack was coming, how was it he didn't know anything else about the enemy? Abdul didn't think it was a good idea to nail him with that question. Instead, I was noncommittal and made no promises about more weapons. I told him that my platoon had plenty of firepower and access to even more should the enemy launch an assault on us. He didn't care about that. He wanted guns. Badly. And my refusal to promise him any taxed his acting abilities. He made an attempt to mask his frustration with fake smiles. His joviality grew forced.

How could I keep him happy without giving him stuff he'd just sell to the enemy? My orders to foster ties with Major Ghul and his unit seemed impossible to fulfill. I kept hammering on the strength of my platoon. It would be his force multiplier. I had no other card to play.

Time passed. The conversation went nowhere. Outside, the moon rose over the mountaintops and cast silvery shafts of light into the basement through the ventilation slits in the walls. I fidgeted, never quite finding a comfortable spot. I think it irritated Baldwin, who somehow managed to give the two bodyguards a run for their money as he sat still as a statue.

In the end, we got nothing out of Major Ghul. He got nothing out of us either. Deadlock. His men would remain poorly equipped, which meant that morale would stay low here and those who were pushed out to cover checkpoints down in the valley would be very vulnerable to an attack—especially ones launched by the actual enemy.

I tried to imagine how his men must have felt, knowing that their commander had sold all their best equipment, leaving them to face the enemy with castoff weapons. No wonder everyone here looked so morose.

Sometime before midnight, we finally managed to extricate ourselves. The major had become overly flattering in the final lap of our conversation, clearly hoping to get something out of us at the last minute. It didn't work. With the combination of his used-car-dealer persona and my professionalism, I sensed an undercurrent of hostility blooming between us. This had not been a good start to a relationship that the battalion had told us was vital to our efforts here.

As the cooking fire died down, we rose for the meeting's final formalities. Handshakes all around, a few last words, and then Abdul guided us back upstairs into the barracks. As the major stayed behind with his men, we stepped into the night. The cold air felt wonderful, and I took deep, cleansing breaths to purge my lungs of the basement's stench.

Cleansing breath. Yeah, right. The place smelled like shit.

We threaded our way through the base in search of my Humvee, passing along the way a few Afghan sentries. One sat in his fighting position snoring, his AK propped beside him.

We found my rig on the southeast side of our perimeter. Chris Brown was still in the turret, helmet still covering his dark brown hair as he peered through night-vision goggles in search of potential threats. Brown was skinny and had an incongruously deep voice colored with a subtle southern accent. He was sensitive and emotional, and I had also found him to be very conscientious. I relied on him a lot. At the same time, he was the platoon's comedian, the spark plug for many jokes and silly scenes. He could do an impression of Rocky Balboa, complete with Philly accent, that would leave the men in stitches.

While Brown kept watch over his sector, Pinholt sat in the driver's seat, door open. He'd given up on Steinbeck for the night to pour over a dog-eared copy of *Forbes*. I was about to say something to him when Sabo materialized out of the darkness. Baldwin looked happy to see him.

"Druid," Baldwin greeted him,

"Fuck you," Sabo replied with a grin.

"Tree fucker," Baldwin retorted.

"I'm no Wiccan," Sabo said with a mock snarl.

"Whatever. Heathen," Baldwin said.

"Okay, I can live with that."

Sabatke had covered himself with satanic tattoos, including a pentagram strategically etched into the back of his neck. With his shirt off, his muscular frame resembled a Wikipedia entry on pagan symbolism. Truth was, the shocking body imagery formed the outer core of Sabo's defenses, under which he nourished a huge and easily wounded heart. He trusted instinctively; it was his default. His beliefs served as armor, keeping people at bay. But those who made the effort to get to know him found him to be a fiercely loyal and devoted friend.

Baldwin understood that about Sabatke. Though a devout Christian, Baldwin slipped past the satanic shock-value exterior with ease and saw the value of Sabo's passion. It was Sabatke's rocket fuel, and it propelled him through his days at a frenetic pace. In turn, Sabatke recognized Baldwin's natural passion, and he respected it. Baldwin's near-pious dedication to cause and country had led him to sacrifice his family's very way of life. A man like Sabatke valued that above anything else a man could offer. It had not taken long for the bond that sprang up between them to transcend their religious differences.

The infantryman's way of life has a knack for distilling a man's character down to its most essential elements. If he measures up, nothing else matters. That's what bonded those two. They measured up.

Sabo switched into professional mode to give me a quick status report. Then Baldwin, Abdul, and I gave a brief account of our meeting with Major Ghul. I wanted to get into the details and see what counsel they might offer on how to handle him in the days ahead, but I knew my men were exhausted.

"Let's discuss this more in the morning. Go get some sleep. I'm going to troop the line in a few, then turn in."

"Roger, sir. Be sure to get some sleep this time," Baldwin said. He and Sabo disappeared into the night together. I heard them giving each other grief until they walked out of earshot.

I watched them go and missed Abdul's departure. I stood beside Pinholt's door and deliberated. Eat something to settle the burning in my stomach, or troop the line and check on the boys?

I could eat later.

The men seemed to be in good spirits. At the northeast corner of the perimeter, I found Sergeant Michael Emerick in the truck commander's seat of his Humvee, hunched over a sketch pad he'd illuminated with his headlamp.

We greeted each other, and I leaned on his door to peer over his shoulder at his latest creation. Emerick was an outstanding NCO and team leader whose men loved him. He was also a gifted artist, a skill I'd recently tapped by asking him to create an emblem for our platoon. When we had a break in patrolling, we were going to paint it on each of our vehicles.

"Whatcha workin' on, Emerick?" I asked.

He showed me the sketch pad.

"Jesus, man, that's outstanding," I said, looking at his creation. He'd drawn a fierce and toothy skull bursting from the "O" of "Outlaws."

"Isn't finished yet, sir," Emerick said a little self-consciously.

"Emerick, this is perfect. We'll put it on every truck. That way, the enemy'll always know who they're dealing with."

"Thank you, sir." Like Wheat, Emerick hailed from Louisiana, though he didn't have Wheat's deep accent.

"No, man, thank you. That image is going to give us our identity."

When I had first taken over the platoon, I wanted us to have our own unique persona. We'd settled on calling ourselves the Outlaws, and I'd paid out of pocket to have T-shirts made for everyone. We'd also come up with our own guidon—we were the only platoon with one (they're officially for company level and above). By the time we got out here, we were known as the Outlaw platoon throughout the brigade. Now, thanks to Emerick's design, the enemy would get to know us as well.

We talked shop for a while. He detailed the sleep cycle he'd established for the men in his truck and his security plan. He had everything handled. No worries with Emerick, ever. I wished him good night and continued along the line.

I spoke with Baldwin next, and as I left his rig, I noticed a figure in the darkness, sitting alone near the fort's outer wall. I changed course and approached him. Abdul was sitting in the dirt, opening an MRE.

He's with us, but he'll never be one of us.

I took a knee next to him. "Abdul, how you doing?"

"Good, thank you, Lieutenant." He looked away and added, "Better since I have a seat in an armored Humvee."

Since we'd begun operations, there'd been times when we didn't have enough armored Humvees for the entire platoon. That had forced us to use the hated M998s—pickup-truck versions with hillbilly armor bolted on the doors. The beds were protected with plywood and sandbags. They were death traps, and everyone knew it. The first time we'd rolled out with one, Abdul had tried to take a seat in one of the armored rigs. Our platoon sergeant had stopped him, saying to me privately that armored seats could be used only for Americans while they were in short supply.

Abdul had complained bitterly, but I had stood by that decision. Our first responsibility was to our men and their families. It was a very difficult call, and I knew it made Abdul feel like a second-class citizen. Given all he'd done for the coalition, it was a painful sight to bear.

"Well, we won't have to worry about that anymore, Abdul." A few weeks ago, Lieutenant Colonel Toner had heard of our plight and gone ballistic. Extra armored Humvees had showed up soon after. They'd been dribbling in ever since, and the whole company would soon be able to dump the Jed Clampett M998s. This mission to Bandar was the first time our entire platoon was properly protected.

"Tell me something, Abdul?"

He looked back at me. Making eye contact with him provoked a pang of guilt in me. "What's that, Lieutenant?"

"Why do you do this job?"

He didn't speak at first. Instead, he dug into his MRE pouch and found a package of crackers. As he opened them, he said, "At the beginning of the war, my father worked for the Americans at FOB Shkin."

I couldn't conceal the surprise in my voice. "Really? Doing what?"

"Interpreter."

His answer intrigued me. "Is he still working there?"

More silence. Abdul studied his exposed cracker, took a bite, then glanced back at me. "He's dead."

I didn't know what to say.

"He was killed by the Taliban four years ago. We received night letters."

I sat down, peering at Abdul intently. "Is that why you do this?"

He nodded. "Every mission I go on, I avenge my father's death. I am the head of my house now. It is my duty."

That explained everything, his courage under fire, the trust Captain Canady had placed in him, his standing with the locals. I understood why he didn't cover his face. He wanted the enemy to know what he was doing.

"How about you, Lieutenant? Why are you here?"

I opened a bottle of water and downed half of it, thinking back to the day I had found purpose in my life. Unconsciously, I touched the St. Christopher medal at my throat.

"September eleventh," I said simply.

I remembered back to the night before the attacks. It had been a typical college Monday. We had studied, drunk, and eaten pizza until I staggered off to bed long after midnight. The next morning, I'd awoken to an apartment scattered with empty beer cans, clicked on the television, and watched the towers collapse.

I flashed to a moment a few weeks after the attacks. I'd been drifting through life without purpose, studying elementary education at Clarion University. My heart hadn't been in it. I'd gone down to a recruiter and talked about joining the army. I mentioned it to my father, who objected to the idea of his oldest son dropping out of college to enlist.

"My father was a good man," Abdul said quietly. "He worked for your Special Forces."

I had no words for that. How could we ask a man like Abdul to have faith in us when our most elite warriors could not protect his father?

My own father's face came to me right then. He was frustrated with me that day, and the words that had passed between us were bitter ones. He wanted me to finish school first, then go in as an officer. I wanted to get into the fight right away. I had found my mission, I knew it in my heart, and I didn't want to wait. I was going to seize the moment, and I was angry that my father didn't support my decision. He had supported me through everything else.

Finally I couldn't take it anymore. I shouted at him, "Well, what the hell have you ever done to be proud of, Dad?"

The moment the words came out, I regretted them. His face broke. We stared at each other, both of us aware of the line I had just crossed.

"I have four kids that I'm proud of every day of my life, Sean."

My dad's childhood dream had been to become a naval officer. Two years into Annapolis, he had given up that dream after my mom became pregnant with me. He'd never once complained or mentioned any regrets.

I sat in the dirt 13,000 miles from home and felt the abiding guilt of that moment return to me. In the end, I had agreed with my dad. I'd transferred from Clarion to Duquesne University so I could join the ROTC program there. Two years later, I'd completed my coursework, earning a degree in history, and the army had commissioned me as a second lieutenant.

After I'd made it through Army Ranger School, my dad had come to my graduation and pinned on my tab. I'd seen the look in his eyes as he approached me, and I'd realized that there would be no prouder moment in my life.

Abdul and I sat in silence for a few minutes, two men whose lives had found purpose in the same tragedies that had befallen our people. Had it not been for 9/11, I would have continued to drift. Abdul's father would still be alive, and he wouldn't have sworn a blood oath against our mutual enemy. Two men. Two cultures. Same mission.

"Someday, I would like to bring my family to New York," Abdul said. He sounded resigned about it.

"Maybe we can make that happen. There's a program that gets 'terps to the States," I said.

"Lieutenant, I would like that very much."

"I'll see what we can do. In the meantime, we've got the contract set for your brother. He should be able to start working in the chow hall in a few weeks."

"Thank you, Lieutenant. My family needs the income."

Abdul's brother was twelve.

"Thank you, Abdul. I couldn't be doing this without you. I appreciate your input."

"Then, Lieutenant, you must listen to me. Yusef is not to be trusted. He is a bad man."

Yusef was one of the other 'terps at Bermel. He was easygoing, laughed a lot, and liked to hang out with the men, telling exceptionally dirty jokes. Several times, Abdul had mentioned his qualms about Yusef. At the same time, Yusef had come to me more than once to complain about Abdul and make his own case for being promoted to the head interpreter on the base. I'd blown it off as politics between the 'terps. But Captain Canady had warned us about Yusef too. I couldn't just dismiss Abdul's concerns.

"I'll keep an eye on him, Abdul. If you see him do anything suspicious, tell me. How's that?"

He looked mollified. "Thank you, sir."

Abdul was my age, but his eyes were much older. He regarded me with a combination of pleasure and sadness, as if he wanted to be one of the team but knew he would never be a full-fledged member no matter how well he did his job.

"Sir? Have I done well enough to get your Ranger tab?" he asked.

I touched the tab on my shoulder and thought about my dad again. The day he pinned it on me I weighed less than a hundred and sixty-five pounds, down from the two-ten I'd been at the start of Ranger School. I'd gone through hell to be able to wear it. "You've gotta do a lot more to earn a Ranger tab, Abdul."

"I guess I'll keep trying, then," he made a melodramatic show of sounding disappointed. He was a good man. I enjoyed his sense of humor.

"Outstanding. In the meantime, get some sleep."

"Roger, sir. Goodnight."

I got up, dusted off, and started to walk away. After only a few steps, I heard him say, "You know, I will earn that tab someday, sir."

"Yeah, I have no doubt you will, Abdul. None."

THREE

THE LONG, DARK REACH

★ ★ ★

WE'D BEEN BACK AT BERMEL FOR ABOUT TEN DAYS WHEN Abdul interrupted a company meeting to say he needed to speak with our commander. Our six days at Bandar had been a complete waste of time. After that first night, we'd never seen Major Ghul again. Apparently, night letters or not, he had returned home or was just deliberately avoiding us. His men continued to slog through their days, their lethargy deepening by the hour. We patrolled at times, though we had to be very careful about doing so. Bandar had no diesel fuel, and though we'd brought seven gas cans each for our Humvees, their thirsty engines burned through our supply at a rapid rate. When we did sortie out into the valley, we found it devoid of human life. There were perhaps three villages within fifty miles of Bandar. Just getting to those villages drained our fuel supply to dangerously low levels. In the end we spent our final few days sitting around the fort running through some training exercises.

By the end of our time there, we had failed to build much of a relationship with the Afghan police. We sat around their shit-strewn outpost, watched these slovenly, dispirited cops, and wondered how on earth such a group could ever be molded into an effective force. Certainly it was beyond our means, especially after Major Ghul took a powder. We spent our days mired in futility.

I think all of us were relieved to head back north to FOB Bermel, where mail, showers, and hot chow awaited us. After a week without even an outhouse, sleeping in our Humvees at Bandar, Bermel, our home away from home, seemed like paradise.

Now Abdul looked shaken as he stood outside the door of our operations center. First Sergeant Christopher told him to wait outside. When we wrapped up the meeting, he and our commander went to go find him.

Abdul's mom had received a night letter. Abdul had known there was a bounty on his head, but this was the first time his family had been threatened directly. Anxious for the safety of his younger brother and mom, he asked our commander, Captain Waverly, if the company could send a platoon down to Shkin to check on them.

Captain Waverly rejected that idea. He told Abdul that he couldn't change the patrol schedule. Besides, the Shkin area was owned by the Special Forces unit stationed at the base down there. Sending a platoon into their battle space would have required coordination, and Captain Waverly just didn't want to jump through those hoops.

Truth was, Waverly didn't want to make any decision that could get him in trouble with Lieutenant Colonel Toner. Waverly had not impressed Toner in training before our deployment and had earned the battalion commander's wrath more than once. The relationship had frayed completely within our first month in Afghanistan. Captain Waverly had become so paranoid that at times it paralyzed his ability to make a decision. Earlier in the month, our base had come under rocket fire. Even though our sentries could see the launch points on Rakhah Ridge and reported that there were no villages or dwellings anywhere near them, Waverly could not bring himself to order our guns to return fire. He had been immobilized with the thought that he could cause an incident if one of our shells inflicted a civilian casualty.

Though his fear of collateral damage was certainly valid—especially within the context of counterinsurgency operations—it incapacitated his tactical decision-making ability. Knowing when to engage the enemy or back off to protect civilians was a cross that all commanders had to bear in combat. Any disruption in this delicate balance could prove disastrous for a new commander. For Waverly, it would be the final straw with Lieutenant Colonel Toner.

As Waverly had dithered, we had taken forty 107mm rockets without firing a shot back. The rest of the command group had been so upset that a shouting match had erupted. Eventually Waverly had ordered our 105mm guns to send rounds back at the enemy, but by then it was too late. We'd been battered for hours, with everyone's lives in danger, and when the attack finally ended, Waverly's actions had destroyed his leadership presence within the company. From then on, the men had whispered that Waverly's indecision was someday going to get one of them hurt or killed.

Abdul knew how the men viewed Waverly. He'd been with many units before and had seen good leaders and bad ones. He would not have gone to Captain Waverly unless he was desperate and took the threat seriously. Since Waverly was the commander, Abdul had nobody else he could turn to for help.

Later that night, after deliberating on Waverly's refusal to send a patrol to check on his family, Abdul came back with another idea. He asked Waverly to give him a few days off so that he could return home to ensure his family's safety. Waverly shook his head and told him it would be too dangerous for him to leave the base.

Lieutenant Taylor and I were angered at the decision but could not do anything about it. Part of our stated mission here was to build relationships with the local Afghan communities. If we could not foster a healthy relationship with our best 'terp, how were we going to do so with the villagers around Bermel?

The next morning, Outlaw Platoon rose early to prepare for another long patrol mission. This time we would be out beyond the wire for another six days, tasked with setting up snap checkpoints and observation posts all over our area of operations. We were to be unpredictable, stay mobile, and keep the enemy off guard. That way, we could impede the insurgents' movements as they would not know which infiltration routes were safe to use.

An hour after dawn, we had the trucks lined up and filled to capacity with ammunition, food, water, and fuel. We were ready to roll, but Abdul had not yet shown up. This was highly unusual. Normally, he would be right among the men, loading the rigs and prepping them for the mission ahead. I sent Baldwin off to find him.

We waited. Chris Brown entertained us from the turret of my Humvee. Sometimes, part of his premission ritual included doing a variant of Michael Jackson's "Thriller" dance. The men would watch and catcall as he went through his moves, visible only from his rib cage up. Down the line of trucks, Wheat whittled and Emerick sketched. Sabo stood to one side, chatting quietly with another member of the platoon. Pinholt tried to engage me in a discussion about the Fed's latest change in interest rates, but I didn't rise to the bait this time. Eventually, he gave up and stuck his head in a beat-up copy of *Atlas Shrugged*.

We missed our start time, which made me anxious as we never rolled late for anything. At last Baldwin returned. No sign of Abdul. Instead, he brought Bruce Lee with him to serve as our 'terp.

Bruce Lee had joined the interpreter contingent at Bermel only a few weeks before, and he'd patrolled with us only a few times. But we'd seen enough of him to realize he was a whack job. Obsessed with martial arts, he'd stand by himself and pretend to be grappling an invisible opponent. He'd never had any formal training, and from what we could gather had learned kung fu from watching bad Chinese movies. When he tried out his moves, he looked like he was having seizures. I once saw him attempt a back flip. He almost slipped a disk. Not much of a "Bruce Lee," but that's what we called him nevertheless.

In the field, his attention drifted. We discovered he could not speak the local dialect, which made him almost useless when visiting villages. His translations frequently made no sense, and the ones that did made us wonder if he was telling the truth.

Bruce Lee made me appreciate Abdul all the more. For the next six days, I'd be going into Indian country without my Tonto. I was not happy.

We sortied beyond the wire, heading into our area of operations five Humvees strong. We hadn't gone far when I got a radio call from the base operations center telling us to turn around and come home. There was no explanation.

We swung around and drove back through the main gate. Soldiers were running in different directions, and there was a charged atmosphere that had been lacking when we left.

We dismounted. Sabo and Baldwin linked up with me. "Any idea what's going on, sir?" Baldwin asked.

"No. Let me see if I can find out. Turn the trucks around and make sure everyone stays close."

"Roger, sir."

I walked to the operations center, where I found First Sergeant Christopher overseeing controlled chaos. When I asked what was going on, he said, "Delta found the body of a local national."

"Where?"

"Midway between here and Shkin."

Shit.

First Sergeant Christopher added, "Abdul is missing. We're trying to determine if it's him."

Focus.

"What can we do to help?" I managed.

"Captain Waverly is out there right now. He'll need you out there with him."

"We're ready to roll."

I walked back to my platoon, my mind a frenzy of activity. All I could think about was Waverly's refusals to help Abdul.

By the time I returned, the men had already heard the news. Everyone had gone quiet. Baldwin and Sabo had returned to their respective trucks. Wheat had ceased his whittling; Emerick had stowed his pen and pad. Chris Brown sat behind his gun and stared straight ahead. I climbed into my rig and exchanged a glance with Pinholt. His jaw was set, but I could see anger in his eyes.

The call to leave the base and join Captain Waverly came a few minutes later. We saddled up and sped out to the scene.

Maybe it isn't him.

Thirty minutes later, we reached Captain Waverly, who directed my rigs to establish outer security. As soon as we were emplaced, I went to talk with our company commander.

He looked pale, but otherwise he showed no emotion.

"Sir, what's the story?" I asked.

Waverly told me that another patrol had discovered a dirt bike lying beside the road. It looked like one of the red Yamahas the 'terps used for transport. A body lay next to the road about a half kilometer south of the motorcycle.

"Let's go take a look," Waverly said.

My throat went dry.

Uncle Matt warned you about this moment.

"Roger, sir."

Lieutenant Marbury, our half-African-American, half-German

fire support officer, joined us. Apparently he'd already seen the corpse. He offered, "He was shot in the leg."

At our family's last Christmas together, I had found myself alone with a beer, standing at the threshold of the kitchen. The rest of the adults had congregated in the kitchen. I had lingered on the periphery, listening and wondering if I'd be around next Christmas for a repeat of this moment.

Marbury pointed the way. "He's down a ways, around the bend in the road over there."

We began to walk that way. Not a word passed between us.

I had just finished off the can of Miller Lite in my hand when my uncle Matt approached. He was the cop in the family and had served with a department just outside Pittsburgh for more than twenty years. He was the kind of man who could walk into a room and command instant respect without ever saying a word. He was a presence.

"How's the beer?" he had asked.

"Awful. Next time, we gotta get Bud Lite," I had replied

Over my uncle Matt's shoulder, I saw my dad edge a little closer to us.

"Sean, with where you're going, there's something you need to be aware of."

I waited for him to continue. He struggled to find the words he wanted.

"What's that?" I asked lightly, hoping that would get him over the hump.

"Look, Sean, I will never forget the first time I saw a dead body. It affects you. A lot."

At the edge of the kitchen, my uncle Matt had told me the story of the first corpse he'd encountered. The man had been murdered and dumped in a puddle of water. He was bloated, and the pool had turned crimson with his blood.

"At some point, you're probably going to experience something like that," he had said in a low voice. I'd nodded, thinking I understood what that meant. Perhaps intellectually that was even true.

"Sean, you need to steel yourself for that moment. Be prepared."

My dad had hovered, pretending not to listen. His face looked torn. He had wanted to hear, but he didn't. Beneath the conflict, I had sensed that he felt a low-grade form of panic. The unknown awaited his son, and there was nothing he could do but stand and watch me wade into it.

Actually, the unknown awaited both of us.

I KEPT PACE ALONGSIDE CAPTAIN WAVERLY AND LIEUTENANT Marbury. The walk to the victim seemed to take forever. With each step that drew us closer my mind screamed at me to stop.

Could this actually be Abdul?

We came over a rise and could see down the road. Fifty meters away, the body lay sprawled in a drainage ditch. The man was wearing old-style desert camouflage pants and khaki man jams. When I saw his pants, my feet stopped and I sucked air.

Keep walking. Be ready.

Be ready? My uncle Matt had warned me, but in this moment I realized he'd never told me how to be prepared. I guess he knew that each man would have to prepare and cope in his own way.

The corpse had fallen facedown. A red motorcycle helmet concealed his head. We were going to have to take it off to identify him.

We drew alongside and stopped. Lieutenant Marbury had been right. The cyclist had been shot in the leg. It was twisted under him in an awkward position.

"What do you think happened?" I asked.

Waverly said nothing. His eyes were devoid of emotion. But I knew him to be a sensitive man. Inside, he must have been reeling. Leaders make decisions based on the best information available and a thorough game boarding of possible outcomes. But even the most competent leaders cannot account for everything. Life has a way of breeding unintended consequences. If it was Abdul, he would shoulder the guilt of this day for the rest of his life.

Lieutenant Marbury looked back up the road and spoke softly. "I'd say he was coming back north out of Shkin and was ambushed here. Maybe he tried to drive through it, but he got hit in the leg and fell off the bike."

I nodded. Made sense so far.

"See how his leg is broken too? Probably happened when he hit the ground."

Blood had congealed around the leg wound. Flies were lapping at it.

Marbury continued, "He tried to get away. But they caught him. Executed him. See the bullet hole in the back of his head?"

I hadn't seen it. I couldn't take my eyes off the flies.

You have to look. If it is Abdul, at the very least you owe him that.

Some of the squad leaders had called Lieutenant Taylor and me "'terp lovers." They'd been through a tour here already and had come away with disdain for and distrust of all Afghans. They'd seen betrayals. They'd seen that here; loyalty shifted like the desert sands. As armor from such things, they'd built a wall between themselves and the people we were sent to protect.

We bent down and unstrapped his helmet. When we pulled it off, black-red pudding drizzled out of it. The lifeless head flopped into the dirt.

Lieutenant Marbury was right, the man had been shot in the back of the head. I could see the entry wound surrounded by matted black hair.

It was Abdul.

Marbury exhaled sharply. "Fucking sons of bitches."

Captain Waverly went still and said not a word.

The bullet had exited above his right eye. It had blown a half-dollar-sized chunk of his skull out. At least he had died instantly when the last bullet was fired.

I stared at my friend, and my mind filled with white noise. It was difficult to process what I was seeing.

Steel yourself, Sean. Be prepared.

Nothing can prepare you for seeing the corpse of a man you called friend, not even the death of a little girl in your arms.

Unable to sit idly by with his family in danger, Abdul had done the only honorable thing. He'd gone AWOL in the night, slipping out of the Afghan side of our base on the dirt bike, speeding south to his home in Shkin.

He'd reached his family. But there must have been eyes watching their qalat. When he'd approached, a few furtive cell phone calls had set the ambush in motion. The enemy had picked a spot equidistant between Abdul's home and our base. As he'd rushed back to us and the morning mission he knew we would need him on, they had struck out of the darkness.

Gunfire had knocked him off the bike, which had stayed upright and continued north a ways before finally tipping over. With his broken, bullet-torn leg, he could not have hoped to get away. Had he fought? His AK-47 was missing, as was his chest rack full of extra magazines for it. I saw no spent shell casings to suggest a last stand.

As he'd lain crippled in the dirt, the enemy had reached him, flung him onto his belly, and executed him with that single shot to the back of the head. They'd stripped him of all valuables and left him in the ditch for us to find.

They're sending a message to us.

With one cunning move, they'd just taken out our best 'terp—

the man who had been my bridge to the people I had hardly begun to understand.

Message received. They know us. They know our weak points. And the enemy has a long, dark reach.

Yusef would be our head 'terp now. Nobody else had enough experience and the languages to hack the job. Bruce Lee was a train wreck. Shaw was okay, but he was shy and never volunteered for anything. He offered the bare minimum. Abdul had been my guide.

We gathered up his body, and part of the company escorted it back to Bermel. The rest of us made a mournful journey south to Shkin, where the family waited. When we arrived, Captain Waverly and Lieutenant Marbury went to the blue metallic front door with Bruce Lee. I stood next to my Humvee some distance away, watching as Abdul's mom answered their knock.

She knew without any translation needed. A wail escaped her lips. She collapsed inside. Marbury, Waverly, and Bruce Lee stepped in after her. Marbury did most of the talking.

As his mother cried, my men stood guard around Abdul's family's home, their eyes cold and filled with anger. For all the danger the rocket attacks had posed for us, they were impersonal. Getting hit with a 107 was akin to being struck by lightning. If it happened, it was your time, like an act of God; or, for the atheists among us, a random moment of chaos.

This assassination made the war personal for all of us.

Suddenly, Abdul's younger brother bolted through the front door and ran to a nearby woodpile. He dropped to his knees, covered his head with his arms, and began to sob. The moment had no end. We stood our vigil, game faces secured. But beneath them, we seethed.

I thought about Abdul's brother all the way back to Bermel. The image of him by that woodpile lingered with me long after the rest of the platoon turned in. I stayed up, typing out my report of the day while suppressing the grief I felt. My words describing Abdul's murder were stilted, formal, remote. Army-speak. I stared at my laptop's screen, editing my sentences to further scrub them of any emotions. When I finished, I felt a sense of shame. Abdul's death deserved something more than this sterile retelling, but I had nothing else to offer him.

It was after 0100 when I finally put my report onto a jump drive and walked over to the company operations center, where I sent it to Lieutenant Colonel Toner. When I returned to my room, I discovered a plate of food sitting on my desk. A steaming mug of coffee sat beside it. Not a soul had been moving outside when I had come back from the operations center, and everyone in my hooch was snoring, sound asleep.

The food looked inviting. Whoever prepared it had heaped the plate with cold cuts, cheese, and bread. I sat down at the desk and reached for the meal, suddenly feeling famished. I hadn't eaten after we returned to Bermel, and the paperwork had kept me from dinner that evening.

Could Dave Taylor have done this for me? We'd both been so busy recently that we'd barely had time to talk to each other, even though his room was only a few doors down. What about Baldwin or Sabo or Campbell? I thought about it as I chewed each bite. Finally I quit speculating. What was the use? There was no way to know for sure who was responsible. What mattered was that some-body had cared enough to make the gesture. And that felt good. Frankly, after the day we'd experienced, I needed a few minutes of feeling good.

Two days later, we held a memorial for Abdul. Captain Waverly had scheduled us to carry out the patrol we had been forced to abort, so we were not going to be able to attend the service. But as we prepared to leave that morning, I stole a few minutes for myself and Abdul.

The grief I'd felt as I stood in the ditch next to his body had given way to a slow burning rage. Rage at the enemy. Rage at the decisions that had led to his death. Rage that we had been unable to save the one Afghan upon whose loyalty I could always depend. Left without him, I feared what would happen the next time I had to interact with Major Ghul or anyone else of his ilk.

His coffin had been placed in the 'terp hooch. As I walked over there, I ran into Yusef.

"Good morning, Commander Sean," he said to me.

Abdul called me Lieutenant Parnell.

"Good morning," I replied awkwardly. I asked how Abdul's family was doing.

Bitterness filled his voice. "How do you think they are doing?"

Before I could answer, he pulled a small, yellowed piece of paper from a pocket. It looked like parchment, and for a disorienting second I thought of pirate maps and buried treasure.

He held it out to me. "The night letter," he said coldly.

I couldn't read it. But the scrawled words looked angry.

He tucked it back into his front pocket and abruptly walked off.

Alone, I entered the 'terp hooch and stood beside Abdul's coffin. It was simple, made of wood. A pauper's burial vessel.

Abdul had been trapped between two cultures the moment he elected to avenge his father's death. Never one of us, no longer able to fully trust his own people or be trusted by them, he'd existed in a never-never land where we returned his loyalty with constant reminders of his second-class status.

I put a hand on the lid. The wood felt cold to the touch. To my dismay, there had been no effort to prepare Abdul's memorial as we would a soldier's. There was no photo of him propped on a stand. There was no rifle propped between his boots, no rack of medals on his body armor's chest plate. There was nothing save this bland coffin that revealed nothing of the man laid to rest inside.

He had worn the Combat Infantryman Badge with great pride.

Though reserved for U.S. infantrymen who have undergone direct fire from the enemy, the 173rd had bestowed this honor on him after he had fought alongside them so valiantly. I hoped that somebody had given it to his family and explained its significance.

No tears came; I felt no depression. The shock and disbelief had worn off. But I could not escape the rage.

Abdul and I were kindred souls, bonded by a similar sense of purpose imposed on us by Al Qaida's 9/11 attacks. His mission had cost him his life. Now I knew in my heart that it could cost me mine as well. Or worse yet, the life of one of my men.

I lifted the coffin's lid. I saw the outline of his body but could not bring myself to look at his face.

With my other hand, I reached to my left shoulder and removed the Ranger tab my father had placed there at graduation. It felt light in my palm. I stared at it and thought of the pride I'd seen shining in my dad's eyes that graduation day.

"You earned this, Abdul."

I reached into the coffin and placed it between his fingers.

I understood his blood feud and the burn inside that it had caused. I understood it, because it had now become mine.

I eased the lid closed.

Without a word, I slipped out of the 'terp hooch into the warm spring morning. The burn inside suddenly felt good, like energy waiting to be harnessed. Maybe it was hate. Maybe it was fear. Or perhaps a combination of both. Either way, Abdul was dead and this war had suddenly become personal.

PART II

THE SPRING OFFENSIVE

★ ★ ★

FOUR

ONLY DO, OR DO NOT

★ ★ ★

May 7, 2006

WE WERE ON THE ROAD AGAIN, THIS TIME SCHEDULED FOR a six-day patrol behind Rakhah Ridge. With the good spring weather had come increased enemy activity. In Afghanistan, warfare has traditionally been seasonal. Winter is the time to heal, train, and prepare. The spring sunshine draws the enemy from their lairs. It has been that way since Alexander the Great.

Our base had a Prophet Section composed of signals intelligence spooks. Its job was to listen in on the enemy's radio chatter to detect patterns, probable intentions, and location. Our 'terps also listened to the enemy's conversations and translated them for the Prophet spooks, who passed that information to us while we were in the field. In the past week, they had heard a lot of talk on the enemy radio net. Something was afoot.

For this patrol, we planned to head out to the south, check out a village down there, then swing around Rakhah Ridge and set up outposts on a couple of hills overlooking key intersections in the road leading out of Pakistan. If we controlled those choke points, we'd disrupt the enemy's ability to move into Afghanistan. A company of Afghan soldiers had sortied with us and led the way with a small cadre of marines to serve as their embedded trainers. They bounced along in Toyota pickups a half kilometer or so in front of us.

Our five Humvees rattled down the narrow dirt road through the village of Malakshay. Not a soul greeted us. Windows were shuttered, doors closed. The bazaar was empty. The place looked like a ghost town. We drifted through the main drag, gunners scanning the empty alleys with nervous anticipation. Not even a cat roamed the streets.

We reached the far end of town and broke out into open country to the east, where we picked up speed. Pinholt and I sat side by side in silence, our usual financial and political banter killed off by the creepy feeling we'd gotten in Malakshay. Ahead, the road headed straight into a series of ridges and hills. We were in for another long stretch of moving at school-zone speed.

Pinholt eased off the gas as Baldwin's truck, which was on point, wound around a corner created by a massive butte that my map identified as Gangikheyl Hill. Rising nearly straight up for 2,500 feet, the feature dominated the landscape. Inching around the corner, we followed Baldwin's truck to the back side of the butte. Behind us, our other three rigs and their alert drivers maintained the proper spacing as we slowed down. As we came around the bend, we could see that the road dropped into a narrow valley behind Gangikheyl Hill.

After only four hours on the road, we were already broiling in the sweatbox the armored Humvees became after any duration under the sun. After a day in such heat, it was not uncommon for our body temperatures to hover at 103 degrees. We called it "baking brain cells." Within hours, our temples throbbed; our bodies leeched salt and fluids. No matter how much Gatorade or water you drank, there was no way to replace everything you lost. When we stopped to pee, our urine looked like apple juice, a sign of perpetual dehydration.

The dust our vehicles kicked up caked our faces and hands. We had to be careful when wiping the sweat off our faces, lest we contaminate our eyes with grit. My gunner, Brian Bray (Chris Brown was in Sabo's truck that day), already sported so many layers of Afghan moondust that he looked like the albino character from *The Da Vinci Code*. We'd learned that to keep from passing out from dehydration or heat exhaustion, we had to eat or drink constantly. We carried beef jerky and potato chips to replace the sodium our bodies dumped out our pores. To keep our electrolytes in balance, we alternated two liters of water with every liter of Gatorade.

With one grimy sleeve, I wiped the sweat off my brow. I'd just finished a liter of Gatorade; time to switch back to water. I found a bottle in a case sitting on the flat space between the front seats.

Pinholt kept us crawling along at ten miles an hour. We reached the dip in the road and had a roller-coaster moment as the Humvee's nose pitched down. A solid cliff ran straight up to our left—the back side of Gangikheyl Hill. To our right, another cliff plunged down into a wadi. A few hundred meters beyond the wadi rose a series of sharp ridges.

The road continued its steep descent for several hundred meters before flattening out. It then followed the lip of the wadi before climbing precipitously up to the top of a knoll that grew out of the back side of Gangikheyl Hill. It was going to be like driving to the bottom of a gravy boat, then up and out its spout.

Looking at the slope ahead, I wondered if it was too steep for us to navigate without each truck getting a running start first. In earlier patrols, we had found that the heavily laden Humvees simply didn't have the power to get up some inclines without getting up a head of steam first.

The hackles on my neck suddenly stood straight up. My nerves jangled, spellbound by a sensation unfelt before.

What the hell?

Perhaps I was getting seriously dehydrated. I opened the water bottle in my hands. My lips curled around its plastic rim just as Baldwin's Humvee exploded. For a split second, a bubble of orange flame sprouted from its right side. The rig lurched hard left as its shocks absorbed the violent blast. Another flame ball boiled underneath the Humvee. Gouts of dirt and smoke spewed horizontally from out between the tires.

An instant later, the fire vanished, replaced by curls of black smoke haloed by swirling dust. McCleod, Baldwin's gunner, disappeared out of the turret, leaving the barrel of his M2 .50-caliber heavy machine gun pointing skyward.

"Baldwin!"

I dropped the water bottle. Before it hit my lap, a third bloom of fire spawned midway between our two Humvees. My truck trembled, and suddenly it sounded as if somebody was making popcorn.

Shrapnel on the armor plate.

The smoke and dirt shrouded Baldwin's Humvee from view.

I heard a sharp explosion behind us, quickly followed by several more. The ground quaked again. The water bottle shifted, fell over my left thigh, and spilled down my pant leg.

Pinholt sat next to me with his gloved hands tight on the Humvee's steering wheel. Sweat trickled down the side of his head; more beaded on his forehead just below the rim of his helmet. He looked at me, his face tense but his eyes determined. He was waiting for me to make a decision.

Ahead, more smoke swirled around Baldwin's Humvee. Beyond

it, I could see our Afghan National Army (ANA) cohorts bailing out of their Toyota Hilux pickup trucks toward the top of the knoll. The Afghan soldiers, never pictures of discipline, ran this way and that with their weapons held at low ready. A few flopped into the dirt on either side of the vehicles. Others vanished off the road, sprinting as they fired randomly from the hip.

Between the explosions, the drumbeat of machine guns rang out from both sides of us.

Gunfire has its own language. Suppressing fire, the purpose of which is to pin you down, sounds undisciplined; it wanders back and forth over you without much aim. It is searching and random and somehow doesn't seem as deadly.

Accurate, aimed fire is a different story. It has purpose to it. You know as soon as you hear it that somebody has you in their sights. The shots come with a rapid-fire focus that underscores their murderous intent. Somebody is *shooting at you*. It becomes intimate and fear-inducing.

Gunfire can also telegraph the trigger puller's emotional response to a firefight. When a squad is surprised, you can tell they're jumpy and startled by their return fire. There's no rhythm, just a crash of noise jumbled together that gradually settles down as they recover their composure.

There are the pros, men who have waited with cold calculation for other men to venture into their sights. They take their time. They space their shots like drummers setting a band's beat.

And then there are the haters, men brimming with passion, controlled only by long-instilled discipline. But when time comes to pull the trigger, the very act becomes an unbridled emotional release, volcanic, furious—terrifying.

The enemy machine gunners hammered at us with accurate bursts. As their bullets struck home, they spoke to us infantry-men as clearly as if they had used our native language. Message received: these were not amateurs hiding in the hills on our flanks.

I reached for my radio handset, remembering that the radio is a lieutenant's best weapon.

"FOB Bermel, this is Blackhawk three-six," I said in a voice as calm as I could manage.

No response. Before I could try again, Sabatke came over the platoon net: "Three-six, this is three-four! We're getting tore up back here! We have to get outta the kill zone!"

"FOB Bermel, this is Blackhawk three-six, troops in contact . . ."

A VOICE BROKE THROUGH THE STATIC. I RECOGNIZED IT AS FIRST Sergeant Christopher. The transmission was weak and garbled. I called the company one more time but received only a broken response again.

"We're getting fucked up back here!" Sabo reported.

Another explosion rocked my Humvee. The enemy machine gunners concentrated on killing the men in our turrets. They knew our Humvees served as mobile firepower platforms. The lone soldier in the turret manned a heavy weapon such as a machine gun or grenade launcher, which were our best casualty-producing assets. Take those out, and we would be virtually defenseless.

A SPRAY OF BULLETS TORE ACROSS BALDWIN'S EMPTY TURRET. I heard a round spang into ours and ricochet around.

"Blackhawk three-six . . ." came First Sergeant Christopher, but the rest of his words were swallowed by static.

Fear assailed me. We were in a kill zone perhaps 350 meters long. To our left was the rocky cliff side of Gangikheyl Hill. It rose about six feet over our Humvees, then flattened out into a short plateau before running nearly vertical to the 2,500-foot summit. The hill was between us and our base, which was the reason for our terrible radio reception.

To the right, the road extended only a few feet beyond my door before dropping into the wadi. Looking out the bulletproof window in my door, I could see muzzle flashes on the conifer-stippled ridgeline.

The abandoned Afghan Toyota Hiluxes made forward movement impossible. We couldn't drive right or left. We couldn't even dismount and attack into the ambush; the terrain was just too rugged. Backing up while taking rocket and machine-gun fire was not going to work either. Our trucks probably didn't even have the power to reverse up the slope we'd just negotiated.

The enemy had used the terrain brilliantly to trap us in their kill zone. The amount of tactical acumen it had taken to conceive and execute this ambush sent a surge of pure terror through me.

We needed artillery. We needed aircraft. But I couldn't talk to the FOB, and we couldn't drive out of the fight.

Another explosion blossomed near Baldwin's Humvee.

Bullets stitched across my rig's turret. A 7.62mm round center-punched our windshield. Two more struck home, and the ballistic glass spiderwebbed with cracks.

I switched to my platoon net and called out, "All elements, this is three-six. The ANA is blocking our path. We're going to need to stand and fight it out."

Silence greeted this.

Again, I peered through the armored-glass window in my door. I could see perhaps twenty muzzle flashes on the hill there. Some appeared to be coming from the trees, some from bushes. I looked left. High up Gangikheyl Hill, I made out another rash of muzzle flashes. The enemy was emplaced in force on both sides of us, plunging fire down on our vehicles.

The FM radio we used to talk to the FOB was useless. My

rig also had a tactical satellite radio, but it didn't work unless we turned off our electronic jamming systems, which were designed to prevent the enemy from detonating roadside bombs on us with a remote device such as a cell phone. If I ordered the jammers shut down, then lost a vehicle to a bomb, I would never be able to live with myself. Surely there had to be another solution.

Baldwin's voice came over the radio, "Three-six, this is three-two, my gunner can't engage. We don't know where the ANA is."

Baldwin's alive! So is McCleod!

Relief cooled the terror I felt. My head cleared.

Think this through, Sean.

The enemy had anticipated our tactics. They'd picked this ground because they knew it was a dead spot for our radios. Without communication we could not call down artillery and an air strike on them. That one calculation had evened their odds against us considerably.

They knew that our field manuals taught us to assault into an ambush like this. But the rock wall to our left and the steep drop into the wadi to our right removed that option from our playbook. They might as well have been behind a moat or a medieval castle wall.

Within this deadly stretch of ground, they targeted our lead and trail vehicles first. Baldwin and Sabatke. Destroy those rigs, and our remaining ones would be trapped in a kill zone dominated by enemy machine gunners and rocketeers.

Okay. There would be no driving out of this fight, certainly not with the ANA blocking our way ahead.

That left something out of the box. Something not in the field manuals. But what? I clutched my rifle, reached for my portable radio, then closed my eyes for just a moment. In the darkness, the firefight drained away and I could see my parents' faces. They were crying in their doorway as a contact team reported my death. Was it a vision? Or just a warning?

Sean, it's time to prove yourself. You have to lead.

The cold, flat ring of lead on armor filled the air. The window in my door splintered.

Suddenly, I was thirteen again, sitting on the school bus home. That year, a fat brute had made it his personal mission to terrorize, humiliate, and pound on me at every turn. Those bus rides became a nightmare. Even my home wasn't safe. After I built a fort in my backyard, the brute and his pals wrecked it one day when we were gone. It grew so bad that I moved through my neighborhood as if I were stealing through enemy territory, fearing that I'd be discovered, chased down, and beaten raw again.

On that particular afternoon, I sat next to a pretty girl and had momentarily dropped my guard. She spoke to me with a soft, inviting voice. I rode along, listening with joy I had not felt in months.

Something slammed into the back of my head and drove my chin into my chest. I saw stars. The brute had thrown his backpack at me. "You better pass that back to me, bitch," he sneered.

Half his size, I knew I had no chance against him, especially since four of his cronies were staring at me. One act of defiance, and they would make an example of me.

My stomach lurching, I reached down, picked up his backpack, and handed it to the kid behind me. He passed it back to the brute.

He threw it at my head again. That time, he caught me even harder. My head jerked forward, and I bounced off the girl who'd been talking to me.

"Give it here, bitch," he called through peals of cruel laughter.

I looked around. Wasn't anyone going to stand up for me? My best friend sat across the aisle from me. I looked pleadingly into his eyes. He looked away. Everyone did. The girl moved.

I passed the backpack to the kid behind me. Moments later, it struck me in the back of the head again.

The bus driver saw it and told the brute to stop. He ignored him, and the driver did nothing. Not a soul rose to my defense.

The bully had terrified everyone, and they just wanted to stay out of his way.

The bus remained silent as the torment continued, until my stop mercifully arrived. I fled, humiliated and more alone than at any other time in my life.

That night, as I thought of all those kids watching and doing nothing, I swore I would never stand idly by while somebody needed help.

That moment propelled me down a path that led me to the army.

I grasped the Humvee's door handle. Pinholt noticed the movement. He turned his head in surprise. "Sir, what the fuck are you doing?"

Be their leader, set the example.

Since training, I'd seen the platoon's dynamic change. Some men had risen to the challenge of Lieutenant Colonel Toner's grueling pace; others had failed or set forth bare minimum effort. That dichotomy had rewritten the social fabric of the platoon. Friendships had faded; new ones had bloomed that were based on success. Those who measured up to Lieutenant Colonel Toner's standards had grown into the heart of our platoon.

So far, I was a member of the platoon's inner circle—not by what I'd done under fire but for those moments back in the States when I had stood up for my men in the face of garrison politics. I had earned their respect, but a moment like this one would break that forever if I didn't take the right path.

I remembered Captain Waverly's decisive moment. Rockets were exploding all around our base, and he had failed to make a decision. Sweating in the ops center, he had been a deer in the headlights. He'd lost the men that day. Not long after, Lieutenant Colonel Toner had replaced him after finding him inside the wire when he'd reported to battalion that he was going out on a patrol.

In combat, men measure up. Or don't. There are no second chances.

I held on to the handle. Another spate of bullets carved their way along the side of the Humvee. Baldwin's rig took another near miss from a rocket-propelled grenade. I could hear my gunner, Bray, shouting something, but his words were unintelligible over the din of battle.

My hand hesitated on the door handle.

Do it. For them.

Just before we'd left Fort Drum, the platoon had gathered for one last night out on the town. Long after midnight, the liquor had made me relaxed and loud. I was happier than I had ever been, surrounded by men I'd come to care so much about.

Then I'd made a snarky comment to a woman who had insulted one of my men. She'd reported it to her boyfriend, a townie with a chip on his shoulder. He and four of his buddies had ambushed me in the bar's bathroom. As they'd grabbed me and carried me outside, I'd laughed and said, "You picked the wrong night to do this."

They'd dragged me into the parking lot, ready to go to work on me. Before they could throw a punch, my entire platoon had poured through the front doors, pounced on the townies, and turned them into bleeding, bellowing wrecks.

"OUTLAW PLATOON!" we'd celebrated with high fives, back slaps, and hugs. It was our first engagement. We'd won a decisive victory, and my men had proven they had my back.

In that drunken parking lot beat down, my bond to those men had become complete. For the first time in my life, I had experienced what loyalty returned felt like. And I knew that I would rather die than lose that.

I yanked the door open and stepped into the storm.

FIVE

GAUNTLET

★ ★ ★

May 7, 2006

SUNLIGHT SHONE HOT ON MY FACE, BUT THE ST. CHRISTO-pher medal felt cool against my chest. I stood on the lip of the wadi as the firefight raged around me.

Something cracked, like Indiana Jones snapping his whip. It happened again. Then again. The noise seemed to be coming from everywhere. It had no focus, no direction or distance. It just en-gulfed me in sensory overload.

On the ridge, I could see the muzzle flashes of machine guns. Perhaps two hundred meters away, maybe less, the men manning them held the advantage. They had cover, concealment, and eleva-tion. They were winning the fight.

A bullet struck the door as I started to close it. The heavy armor shuddered from the impact. I took a last look at Pinholt, who was still yelling something at me, then slammed the door.

A puff of white smoke wafted from a patch of brush halfway up the ridge. Over the gunfire, I heard a hollow bass drumbeat. A split second later, an RPG struck the wadi's rim perhaps five meters up the road from me. In that instant, some primal instinct took over and I felt my body duck just as the heat wave surged over me. It burned the hackles on my neck and singed the exposed hair below my helmet. Before I could even process a thought, the heat vanished and the concussion wave struck as shrapnel splashed overhead.

Every training exercise we'd been through emphasized moving under fire. Stay in place, the enemy wins. You become easy meat, or you allow yourself to be pinned down, unable to fight back or escape.

Another bullet ricocheted off the Humvee. Fear gripped me. Nothing moved. Nothing worked.

I stood in the funeral home's doorway, my grandfather's coffin on the other side of the room. Between us sat our family and friends. They stared at me in my sweat-stained ACUs. I'd driven all night to be there for that moment. And on the threshold, the sight of his coffin and the eyes upon me bred fear my feet could not overcome.

The shroud of dirt elongated as it drifted across the road. Soon it would thin out and offer no concealment at all.

From somewhere to my right, I heard a distinctive boom, different from the other weapons already in the fight. It was like thunder, louder and more throaty than an AK. The sound of it echoed down our narrow valley.

Dragunov.

Sniper rifle.

Something pulled at my pant leg. For a crazy moment I thought of my cousin Freddie when he was a baby, tugging at my pants to get my attention. But when I looked down, I didn't see the child who'd been named after my grandfather. I saw a bullet hole in my ACUs just above my right boot. There was an exit hole in the fabric at shin level. The sniper had his crosshairs on me.

I couldn't move. I stood in the doorway, my family waiting for me to react. Then I saw my father's eyes. They broke fear's grip on me. My feet shuffled forward. I made it down the aisle and fell to my knees alongside the open coffin. Head down, as if in prayer, I waited for words to come. In that moment, I knew I needed to say something profound. How do you say thank you for a lifetime of support and love? The words would not come.

Through the riot of noise, I heard the Dragunov again. Bits of debris—rocks, clods of dirt—rained down around my Humvee as the last pieces of the RPG impact fell back to earth.

How much time had passed? Five minutes? Five seconds? In such moments, time has no traction. The chaos kaleidoscopes around you and scrambles your senses. In later fights, I learned to stay grounded. In this one, I didn't know enough to do anything but to be a prisoner of the chaos.

The dust swirled. The Dragunov boomed. AKs rattled, the machine guns poured cold fury. Indy's whip cracked repeatedly. My boots were made of iron.

Then I saw Baldwin's rig again, forty meters and a continent away. The sight of it filled me with dread. What would I do if I closed on it to find Baldwin wounded? He was just the selfless type of NCO to ignore his own wounds for the sake of his men and the mission. He had sounded fine over the radio, but until I laid eyes on him, I couldn't be sure.

What would I say to his wife, Regina, or his children if he were hurt or dying? Seeing that scene play out in my mind, I couldn't think of Baldwin as my stalwart NCO; he was the bear-sized, loving family man and husband I'd seen back in New York.

The hospital bustled with activity. Nurses moved purposefully about; doctors in long white coats carried charts. A woman cried

softly, alone in a waiting room chair. I made my way down a cor-
ridor until I saw Baldwin, standing near an open door. His face
registered surprise when he saw me. He extended his hand, and I
felt connected to this man by the warmth of his handshake.

"Thank you for coming, sir."

He pushed open the door to the private room. Regina lay
propped in bed, their newborn daughter in her arms. A weary
smile. A father's pride. A family moment of which I was a part.

Looking now at the smoking Humvee before me, I had one
thought: *Get to Baldwin.*

The fear broke, and my legs flew into action. Hunched down, I
sprinted forward.

Do not let your brothers down.

Bullets spouted in the dirt around me. I felt another tug on my
pants. I crossed the open ground to the rocket-hammered Humvee
with what felt like every insurgent in range targeting me. Somehow
I made it.

Alongside Baldwin's Humvee now, I could see that the rig's
armor had held and everyone was okay. The thoughts of home and
family vanished. We had a job to do, and I needed my stalwart
NCO.

I slammed my fist against the armored glass in Baldwin's door.
In the backseat, I saw Bruce Lee curled up and cowering on the
floorboard behind Baldwin's seat. I needed a 'terp right then, and
seeing Bruce Lee incapacitated by terror reminded me again how
dearly we missed Abdul.

I didn't stop. I didn't issue any orders. I had momentum. My
feet were working.

Either Baldwin would follow me, or he wouldn't. Either way, I
had to get to the top of the hill and get the Afghan troops to clear
the road for us.

My lungs ached. My head swam. I kept running, carrying my
rifle by its ACOG scope as if it were a briefcase. A machine-gun

burst ripped the dirt around me. I was flying now, running flat out like a kid fleeing a graveyard. The road steepened, and I forced more energy from my body, afraid that if I slowed, the bullets would catch me.

There was almost no cover or concealment until I reached the top of the knoll and the abandoned Afghan pickups.

The Dragunov spoke again.

How was I going to get the Afghans to get out of the way without Abdul or Bruce Lee? The only other way was to find the marine trainers embedded with the unit. I could see a few Afghan troops taking cover behind boulders alongside the road at the top of the knoll. A few lay prone behind the pickups. Others darted this way and that, streaming along the crest and disappearing over it. Finding the marines was going to take time we didn't have.

Fucking Bruce Lee.

Right then, I needed Baldwin. His steady presence, his patient council—he'd be able to figure out what to do. He was a combat vet; he'd mastered this chaos. He'd show me the way.

The nearest Afghan pickup was about fifty meters away. I reached the steepest part of the road. In the high-noon sun, kitted in full battle rattle, my full-speed dash was sucking my energy reserves dry. My ACUs were drenched with sweat. Another ten meters left me gasping, lungs afire.

What if Baldwin doesn't follow me?

The thought sent a thrill of fear through me. I'd never given him an order.

To my left, a couple of conifer trees screened me from the enemy gunners on Gangikheyl Hill. That didn't stop them from sawing bursts through the pines. Branches snapped and tumbled into the road. Needles fell. Bullets slapped into the trunks.

If he didn't follow me, I had two options: keep going, or run back and get him.

I broke out beyond the row of pines, feeling slower now. Each stride grew heavier and required more effort.

I didn't have it in me to go back. Either he'd follow me, or he wouldn't. The time to establish the sort of bond that made men like Baldwin trust a man like me had long passed. If I had failed to forge that bond, I would know it now.

You cannot lead men who are unwilling to be led. You must inspire them to give you the power to do so. That power comes only from their minds, their hearts, not from discipline or devotion to army regulations. When death lurks, nothing else matters but that bond of trust, or lack thereof, between soldier and leader.

In college, I memorized a passage from Xeones as he described King Leonidas, the Spartan leader made famous by Steven Pressfield's *Gates of Fire:* "A king does not require service of those he leads but provides it to them. He serves them, not they him."

Did my men know that I served them?

Random AK rounds popped and skipped around me. Twenty meters to go. I was almost through the gauntlet.

As I staggered the final meters to cover, I burned with self-doubt. Had I just sifted myself from the inner circle? Would I end up like Captain Waverly for this decision?

I had to know. I broke stride to look over my shoulder, praying that I would see Baldwin's fullback figure charging up the hill behind me.

SIX

WELCOME TO THE FAMILY

★ ★ ★

THROUGH THE SMOKE AND SPINNING CLOUDLETS OF MOON-
dust, I saw the Illinois father of three racing toward me. Bullets scored the road around him. A stitch of machine-gun fire split
his stride and kicked up a half-dozen fountains of dirt right between his legs. He ran on, jaw set, helmet low over his forehead.

Phillip Baldwin had my back.

And so did the rest of Outlaw Platoon. Wheat and Campbell,
our medic, Doc Pantoja, Travis Roberts with his grenade launcher—
together they streamed up the hill after me, weapons high, beard-
ing the enemy and the rivers of lead pouring onto the road. Over
my shoulder, I counted ten, fifteen, twenty men dismounted. Only
the gunners and drivers remained in their rigs.

The sight shattered all self-doubt and sent bolts of pure energy
through my system. My exhaustion gone, my legs grew light. The
burn in my lungs vanished. Euphoria drove me forward. In that

moment, I knew there'd be no way we'd lose this fight. I almost pitied the enemy. The hurt was about to be laid on them like they'd never known. Outlaw Platoon was going to work.

I bounded the final meters to the nearest Afghan truck, which had been abandoned a short distance below the knoll's crest. An ANA soldier lay in the dust behind one tire, head down, weapon at his side. I passed him without a word just as Baldwin caught up to me.

"Sir, you're absolutely fucking crazy!"

I spun to face my brother, laughter growing into a rapturous victory cry.

"Let's find the marines and get the ANA outta the way."

"Roger that."

A fusillade of bullets chopped through a nearby pine tree. Branches and needles rained down on us. We looked at each other and laughed like teenagers.

"This is fucking awesome, sir! Never had anything like this last time we were here." Baldwin's eyes shone with adrenaline. No doubt they matched mine.

Down the hill, some of the men paused to open up on the enemy with their rifles. A few used the trucks as cover. To my immense pride, nobody fired from the hip. They chose their targets carefully to ensure that no stray ANA would be hit.

Travis Roberts finished the gauntlet and sprinted over to us. He was a crack grenadier. Back at Fort Drum, he had outscored the entire battalion on the M203 grenade launcher range and was quietly proud of his status as 2-87's top marksman with this weapon. I wondered if his gaming addiction had something to do with this feat. He'd honed his small-motor skills with countless hours of Halo on the Xbox 360 and SOCOM on his PlayStation 2. His room at Bermel looked like a Best Buy with all the consoles and monitors he had stuffed into it. He even had a handheld Game Boy, which he hauled around everywhere, like Pinholt carried books. Any free moment, he'd be nose down killing pixilated bad guys.

Baldwin approached Roberts and ordered, "Use your 203 to knock out those machine-gun positions over there." He pointed to the ridge on the far side of the wadi. Roberts didn't bother to reply. He just lunged to the east side of the road, settled down into a firing stance behind some cover, and searched for somebody to kill for real this time.

More men joined us. Baldwin organized them into a perimeter, making sure the east side, facing the ridge, was the strongest. The volume of fire was much heavier from that side of the road, and Baldwin recognized our need to neutralize the enemy there first.

Roberts found a target and squeezed his 203's trigger. The grenade exploded next to some trees midway up the ridge. As he reloaded, I heard him shouting, "Eat that, motherfuckers!"

"Make sure of your targets," I reminded the men. "The ANA are all over the place."

The men had it handled. I grabbed Baldwin, and together we charged to the knoll's crest in search of the marines. Beyond a couple of the Toyota pickups, we found one of their Humvees. Running to the right side, we discovered their commander, a major, slouched sideways in the passenger seat with his back resting against the center console. He silently held a radio's handset against his ear.

"Sir! We gotta move to the high ground!"

He turned vacant eyes my way. I stopped cold at his open door. "Sir, I need you to move your rigs out of the way. My trucks are trapped at the bottom of the hill!"

No response. He was the senior officer on the field. He needed to be coordinating this fight. His behavior surprised me.

"Sir? Either we get up this hill or we die."

He said nothing. His unfocused gaze almost unnerved me. Baldwin and I exchanged a glance. No words passed between us, but we both knew exactly what to do.

The major's checked out. Find his first sergeant.

The sweet sound of M4 carbines firing swelled behind us. My men laid on their triggers. M4 magazines carried thirty 5.56mm bullets and could hit targets up to 600 meters away. It was our standard-issue rifle, and it was deadly effective. The hurting time had come.

I felt a hand grip my shoulder. I spun around to see the marines' senior NCO, First Sergeant Grigsby, standing beside me.

"Sir, whaddya need?" he shouted.

"My trucks are trapped at the bottom of the hill. We need you to clear the road and get your men to the top of the hill. I'll get my trucks up here, and we can consolidate at the crest."

He nodded. "You got it, sir!"

He sped back to his Afghan soldiers, shouting and gesturing as he ran among them. A few rose and began to move toward the pickups.

Baldwin and I returned to the platoon perimeter. *Whomp!* Roberts sent another 203 round into the ridge.

On the ridge, I counted four different machine-gun positions. Two more chattered away from the backside of Gangikheyl Hill.

Those machine gunners were dug in. It would take more than Roberts and a squad's worth of rifles to knock them out. We needed a bigger punch.

"Baldwin," I called out, "where's our mortar?"

He pointed back down the road at Tony Garrett. With the 60mm mortar tube slung over one shoulder, he was sprinting up the slope through a hail of machine-gun fire as his section leader, Sergeant "Bear" Ferguson, matched him stride for stride. Garrett hailed from Atlanta, wore his ball caps sideways, and spoke with a honky gangsta affectation—our version of Eminem but more heavily armed.

The Dragunov barked. AKs rattled. Roberts triggered off another 203 grenade. At last, Garrett and Ferguson reached our perimeter. Both men were winded and bathed in sweat. The three components of the mortar weigh forty-five pounds, and the rounds are another three and a half pounds each. Bear and Garrett were the two most heavily laden men in our platoon.

"Garrett," I said, "start droppin' rounds on those machine-gun nests."

"Yew gottit, sir."

Still standing exposed in the middle of the road, he swung the mortar off his shoulder and planted it. No time for the bipod. No time for aiming stakes and optics. Instead, he licked his finger and held it up to gauge the breeze, then pointed the tube at the enemy on the ridge. Kentucky windage at its finest.

Bear dropped a round into the tube. Garrett eyeballed the nearest enemy machine-gun nest and touched off his weapon. With a hollow *thunk* the mortar round sailed high over the firefight to detonate on the ridge.

"Ya, beetches! Comin' at ya now! How ya like that shee-eet!" Garrett screamed. His gangsta was tinged with a soft southern accent, which made his voice seem ridiculously out of place in the middle of an Afghan firefight.

He and Ferguson worked flawlessly together. Reloading the mortar, Garrett made an adjustment and walked the second round closer to the nest. Alarmed by this threat, the enemy gunners shifted their fire and sprayed my mortar team. Undeterred, Ferguson and Garrett reloaded again even as bullets skipped and snapped past them.

As I moved to the right side of the road to get a better view of the enemy on the far side of the wadi, Sergeant Wheat appeared beside me. As always, a piece of hay dangled out of his mouth. I wondered if he had his folks send him straw from back home in their care packages.

"Where ya need me, sir?" he drawled.

I pointed to the right side of our perimeter. Wheat gave me a thumbs-up and headed off to find a good sniping position.

Up the road, the Afghan troops started to consolidate at the top of the knoll. Some climbed into their Toyotas; others stayed in the fight, mowing through their ammunition with long, full auto bursts from the AKs. We were getting organized amid the chaos at last.

Next play, Sean?

I NEEDED TO GET BACK ON THE HORN AND CALL THE BASE. IF WE could just get the trucks out of the low ground, we could establish contact and call in artillery and maybe even air support.

I thought of Captain Waverly and his refusal to fire back at the enemy rocket teams that had pounded Bermel a few weeks before. If he were on the other end of the radio, I had no confidence he'd clear fire for us. But he was gone now. Lieutenant Colonel Toner had seen to that. Our new company commander, Captain Jason Dye, was a big unknown to us. We didn't even know his reputation, and he was so fresh to the outfit that I had no idea how he'd respond to any request for fire support.

The first of the Toyota pickups jerked into gear and lumbered up the road. As First Sergeant Grigsby directed it into place, a second Toyota followed. His perimeter was taking shape.

I turned to tell Baldwin my next move. I noticed a bullet hole in his chest rack.

"Baldwin, are you okay?" Concern was evident in my voice.

"Never better, sir, why?"

I pointed at his chest. He reached into a bullet-scarred pouch and withdrew two spare magazines for his rifle. Both had been side-punched by a 7.62mm round.

"Looks like we both had close ones, sir," he said while nodding at my pants. Another bullet had shredded the other pant leg. My ACUs looked as though they belonged to a castaway.

ANOTHER TOYOTA CREPT UP THE HILL, CLOSELY FOLLOWED BY the marine major's Humvee. My drivers saw the progress and spontaneously began to creep forward. The enemy split their fire. Some of the hilltop marksmen focused on our Humvees. Others traded shots with the men around me. In a fight like this one, firepower and accuracy are the components of victory. We didn't yet have the power, but I knew we would be more accurate. I could feel the momentum slowly shifting.

"Baldwin, you got this?" I asked.

"Roger, sir."

I took off for Pinholt and my truck's radios. As I ran downhill, the weight of my body armor, rifle, and gear propelled me into an almost uncontrollable speed. Gravity took over; I was its passenger, and my legs barely kept up.

Just above the base of the incline, I passed Baldwin's rig. McCleod had become outright defiant and now decided to stand up in his turret, practically daring the enemy to hit him.

Mouth dry, heart pounding, exaltation ruling my heart, I crossed the last stretch of open ground to my Humvee. Pinholt touched his brake. The rig was out of the lowest stretch of ground now, and as I reached inside the passenger side door and grabbed the radio handset, I prayed we'd have better reception.

"FOB Bermel, this is Blackhawk three-six."

Captain Dye's voice swelled out of the static: "Blackhawk three-six, this is Blackhawk six, go ahead."

Dye spoke with an impossibly soft tone. I could barely hear him over all the gunfire.

"Blackhawk six, we are at the base of Gangikheyl Hill. We've been engaged by thirty-plus enemy on both sides of the road. Right now, we're moving up the hill. Main focus has been to get the ANA consolidated at the top. We'll join them there."

"Roger that, Blackhawk three-six. Gimme a call when you're in place, and I'll start slinging rounds for you."

"Thanks, six. Three-six out."

Captain Dye just passed the test.

I tossed the handset away, grabbed a bottle of water, and chugged it down. Silently, I thanked Lieutenant Colonel Toner for sending us a commander who thought of us first.

"Pinholt, I'm going back up the hill. I'll link up with you there."

"Roger, sir."

I hadn't taken a half-dozen steps when he shouted, "Sir, Lieutenant Colonel Toner's on the radio and wants to talk to you."

"You talk to him, I need to get back into the fight."

I took a few more steps up the slope before Pinholt yelled, "Sir, he doesn't wanna talk to me. I think you need to come back."

Annoyed, I rushed back to the Humvee.

"Blackhawk three-six, this is Cat six," Toner growled. "If I say I wanna talk to you, don't you put me on the horn with your radio operator. Got it?"

Chastised, I replied, "Roger, six."

"Coordinate closely with the ANA. Make absolutely certain you don't have a blue-on-blue incident. Understood?"

"Roger, that."

"You're doing a great job. Cat six out." The radio went dead.

I stared at the handset.

Note to self: next time battalion commander calls, don't palm him off on poor Pinholt.

As I left the truck again, Pinholt said, "Sir, take a radio." He tossed me a portable one.

"Thanks!"

The Dragunov cracked. I ducked and waited. Apparently, the enemy sniper had picked a new target. A surge of fury went through me.

He's shooting at one of my men.

We needed to find that guy and kill him. Snipers are significant force multipliers. One good sniper can pin down an entire company. Fortunately, this one didn't seem to be very good. So far . . .

"Hey, sir, what's happenin'?" The voice cut through the din of battle like no other.

From out of the dust and smoke billowing behind my truck, a short, wiry figure emerged. Cigarette hanging from the corner of his mouth, a can of German Bitburger near beer in one hand, freshly promoted Sergeant First Class Greg Greeson strolled serenely through the storm of shot and shell, a pair of ballistic sunglasses concealing his eyes.

I gaped at him. A burst of machine-gun fire ripped up the ground between us. A few scattered AK rounds Indy-whipped overhead. He seemed oblivious to the threat as he waddled, bowlegged toward me. Greeson always walked with his toes pointed out at forty-five-degree angles, as if he'd spent a lifetime in the saddle and felt uncomfortable with his heels on the ground.

"What's goin' on, sir?" he asked again in his Sling Blade meets Sam Elliott voice. Though he'd been in the army for more than twenty years, he hadn't lost his Arkansas twang. I was at a loss for words.

As he reached me, he unrolled a long, mirth-filled laugh. "Hey, sir, you just need to calm the fuck down!"

He chortled again, like a man watching his son play in his first Little League game. Perhaps he was fondly reminiscing about his first moments under fire as he watched me.

"What the hell are you doing?" I asked, still unable to process the spectacle that was my platoon sergeant. Greeson had just been promoted into that slot. As the senior noncommissioned officer, his main job was to handle any casualties and ensure the men had plenty of ammunition and water. He was also my second-in-command. If I went down, the platoon would be his.

He took a long pull from his can of near beer, then smiled. "Comin' to see you, sir."

Greeson had been in every shithole post the army can send a career NCO to. Before I graduated from grade school, he had already earned his first CIB while fighting with the 7th Infantry Division in Panama. His face was furrowed from decades of hard living—he drank hard and smoked three packs of cigarettes a day. He'd seen everything more than once, and his icy calm in the midst of chaos had made him a hero to the company's young privates.

"Where's the CCP?" I asked, referring to our designated casualty collection point. It was the place any wounded men would be carried to for treatment and evacuation.

Greeson looked down the column of Humvees and drawled, "Hell, sir, we're surrounded. How 'bout right fuuuckin' here?"

"Fair enough," I said.

He let out another *I remember those days* sort of cackle that got drowned out with another swig of Bitburger. When he'd first come to the platoon in April, I had asked him what he wanted to do once he retired. "Gonna be a part-time gunsmith, full-time alcoholic, sir."

A 7.62mm bullet pinged off my Humvee. I ducked.

"Don't worry 'bout nothin', sir. Yer doin' great."

He exhaled a cloud of cigarette smoke, quaffed the dregs of his near beer, and pitched the can into the dirt.

"Thanks," I managed. I went on to explain what my plan was. He listened and nodded his head. After I finished, Greeson regarded the ridge beyond the wadi as if noticing it for the first time.

"Fuckers," he muttered with all the menace of a cagey old lion about to thin out a herd of gazelles.

"I'll see you on the high ground!" I shouted as I started back up the incline.

"Go get 'em, sir!" Greeson headed off to confer with Sabo, who was moving between the trucks and shouting instructions to the gunners.

I broke into a trot. I could hear more M4s banging away from Baldwin's perimeter.

More of my soldiers streamed up the road with me. Aleksandr Nosov, our Russian M249 light machine gunner, ran past me, hefting his twenty-pound weapon as if it were a child's toy. About my own age, he was a born infantryman. Close on his heels came Sergeant Bennett Garvin, one of Baldwin's team leaders.

The incoming didn't seem as intense on this last passage through the gauntlet. Smoke and dust shrouded much of the ridge, and every few seconds a mortar round or 203 grenade pounded the enemy's fighting positions.

A moment later, I found Baldwin in the middle of the road, not far from Garrett and Bear Ferguson. The pickup we'd been using for cover in the middle of the perimeter had disappeared over the crest of the knoll.

"How's it goin' here?" I asked.

Baldwin took a swig of water, "It's all good, sir. We got things under control. Garrett 'n' Roberts are wipin' guys out."

Sergeant Campbell staggered into our perimeter, his face shining with sweat. "Mother of God!" he exclaimed, "This shit is heavy." He was carrying an assault pack full of extra 60mm mortar rounds for Garrett. Now he slipped the straps off his shoulder and uttered an indignant curse.

"Check this out, I almost got my ass shot off," he said as he held up the pack for us to see. Several 7.62mm-sized bullet holes had punctured its side.

"How the hell did those not detonate one of the mortar rounds?" Baldwin marveled.

"Crazy shit," Campbell replied. He dragged the pack over to Garrett and started unloading the rounds for him.

"Where are the ANA?" I asked Baldwin.

"Grigby's got 'em all wrangled up and squared away at the top of the hill," he replied.

Excellent. The road was clear. Our trucks could get out of the low ground.

Campbell returned to us and we had a quick leaders' meeting, our first while under fire.

"Okay, guys, let's get everyone to the top and link up with the ANA. Once we do that, we'll get some artillery support."

I looked up the road. The platoon's perimeter was about 150 meters from the crest of the knoll. I noticed that the road above us was much less exposed. Trees, rocks, and dirt berms lined either side and would provide us with ample cover as we moved.

I returned my attention to my squad leaders, "Okay, I'm pretty certain I heard a Dragunov out there. Means we have a sniper."

Wheat overheard me. He was lying prone behind a rocky outcropping. "Yes, they do, sir. I heard the Dragunov, and I'm searching for the sniper now."

"Good job. Stay on him, Wheat."

"Roger, sir."

Below us, the trucks inched up the incline. Underpowered and without a running start to gain speed, they crawled forward with engines roaring. I could see McCleod in his turret, racking the bolt of his M2 .50-caliber machine gun, his face contorted by rage. Behind him, Bray was shouting something, but his words were swallowed in the din.

"Okay," I said, "We'll move out in just a minute. The trucks can meet us at the crest."

Baldwin and Campbell nodded in unison.

"Then what?" Baldwin asked.

"We attack."

SEVEN

THE BECOMING

★ ★ ★

O KAY, LET'S MOVE TO THE TOP OF THE HILL AND SECURE A perimeter before the trucks get up there."

Baldwin and Campbell sprang into action.

"Bennett!" Baldwin shouted to his team leader, Sergeant Garvin, "Grab your guys and let's go!"

Campbell returned to his men. "Okay, first squad! Get yer asses up!"

Baldwin dashed for the knoll's crest, Garvin and the rest of his squad in trail. A few seconds later, Ferguson and Garrett went after them. Garrett ran like a jackrabbit, despite hefting the mortar tube over one shoulder again.

Campbell's men rallied to him. They waited until Baldwin reached the top of the hill before following Second Squad. Their boots kicked up miniclouds of moondust as they ran. Without our guys shooting back, I feared that the volume of enemy fire would increase. I listened for the expected uptick, but it didn't happen. They still swept the road with their machine guns, but the bursts came in longer intervals now. Maybe we had already inflicted damage on them.

Down the road, the trucks continued to rumble toward us. I stood between the two elements of the platoon, rifle in one hand, radio in the other. After taking a last look around to make sure we hadn't left anyone behind, I tacked on to the rear of Campbell's squad. When I reached the top of the knoll, I found it flattened out onto a broad plateau that would allow us to spread out and maximize our platoon's firepower. No more being bottled up on the road.

Baldwin was already emplacing his men. Garvin was shouting orders to his team. Campbell pointed out where he wanted his squad. The men scrambled off the road to find good fighting positions among the trees and rocks. Wheat, unflappable as ever, hefted his M4 and strolled through the firefight, eyeing the ground professionally in search of the best possible sniper hide.

Back home, we had trained hard for this exact moment. But all the rehearsals and drills can never prepare you for what combat *feels* like. That is battle's great trap. There is no way to psychologically prepare a man for that first clash. The literature of combat is riddled with examples of men panicking in their inaugural firefight. Some lose all reason and cannot function, curling into a protective fetal position. But a few, the hardy few, find in battle a home that has eluded them elsewhere in their lives. A man's psychological composition determines his reaction; most of the time even he won't know how the threat of death will play upon his psyche until the first round cracks by his head.

That day, as the afternoon shadows grew long, I watched my men perform everything asked of them with flawless precision. Roberts had ducked down behind some concealment and had already touched off another 203 round. Garvin moved between his team members with complete disregard for his own safety. Garrett unslung the mortar and prepared it for action. He and Bear Ferguson made an incredible team, though in the civilian world they were such different individuals that I doubt they'd have even had anything to say to each other.

Down the line, Nosov popped his bipod down, dived into the dirt behind a rock, and set his light machine gun in position. Born and raised in Murmansk, Nosov had come to the United States only a few years before. Back at Fort Drum, when I had been trying to get to know the men, I had asked him why he joined the army. I expected to hear that he'd done it to gain citizenship. Instead, he earnestly replied, "I want to go to war."

He was getting his wish now, that was for sure.

The sight of every man rising to the occasion generated a wave of pure love in me. A good leader is supposed to inspire his men. But great men inspire their leader.

Baldwin's rocket-scarred Humvee limped up the rise. McCleod stood high in the turret as usual, his face telegraphing his emotions. His pissed off meter was pegged. Holding his .50-caliber's handles, he scowled and shouted epithets at the enemy.

My machine gunners were a prideful lot. They judged themselves by their marksmanship and attention to detail. I'd learned in training that their identities were grounded in their skill with their weapons. On the range, second place was unacceptable. They were not graceful in defeat, and they competed furiously against one another.

Right now, they'd been getting the hell pounded out of them by their enemy counterparts. Instead of inspiring terror the beating evoked angry indignation in McCleod. I could see his impatience to fight back wrestling with his innate sense of discipline. It takes a special kind of man to let the enemy target him and not shoot back.

That was about to change. First Sergeant Grigsby had his entire Afghan force assembled on the hill. There would be no blue-on-blue fratricide now. Weapons free time.

I motioned to Baldwin's rig to take up a position facing the ridge. "Orient east!" I shouted to McCleod. He nodded sharply and petted the receiver of his Ma Deuce. He knew his moment was about to come.

Next in line came Pinholt, driving my Humvee. Bray was in the turret, watching me intently. His face mirrored McCleod's. I pointed to the east. We'd pit his fifty cal against the enemy gunners on the ridge.

Down the road, Chris Brown emerged from the turret of Sabo's Humvee, his owlish eyes full of conflicting fear and anger. Chris was a tremendous young man, full of life, deeply sensitive, and possessing a sharp intelligence that I had come to appreciate in our countless hours on patrol together. Usually he gunned my truck, but for this mission he had swapped with Bray.

He'd come to be almost like a younger brother to me. Right now I could see him struggling, and I wasn't sure how to help him.

HE BUCKED BACK AGAINST HIS FEAR. WHEN HE SAW BRAY AND McCleod seemingly impervious to the bullets still cracking around us, he rose a little higher in the turret. Slowly, his right hand reached forward, grasped the charging handle on his machine gun, and racked the bolt.

That's it, brother.

His rig swung to the back side of our new position, ready to deal with the threat on Gangikheyl Hill. The next Humvee rolled up with Mark Howard in the turret. I sent it to reinforce the west side.

Last in line was Greeson's Humvee with Private Erwin Echavez manning the Mark 19 automatic grenade launcher. This was our best heavy weapon, one that when unleashed could cause absolute havoc to the enemy. Already Echávez had swung the turret to the east, ready to engage the second he received the order.

A rash of machine-gun fire ripped across Greeson's Humvee. Sparks flared along its armored hide and walked right over Echavez's turret. He ducked just as three bullets punctured the Mark 19's ammunition feed tray. When he popped back up and checked his weapon, he yelled over to me, "Sir, the Mark 19's damaged. I'll have to single-shot it."

A Mark 19 fired in full auto will burn through a forty-round drum in a matter of seconds, delivering awesome quantities of explosive destruction on its target area. With ours crippled, it would function as little more than a glorified 203.

"Do what you can with it," I said.

"Roger that, sir."

Greeson's driver scooted into position. Our hilltop bristled with firepower. We were organized, and the men were brimming with rage at being on the receiving end of this fight for so long.

It was time. I ordered, "Engage all known, likely, and suspected targets! Got it? Kill these bastards!"

Outlaw Platoon was purpose-built for this moment. In one cathartic spasm, the platoon exploded in violent release. All the pent-up fury we felt burned forth into an unbridled torrent of firepower. Right then, the platoon coalesced into a single entity; I could feel it happen even as the men fired as one. I pumped my fist and moved down the line, shouting encouragement as I went.

Ferguson and Garrett got the mortar into the fight again. Garrett took aim and let fly with another round. It scored a near miss on a machine-gun team dug in on the ridge. Bear reloaded. Garrett made a slight correction and fired again.

"Holy shit!" somebody screamed as the round landed right between the enemy machine gunner and loader. Before smoke and dust obscured the scene, I saw pieces of both men blown sideways out of their fighting position.

Garrett looked up to admire his handiwork. "Yeeaaah. Slayin' yew bee-etches now!"

I shouted in victory. My men were kicking ass. I was euphoric.

A DARK FIGURE SUDDENLY APPEARED ON THE TOP OF THE RIDGE. The man moved fast and fluidly, like a wraith. He caught the attention of Bray, who swung his eighty-pound weapon toward the running figure. His thumbs twitched on the butterfly triggers that sent jets of flame spewing from the Ma Deuce's barrel. His first rounds, traveling at almost nine hundred meters a second, thrashed the ground behind the man. A nudge corrected his aim, and his next flutter on the trigger sent an inch-and-a-half-long bullet right into the man's shoulder. The velocity and power of the hit ripped his entire arm off. Blood arced over him as the impact blew him off his feet. His body disappeared over the ridgeline.

"HELL, YEAH!" somebody shouted.

It was time to call Captain Dye and deluge the enemy with our 105s. "Blackhawk six, this is Blackhawk three-six."

"Go ahead, three-six." Dye's soft voice came across crystal clear this time. My voice competed with the sound of the gunfire, but I was able to give him our latest grid coordinate and update him on our situation.

"Copy that, three-six. Am I good to start firing indirect?"

"Roger that, six."

"Copy. Stand by. We've also got gunships coming your way."

I handed the radio to my forward observer, Josiah Reuter. "Talk 'em in. Your show. Get to it, and give 'em hell."

Reuter flashed a grin and took the handset.

Above us, Bray found a target and hammered at it. "Yooo-ouuuu bet! Like that? Got ya, motherfucker! Gotcha!" His voice was consumed with fury.

I checked on the west side of our perimeter. Using the scope mounted on his machine gun, Brown took aim at something on Gangikheyl Hill. Howard did the same. When they both opened up, their machine guns acted like a thresher, devastating everything in their paths. Men, trees, boulders were shredded by the awesome power of their M240s.

They've got things well in hand. Focus on the most pressing threat—the ridge to our east.

I heard the Mark 19 chug; despite the damage to the feed tray, Echavez had managed to get his weapon working. His 40mm grenade struck the ridgeline, adding to the smoke and dust smothering the enemy positions now.

He reached forward and charged his weapon, his right arm bulging with the effort. He scanned for targets for several seconds until he discovered an enemy soldier partially concealed high in a pine tree perhaps a football field away. He snapped off a shot at him. The grenade struck the insurgent's center mass and buried itself in his flesh before detonating. One leg spun crazily out of the tree, tumbling end over end as branches and needles flew in all directions. His head and arms separated in a fan of blood; I could have sworn I heard the meaty slap as they returned to earth.

The first of the 105 shells freight trained overhead. The ground shook as they impacted on the far side of the ridge. The rate of fire increased as Reuter coached the artillerymen onto their targets. Soon their explosions intermingled, creating a continuous rumble that drowned out almost every other sound.

Echavez tried to fire again, but his Mark 19 refused to function. He tinkered with the weapon. With a quick pull on the bolt handle, he jacked another shell into the chamber manually. The barrel spat a cone of fire, and another grenade pounded the ridge.

Brown unleashed on another target. A puff of red erupted from the man he'd spotted, and down he went in a heap.

"Fuck those guys! They don't have shit on us!" McCleod screamed. He blasted away with another devastating volley. All along the line, the men screamed and taunted in adrenaline-fueled release.

Brown shouted over to me, "Sir, I see 'em running off the hill to the south!"

Bray confirmed it on the east side too: "They're trying to break contact."

We were driving them away. Now was the time to deliver the coup de grâce.

Captain Dye called over the radio to let me know that the base's quick reaction force, a platoon of heavily armed trucks that Lieutenant Colonel Toner had attached to us from Delta Company, would be arriving soon from the north. The Delta element came from our battalion's heavy-weapons company. Originally designed to be an antitank element, these platoons were just large enough to crew their weapons and vehicles. Whereas we rolled with thirty to forty men on each patrol, Delta Company's platoons had fewer than twenty. They wouldn't be able to kick dismounts out to us, but their Mark 19s and .50-calibers would be a welcome addition. I told Greeson to handle that linkup and get them into position to plus up our perimeter.

For us to do this right and finish the enemy off, I'd need the ANA's help. But as a platoon leader, it wasn't my job to maneuver a company's worth of troops. Yet the marine major hadn't left his Humvee. By rank, he should have been coordinating the fight, but he had not even contacted me over the radio. Instead, he'd left First Sergeant Grigsby alone to lead the Afghan troops.

There's nobody else to do it. Get it done.

There was no time for niceties; we needed to act quickly. I found First Sergeant Grigsby and told him what I wanted. He nodded enthusiastically before going off to round up his men.

Captain Dye's voice came through my handheld radio. "Three-six, this is six. Copy?"

"Go ahead, six."

"We just picked up a radio intercept that they're withdrawing to the south."

The Prophet spooks must have heard some enemy radio transmissions. Their tidbit matched with what my gunners were seeing.

"They're carrying ten dead and have at least another five wounded with them."

"Copy that, six."

We had to get after them, now.

On the east side of the perimeter, I found Baldwin and Campbell.

"Baldwin, grab your squad. Campbell, give me a fire team. We're gonna counterattack. Grigsby and the ANA are going to lead out," I pointed to a mud-walled house on the ridge beyond the wadi. It was the only dwelling for miles around, and it looked like a likely place for the enemy to be. "They'll clear that building while we take the top of the ridge."

Baldwin broke into a smile. He looked almost rapturous, and I remembered how a few weeks back, he'd asked Lieutenant Colonel Toner, "Sir, when the hell are we gonna get to kill bad guys?"

Toner loved that sort of question. "Sergeant Baldwin, don't you worry, I have a feeling it'll be real soon."

Baldwin had not joined the army for college money. He hadn't joined because he couldn't find a job. He'd joined to kill the sons of bitches responsible for 9/11. This was his moment, and it made him positively glow.

Over the thunder of artillery volleys, I heard the Apache gunships closing in on us. I keyed my radio and told Reuter, "Have one of the Apaches sweep south to cut off their exfil route. I want the other one on our shoulder, covering us as we move. Got it?"

"Roger, sir."

Grigsby and the ANA burst out of the perimeter and swept down into the wadi. Here it flattened out into more of a depression than the steep-banked terrain obstacle we had faced back on the low ground. They negotiated the slope with ease as some of the Afghan troops fired from the hip while they ran.

I turned to Baldwin and Campbell. "Okay, follow me."

Our gunners poured the lead out, covering our movement with a barrage of fire. Baldwin and Campbell motioned to their men. As one, we rose and streamed off our hilltop straight for the enemy's positions, our weapons up, ready to engage should any insurgents appear before us.

The Afghans reached the house. They stacked up next to the door, then kicked it in on First Sergeant Grigsby's orders. As their entry squad rushed inside, our section from Outlaw Platoon ran past them and assaulted the ridge. Behind us, Sabo had his gunners shift fire so they didn't accidentally hit us. The Apache buzzed overhead, its crew searching for any threat. Every part of the attack functioned with seamless precision.

We reached the top of the ridge without receiving a single bullet. The enemy had melted away. The men spread out and took up fighting positions. When it became clear that the enemy would not contest us, Baldwin I went back down to the house along with Reuter and Wheat.

Until the enemy showed up, it appeared, the dwelling had been abandoned for a long time. Neglected walls and dust and dirt everywhere attested to its disuse. Baldwin peered into one room and gestured for me to join him. I stuck my head into the doorway and saw several stretchers, blood still pooled on them, lined up on the floor. Crimson-stained khaki man jams lay scattered in heaps throughout the room.

"Check this out," Wheat said, looking at a pile of discarded prescription bottles issued by a Pakistani hospital. Soiled pressure dressings, torn packages for other medical supplies, and syringes completed the scene. This was their casualty collection point. They were sophisticated enough to designate one. That took training and a lot of advance planning.

Outside, the firing died down. The artillery barrage lifted. The Apaches went off in search of the enemy. Soon the battlefield, still shrouded in smoke and dust, fell silent. By the time we had all the components in place for our counterattack, the enemy had simply vanished.

The adrenaline in my body drained away. The excitement and high I'd felt evaporated, replaced by sudden exhaustion. The men went through the same change. They grew quiet, and their faces reflected their fatigue. I checked my watch and was stunned to see that it was almost dinner hour. We'd been in the fight all afternoon.

There was no way we could pursue the ambush force. It would be dark soon. We needed ammunition, and my men were smoked. Still, I hated to give the enemy a free pass. Perhaps we could return tomorrow and hunt them down.

In the meantime, we had one final task waiting for us. Along with the ANA, our assault force walked the ridge to search and clear the enemy's fighting positions.

At the nearest insurgent machine-gun nest, we found thousands of spent shell casings piled around their dugout. Inside were discarded snack wrappers, a few empty water bottles. Blood splattered the flattened grass. At the next position, we discovered a red-brown trail leading up over the ridge, indicative of a casualty who had been dragged off by his comrades. Our search uncovered several more. We'd hurt them. Badly.

The nest hit by Garrett's mortar still smoldered from the round's impact. Ragged bits of flesh and bone coated the ground on either side. I didn't see anything larger than part of a boot, a fragment of the machine gunner's foot still inside. Figure at least twelve dead, not the ten reported by the Prophet spooks. There wasn't enough left of those guys for the enemy to carry off.

At the top of the ridge, we located the spot where the RPG teams had been emplaced. Chewing gum wrappers littered the area, and in their haste to escape our firepower, the enemy had left behind their reloads and several launchers. We policed them up and brought them back to our hilltop perimeter.

As we worked, I noticed Yusef moving between the U.S. and Afghan elements. He'd come out with Delta Platoon and had had the stones to dismount. Bruce Lee had never emerged from his Humvee. I made a mental note of that. In the future, I'd want Yusef out with our platoon as much as possible. Short of Abdul, Yusef was the best we had.

Miraculously, only one Afghan soldier had been slightly wounded in the fight. Greeson ordered that he be carried to his Humvee, where he'd established a new casualty collection point. I went over to check on him and saw that our medic, Doc Pantoja, had already bandaged the young soldier. He'd taking a grazing shot to the side of his abdomen. Nothing serious. It amazed me that, given all the small-arms fire we had faced that day, this was all the enemy had been able to achieve.

Long after dusk, we began the slow drive back to Bermel. We needed to repair or swap out our battered vehicles. Somehow, despite all the rockets and bullets we had taken, the vehicles still functioned, but we couldn't continue our six-day patrol without a pit stop at the FOB.

As we drove, I touched my St. Christopher medal, recalling the day I learned my grandfather had died. I got the news just before we were supposed to deploy to Afghanistan, and I had to drive all night to get back to Pennsylvania.

After the memorial, my grandmother had come to me and said,

"Sean, your grandfather let himself go. He said this way he would be able to watch over you while you are in Afghanistan."

She had reached for my hands. In hers she held his St. Christopher medal. My grandpap had worn it every day since she had given it to him on Christmas Day of 1949. "Take this. It will keep you safe."

I should have died today. Perhaps it really had kept me safe.

We rolled through the gate sometime before midnight, our bullet-scarred trucks garnering lots of attention from the guards. Everyone back at base had heard about our fight, and the rest of the men from our platoon had turned out to watch our return.

At our parking area, we dismounted amid a boisterous reception. The men bear-hugged and high-fived as they recounted moments in the fight. Marcel Rowley, our platoon's Southern California skate punk, limped over to me. He'd been stung by a poisonous scorpion a few days earlier and was still recovering from the wound.

"Wow," he said as he greeted me. "Look at you, sir, all victorious."

We shook hands and slapped shoulders. "Wish I could've been out there with you, sir."

"You heal up, Rowley. You'll be out with us soon."

Under his excitement, I could see he was hurting. And it wasn't because of the scorpion sting.

Before I could offer anything else, Cole bounded over and raised his hand for a high five. We smacked palms as he said, "Way to go, sir! Way to go!"

"The men did great today," I replied.

Cole had just arrived at Bermel. Prior to our departure from Fort Drum, Lieutenant Colonel Toner had ordered all men whose wives or girlfriends were in the late stages of pregnancy to stay home so they could be present for the birth of their children. Cole's young wife had been due in January, so he had remained behind to be with her. Watching us depart was a crushing blow to Cole. He was all heart.

"You guys kicked ass today!" he said. Then, with a mix of guilt and shame in his voice, he added, "I'm sorry I'm not out there with you yet, sir. This is killing me."

I gave Cole a man hug. He had come to Bermel overweight and out of shape. Caring for a newborn will do that to a person. First Sergeant Christopher had told him that he would have to drop twenty pounds before he could leave the wire. Since then, Cole had been hitting the gym three times a day so he could get out there with us.

"Cole, listen to me," I said to him. "You are a member of this platoon no matter what. Got it?"

Behind his jovial smile, I could see in his eyes that he did not feel that way. His weight had separated him from the rest of the platoon, and that was hard for him to take.

"Yes, sir. I'm losing the weight. I'm working hard. I'll be out there as soon as I can."

"I don't doubt that for a minute, Cole."

He started off to talk to other members of the platoon. As he left, I asked him, "Hey, how's your son doing?"

"Outstanding, sir. He's something else. I'm glad I was there for him." He left unsaid, "Now I need to be there for my brothers here."

Around me, the spontaneous celebrations ebbed as my sergeants got the men to work on the vehicles. They were going to need a lot of attention before they could roll out again; in the meantime, I needed to report to Captain Dye.

I walked over to the tactical operations center, where First Sergeant Christopher greeted me with a wry smile on his face. "Lieutenant, your voice sounded a little anxious over the radio."

My uniform was still drenched with sweat. My hair looked as though I'd just walked out of the shower. A flare of anger welled in me before I realized he was teasing.

"Well, First Sergeant, I was getting shot at!"

"Keep it calm, Lieutenant. Keep it calm," he replied, laughing.

Captain Dye came over and asked for a full report of the engagement. It took about thirty minutes to walk through everything that had happened. By the time I finished, my stomach was growling. I hadn't eaten since breakfast. At last Captain Dye let me go, and I headed off to grab a late dinner. Everyone else on the base had eaten already, but First Sergeant Christopher had made sure that the cooks stayed put to feed Outlaw Platoon when we got back. It was a kind and appreciated gesture, the mark of a great first sergeant.

When I walked into the chow hall, my platoon was huddled together, talking excitedly. When they saw me enter, the chatter stopped. I sensed trouble in the silence.

Baldwin rose from his table, where all my squad leaders had congregated. Staff Sergeant Waites, who had not been out with us, was missing. I ran through our homecoming and realized that he hadn't been there to greet us either.

Before I could think that absence through, Baldwin strode across the chow hall toward me. His jaw was set. All eyes were on us. Not a word was spoken, which made me fear that the men had been talking about me before I came in.

Baldwin stood in front of me, and for a second I couldn't meet his eyes. I felt his hand slam down on my shoulder. "Sir," he said loud enough for everyone in the chow hall to hear, "I just wanted to tell you that you did a great fucking job out there today."

The entire platoon erupted in cheers.

Baldwin escorted me to the squad leaders' table. Greeson, already with two empty cans of near beer next to his tray, echoed Baldwin and grunted, "Yeah, sir. Good job."

There is no finer feeling for a young lieutenant than to receive such praise from his sergeants. Once again, a surge of love went through me. These men were family now, not just brother warriors. Family.

Sabo regarded me, head cocked.

"What?" I asked.

He didn't say anything at first, just shoveled a forkful of food into his mouth.

He returned his attention to me. "Yeah, you did all right, I guess. Just don't get cocky."

Laughter never felt so good. And in that moment, I knew the highest high of them all: victory in combat.

But later that night, as I lay in bed, unable to sleep despite my exhaustion, I felt the flip side of that victory.

Bray's fifty thundered. A man's arm was torn from his body.

I reveled in that moment.

The mortared machine-gun nest was a charnel site. Men blown apart leave a vile, stinking mess. Ruined bowels, the copper scent of blood. Bits and pieces. Nothing more. Defiled by firepower.

I had watched Garrett score that hit and felt enraptured. Victory was evident in every kill. And none of my men had been hit. An infantry leader could not ask for anything more.

But what about the man you are?

I am a warrior.

Where is the human side?

Ugly thoughts boiled within me. Unformed, terrifying, they swirled around in my head as if my mind had tumbled across some truth my subconscious could not face.

Today I watched a man get blown to pieces.

I did what I had to do as a soldier to win a desperate battle.

Yes, but about the man you wanted to be? How did you serve him today?

I tried to drive the thought from my mind.

Can Sean the human coexist with Sean the combat leader?

Today we had felt the indescribable rush created by bloodlust, survival, and victory. It had bonded my platoon in ways I couldn't quite grasp. Now, as I tossed in my bed, I wondered how we could ever return to our former selves after what this fight had done to us.

We were becoming—exactly what I didn't yet know, but just sensing the permanence of the transformation inspired more fear than anything else I'd faced that day.

Restless, I rose from bed and stepped into the black Afghan night. I had never felt farther from home than at that moment.

EIGHT

BRING OUT YOUR DEAD

★ ★ ★

May 8, 2006
FOB Bermel

THE OFF-KEY NOTES OF AN R-AND-B SONG WOKE ME FROM restive sleep. The sun had yet to reappear, and a check of my watch revealed that it was not yet 0430.

The singing grew louder. Delta's platoon sergeant was billeted in the room next to mine. His bunk and mine were separated by only a sheet of half-inch plywood. Recently, he'd taken to slipping on headphones and bellowing along to his music, a source of enduring frustration for me, especially since he rarely seemed to patrol with his men and kept odd hours. As far as I could tell, he spent most of his days hopping flights back and forth to Bagram, which made no sense to any of us. But since he belonged to Delta, his chain of command was at a different base, so he openly blew everyone here off—including First Sergeant Christopher.

He let loose with the chorus to an R. Kelly tune. He possessed the creepiest falsetto voice I'd ever heard. It grated on my ears until I wanted to punch him through the wall.

It wasn't worth it to try to go back to sleep. I had to be up soon anyway, so I climbed out of bed and got dressed. I heard Lieutenant Taylor stirring, and I wandered over to his room. Even though we were neighbors, the two of us had had precious little time to talk in recent weeks due to the demands of our jobs. In half whispers, we caught up. Dave was scheduled to head back home on leave in a few days, but he was going back to a very sad situation. His dad had fallen ill, and Dave had just learned that he was getting worse. He and his father were very close—as close as my own dad and me. We spoke at length about his dad's condition, and by the time the conversation was over, I felt as close to Dave as I ever had.

"Thanks for listening," he said to me. "I know how you and your dad are. Makes it easy to talk about all this with you."

"Anytime, man. Anytime."

I left his room, worried about my friend. I found it hard enough to lead men in battle while totally focused. I didn't envy Dave having to do it while worrying about his dad's medical condition. I was glad he'd get a chance to get home and see the situation firsthand.

Hours later in the tactical operations center, I met up with Captain Dye, who briefed me on the day's mission. Our prophet spooks had spent the night listening to the enemy's radio chatter. Going off the information they had gleaned, Captain Dye pointed to a grid behind Rakhah Ridge just a few kilometers west of the border. "I want you to take your platoon out there and see if you can find 'em," he explained. "Leave at first light."

"Roger, sir."

I headed out to grab a bite before briefing my squad leaders. Yesterday the enemy had brought the fight to us. They'd caught us by surprise, and they'd given us hell until we'd gotten out of the low ground. Today we were going to carry the fight to them. I loved the aggressiveness of the mission.

Stepping into the chow hall, I spotted Pinholt standing by a rack of single-serving breakfast cereal cups. He was proudly holding a cup of Cocoa Krispies. The kitchen crew rationed them out so that only one was put out for our consumption every morning. Pinholt knew how much I loved them and made a point of competing for them with me. At times, he'd get up before anyone else in the platoon just to score my favorite cereal.

"Good morning, sir."

"Pinholt! Dammit, not again!"

Given his intellectual qualities, it was easy to forget that he was all of nineteen. In a different world back home, he probably would've been goofing on his fraternity brothers at some university in Texas.

I grabbed a cup of corn flakes. "At least these are healthy."

Pinholt waved the Cocoa Krispies in front of me. "Oh, but sir, these are so full of chocolate goodness."

"Bastard," I muttered, trying to look pissed.

"Maybe tomorrow, sir, maybe tomorrow."

"Whatcha reading?" I asked as I poured a cup of coffee.

"*Atlas Shrugged*. Ayn Rand," he replied.

"Haven't you been reading that since Fort Drum?"

He shrugged. "Beats *Maxim*."

"Hey, want some coffee?" I asked.

"Sir, you know I don't drink coffee."

"Yeah, well, I figure I couldn't convince you to have a few beers back in Watertown, I gotta find some way to corrupt you."

"Not gonna happen, sir."

I grabbed some sugar and turned to find a table. On the other end of the chow hall, Yusef sat shooting the breeze with some of

Second Platoon's men. He was always asking us to define words and sayings. He loved jokes, the raunchier, the better. He preferred to hang out with our troops, something that unsettled me at times because of the familiarity it bred. That level of closeness could become an operational security issue, and I made a mental note to talk to the men about it.

As I walked past him, Yusef greeted me with all the effusive warmth of a used-car salesman. "Commander Sean, I get an AK-47 today?" he asked.

"No," I said.

"But Abdul carried AK," he said.

"No."

"But how will I defend myself? Besides, I'm senior 'terp now. I should carry AK."

"Sorry, Yusef. Besides, it's not my call anyways. Talk to Captain Dye."

He smiled ruefully and returned his attention to the Second Platoon troops at his table. I heard him ask, "So tell me, what is 'douche bag' mean?"

I walked along the row of tables and found Emerick busily sketching something on his pad. We were going to paint his skull design and stylized words on our Humvees as soon as we finished this patrol cycle.

"Whatcha working on, Emerick?" I asked.

He flashed a puckish grin and held his sketch pad up. With loving detail, he'd drawn two demons having sex.

"That's an interesting new position." I wondered if he had used the Kama Sutra as a reference.

"I'm going to add a few more," he said.

"Demon orgy, eh?"

"The finest kind, sir."

I sat down. Pinholt picked a place next to me. Soon Sabo, Baldwin, and Campbell joined us. Greeson, his tray stacked with near beers and scrambled eggs, slid into a spot across from me.

"What's the word today, sir?"

"We'll brief in fifteen," I said, "but we're going after 'em."

Baldwin lit up, "Right on."

"Sir," Sabo said seriously, "if we catch up to them, can you do us all a favor?"

"What?"

"Kill 'em or capture 'em, fine with me. Just whatever you do, don't show 'em your sack again."

I went beet red. "Did you really just go there?"

"Yeah, I did, sir."

"Again?"

"Hey, sir," Greeson chimed in, "if we didn't love ya, we'd ignore ya."

"Well, that's a comfort."

"When they make a movie about us someday, I can't wait to see that scene," Pinholt said.

"It'll have to be a porno," Sabo noted.

I shook my head and covered my eyes with one hand. I had no defense. I'd been taking this shit for weeks after I'd put in a less-than-stellar performance on our first attempt at reaching out to one of the local villages.

We had rolled into town in our Humvees, all set to meet with the elders to assess their community's needs and address any complaints. We'd just completed our cultural sensitivity training, and I had nervously focused on the key lessons from that class. Take your boots off. Don't maintain eye contact too long. Never show them the soles of your feet. Don't ever use your left hand for anything.

The village elders had gathered for a shura, the Afghan version of a city council meeting. They had greeted us cautiously. Accustomed to seeing units come and go, they had learned that every

U.S. outfit would treat them differently. So they were taking a wait-and-see attitude with us.

After I took off my helmet, I tried to find a way to get seated without showing the soles of my feet to anyone. As I did, I managed to tear my crotch seam wide open. We infantrymen never wore underwear—it chafed us raw and sometimes caused infections. I heard the seam split, felt the sudden rush of cold air where there shouldn't be, and noted the studious nonsmiles the village elders had planted on their faces. Most of them tried to look away but kept casting sideways glances at me and my exposed parts.

Baldwin had been standing next to me. "Did that just happen?" he asked incredulously.

"Talk to them, Baldwin! I gotta cover up."

"What the hell do you want me to say to them?" he asked.

Everyone had been sitting cross-legged. I couldn't pull that off anymore, and I was frantically trying to figure out a way to conceal myself.

"I don't care. Anything!"

One of the elders broke his facade. I saw him cover his mouth as he smiled. Two more exchanged glances. Abdul was our 'terp that day. He kept his eyes fixed on the floor and tried hard not to snicker.

I sat on my knees and covered my thighs with my body armor. As unobtrusively as I could, I scooted back against the nearest wall. One of the elders leaned over and took a sideways gander at me. He looked back at one of his pals, and they both smirked.

After the meeting, Baldwin came up to me, his face deadly serious. I expected him to ask me something about what the elders had discussed. I had no idea what had gone on. I'd spent the entire time petrified that I was still exposed.

"Sir," Baldwin called to me, "you really have a unique way of establishing rapport with the locals."

"Thanks."

Straight-faced, he added, "Yeah, not many people have the balls to pull that off."

Now, as I sat in there in the chow hall, I realized I had a long way to go yet before I would live that episode down. Campbell polished off the last of his eggs, wiped his mouth, and decided to join in on the fun. A broad, shit-eating grin striped his face as he leaned forward to ask, "Sir, you gotta tell me how it felt when the village elders checked out your junk?"

"I don't know, Corky, you tell me. You're the one who's used to showing your balls to other dudes!"

He stared at me, surprised that I had used the nickname his fellow squad leaders had given him. His brain searched for a pithy comeback. He gave up, scrunched his brow and fired back, "Shut the fuck up, sir!"

I loved how he added "sir" at the end of that. Four months ago, we could never have shared an exchange like this one. He was my enigma, a hard man to get to know. Initially, he'd been an almost fanatical hard-ass on his men, but he'd eased up as they accepted him. I'm not sure that had ever happened to him before, and their loyalty surprised him. He'd responded in kind. I couldn't crack his solid-steel defenses. I could tell that the man behind them was significant, but he cut me off every time I tried to get through to him. Then, just before we left Fort Drum, his wife gave birth to a baby girl. I visited them in the hospital, held his daughter, and spent time with his young family. That broke the wall down. Ever since then, we'd been open to each other, and we'd grown close.

These moments in the chow hall gave me a chance to take the platoon's pulse, for us to decompress and just be ourselves. This morning, despite lack of sleep and knowing we were about to launch our own offensive to catch and kill the remaining enemy ambush force, the men exuded happy confidence. No doubt the lingering effects of our first victory had a lot to do with the mood around the table.

An hour later, I took five trucks and thirty men out the main gate. Baldwin led the way. We looped behind Rakhah Ridge and plunged into the sawtooth ridges just west of the international frontier. The road grew treacherous as it wound around towering mountains. At times it became so narrow that we would have had a hard time dismounting had we been attacked. Sheer cliffs ran straight up on one side. Dizzying drops into vast canyons greeted us on the other side. We crept along, everyone vigilant for the enemy.

Five kilometers from the border, one of our gunners spotted movement on a mountaintop about a thousand meters away from our column. Through my binoculars, I could make out a group of men, all with rifles slung over their shoulders, loading long tubes into the back of a flatbed truck. A few of them peeled off from the crowd and walked over to a dark patch of the mountainside a short distance away.

Dark patch, hell. That's a cave.

Several men ducked inside the cave, grabbed more long tubes, and began walking back to the truck. Given that we were a kilometer away, it took some study and patience to recognize the tubes were actually 107mm rockets.

"Greeson, these are the guys that have been barraging the FOB. Probably the survivors of yesterday's fight, too."

"Roger that, sir. Let's pay 'em back."

I called Captain Dye and requested a fire mission. If we could smother that mountaintop with 105 shells in the next few minutes, we could kill the entire rocket team and destroy their stash of reloads.

We waited. Every second seemed like a wasted opportunity. My impatience grew until I could hardly sit still.

Come on, Dye. You had our back yesterday. What's the holdup?

I checked my watch. Five minutes had ticked off. On the mountaintop, the enemy team returned to the cave and carried another batch of rockets to their truck. The stack of 107s on the bed was growing high. The cave must serve as a resupply point. Given the amount of ordnance they were taking from it, they were either clearing it out or planning a major bombardment of FOB Bermel.

The radio crackled. Finally. "Blackhawk three-six, stand by for Mountain six."

Pinholt and I stared at each other in surprise. "Did he just say Mountain six?" I asked.

"That's what I heard," Pinholt confirmed.

Mountain six was the commanding general of the 10th Mountain Division. Why would he want to talk to me, probably his most junior officer?

"Blackhawk three-six, this is Mountain six."

A lump clogged my throat. This was like a cubicle dweller at Microsoft getting a call from Bill Gates.

"This is Blackhawk three-six. Go ahead, Mountain six."

"We've got an air strike coming in. After the bird hits your target, I want you to get up there. Clear the area. If you find anyone alive, take them prisoner. Be careful. Mountain six out."

Apparently we had stumbled across something important. I acknowledged the order and then radioed my trucks that we had an air strike inbound.

A pair of A-10 Warthogs sped off the runway at Bagram, where they'd been sitting at alert status for just such a call. Throttles open, engines thundering, they raced east. The lead pilot's voice came over the radio as they closed in on the target area, and I was mildly surprised to hear a woman's voice. I didn't know there were any female A-10 pilots. My forward observer coached her in the final distance until she called weapons free.

Three five-hundred-pound bombs fell out of the sky at five-minute intervals. Each one scored a direct hit. The men, the truck, and the cave vanished in a storm of smoke, spewing dirt and rock down the mountainside.

"Baldwin, let's go!" I ordered. My column surged forward. According to our map, the road that led to the top of the mountain met ours at an intersection on the east-side slope. We had a couple of kilometers to cover before we could reach that intersection. It was important for us to get to the blast site as soon as possible to ensure that any survivors had no time to escape.

"Three-six, this is Blackhawk six. Enemy is now fleeing east for the border carrying their wounded."

"Roger that, six."

"Three clicks [kilometers] out."

I told Baldwin to pick up the pace.

"They've loaded their wounded into a truck," Captain Dye reported.

They must have had another prepositioned down the mountain; no way had the one we saw survived the bombing.

In front of us, the mountaintop boiled smoke into the crystal blue sky. It looked like a volcano ready to erupt and gave the scene a prehistoric quality.

"Come on, Baldwin. Faster," I urged.

"Going as fast as we can, three-six."

I looked at our dash. We were barely doing twenty-five, but even that seemed extraordinarily dangerous given the road.

"Blackhawk three-six, this is Blackhawk six, enemy is now two clicks from you."

We were closing the distance. We might win the race after all and run them down before they reached their Pakistani sanctuary.

The road steepened, and we negotiated a series of switchback turns that forced us to bleed off some speed.

"Three-six, this is six. One and a half now."

"Roger."

We rounded another bend. The road seemed suspended alongside a rock cliff hundreds of feet above a valley floor. I looked down and saw the edge of the road only a few feet from my door. If Pinholt sneezed, we'd be toast.

Baldwin disappeared around the bend.

"Sir, we have a problem," he radioed.

"What's the matter?"

We motored around the turn. Before Baldwin could answer, I saw a civilian flatbed truck obstructing the way forward. It had been parked at an angle so as to serve as a roadblock.

"What now, sir?" Baldwin asked.

I thought it over. We could try to hot-wire it and move it. That was terribly risky, though. The enemy could have booby-trapped it, and I would not lose a man that way.

"Hit it with your fifty," I ordered.

McLeod racked his machine gun and poured a long burst into the vehicle. Windows shattered, one fender spun away, shredded by the heavy bullets. No explosion.

The clock was ticking. We needed to get on with it. Still, I wanted to be sure we'd detonated any potential booby traps before approaching the truck.

"Hit it with the 203."

Roberts dismounted and sent a grenade directly into the truck. The explosion blew the tires out and set the rig on fire. But it did not trigger a secondary blast. Convinced it was safe, we moved forward and pushed the vehicle out of our way.

"Let's go!"

But it was too late. The roadblock had given them just enough time to scamper back across the border. Losing the race didn't sit well with any of us.

A few minutes later, we reached the intersection and drove to the top of the mountain. As I dismounted, I was astonished by the view. Our entire area of operations, including FOB Bermel on the other side of Rakhah Ridge, could be seen from this vantage point. Short of having eyes in the sky, this was the best observation point I'd seen in country.

The enemy had turned it into a forward base. Though the bombs had collapsed the cave's entrance, we discovered the remains of an enemy camp a short distance away. Torn tents and teepeelike lean-to structures dotted a stretch of flat ground that had been concealed by a grove of conifer trees. The pine trees were now broken like matchsticks, their trunks burnt, needles blown from shattered branches. They looked like skeletons set against the azure backdrop of the midday sky.

Here and there we found scraps of bloody clothing, all that was left of an insurgent after the air strike had caught him in the open.

We searched the camp and found a few personal stashes with Afghan and Pakistani passports. Baldwin brought me a photo he'd discovered. "Check this out, sir."

The picture showed a grinning fighter holding an AK-47. Two smiling children flanked him. They didn't look like Afghans.

"What do you think, Baldwin? Arabs?"

"Yeah. This was a foreign fighter camp."

Next to a couple of charred tree trunks, the men found a cache of 107mm rockets. Crates of ammunition, a few scattered AKs, and provisions completed the scene.

At the cave entrance, we found the remains of the flatbed truck we'd seen. When the bombs struck, a landslide of rocks and dirt had swept over the area. Now the remains of the rig lay half buried; its load of rockets in the bed looked to have detonated in a secondary explosion.

Then stench hit us. Offal. Blood. The reek of humans defiled by firepower.

The men began to try to dig out the cave entrance. As they dug, they unearthed pieces of the men killed in the attack. I told them to stop. The gruesome work would not do any good, anyway. The entrance was under tons of dirt and rock and would take hours to uncover again.

I noticed a boulder that had plummeted down from the mountain's peak, propelled by the triple bomb blasts. I went to investigate. It had landed on an enemy fighter. His left side lay crushed beneath it. His right side was still exposed, and I noticed that he was naked. That was not an uncommon discovery; a bomb's concussion wave can blow clothing right off a person in its blast radius.

The sight prompted an idea. We Americans pride ourselves in never leaving a comrade behind. Soldiers will risk their lives to recover the body of a fallen brother. After some of the Rangers killed in the Bloody Sunday firefight in Somali back in 1993 were dragged through the streets of Mogadishu by the enemy, a determination to ensure that none of our men suffered such defilement again became ingrained in the army's culture. Since 9/11, it had been tested time after time. The enemy would not get our fallen.

In this one respect, our enemy shared our values, if for different motivations. Muslims believe that the dead have to be buried within twenty-four hours, lest they lose their opportunity to enter Paradise. That was why they carried their dead out with them as they escaped from us the day before. This was why, after years of fighting in Afghanistan, it was rare to see dead lying exposed at any time other than the immediate aftermath of a fight.

I looked at the corpse.

If that was Baldwin, would I be willing to risk my life to come back and get him?

Yes.

Maybe we could exploit that. Maybe the bodies here could be bait.

We cleared the site and set up a platoon perimeter on a neighboring hilltop that afforded a prime view of the enemy base. Captain Dye came out to join us with the Delta Platoon, and we settled down to wait.

At dusk, the enemy telegraphed their intentions. Radio chatter increased, and the Prophet spooks reported that they had crossed the border into Afghanistan again. Dye ordered our 105s to open up. Scores of rounds pummeled the mountaintop's approach. The enemy frequency went silent.

A few hours later, they tried again. The 105s split the darkness, their huge explosions igniting the night sky with red-orange flashes like hellish lightning. The ground shook. It began to rain. A Predator drone buzzed overhead, sending back real time imagery of the target area for the men at the base. I sat in a shallow foxhole with Captain Dye and watched the fireworks.

"This is what it's all about," he whispered.

"What, sir?"

"Being in the infantry. This is what it's all about."

"It is," I managed, thinking back to hockey games and history classes, moments with my grandfather, dinners with my family. Here on the other side of the planet, the rain chilled us to the bone. We shivered under our ponchos and didn't say another word.

I thought of the photograph Baldwin had found. Those kids, were they the soldier's sons? I hadn't even thought of that when I'd first looked at it. I'd just eyed the image with a professional eye, trying to glean some useful intelligence from it. Now I wondered if their father was out there in the rain, trying his honorable best to recover his comrade's corpse.

Or maybe he was our bait.

The shelling continued, and the night seemed without end.

NINE

THE MORAL HIGH GROUND

★ ★ ★

I N THE DAYS FOLLOWING OUR DESTRUCTION OF THE ENEMY'S cave network, a series of Taliban-led offensives conspired to change the focus of our operations. In southern Afghanistan, coalition forces virtually lost control of Kandahar and Helmand Provinces, forcing the army and marines to counterattack to regain the lost territories. With the U.S. military heavily committed in Iraq, the only way to reinforce our units around Kandahar was to strip troops from other sections of Afghanistan. Our battalion bore the burden of that sudden redeployment. By mid-May, Lieutenant Colonel Toner possessed little more than a company's worth of combat troops to patrol a section of the border region the size of Rhode Island. My own platoon gave up a four-man fire team to augment our troops who were sent south. Right when I needed them most, I lost some of my most stalwart men, including Aleksandr Nosov, Erwin Echavez, and Khanh Nguyen. Short and built like a bulldog,

Khanh was a quiet, dedicated soldier whose father had served in the South Vietnamese Army.

To compensate for the lack of combat power left to us, Lieutenant Colonel Toner ratcheted up our operational tempo until it pushed our remaining men to the breaking point. We patrolled nonstop, returning to the base only to refuel, rearm, and grab more supplies. Days off became distant memories as we tried to mask our numerical weakness with a constant presence out in the neighborhood.

Even with this effort, there was no way we could continue to support all the operations we'd undertaken earlier in the spring. The Bandar checkpoint and Major Ghul's police battalion dropped to the bottom of our priority list. They would have to fend for themselves while we took care of business closer to FOB Bermel.

The frantic pace wore us out and degraded morale, but it did serve to get us intimately familiar with our battlefield. My platoon walked every hill, mesa, and ridge for fifty miles in all directions around Bermel. We drove the wadis, discovered goat tracks that could handle our Humvees, and used them as shortcuts to get around potential roadside bombs. We documented every trail, hamlet, qalat, and compound until we had rewritten our army-issued maps to reflect the changes years of warfare had wrought on the landscape.

Signs of the enemy abounded. Hidden in swales or within groves of pines, we found more teepeelike shelters, which we searched before destroying. In other places, the enemy had prepared fighting positions that overlooked roads our company frequented. Usually they consisted of shallow pits rimmed with rocks stacked like sandbags. We filled them in with our boots or entrenching tools, though we knew the enemy could just dig new ones. But I would be damned before I'd give the insurgents a free pass at anything.

In several places, we discovered more sophisticated fieldworks, including covered dugouts so masterfully camouflaged that they were undetectable at anything but point-blank range. To thwart our thermal imaging systems, each dugout was roofed with logs buried under three feet of dirt and pine needles. Even a passing AH-64 helicopter, with all its sensors, would have been unable to see the men hiding in those positions.

In some of the dugouts, we found prescription bottles for antibiotics and painkillers issued by hospitals in Pakistan. After passing that up the chain of command, we later learned that the treatment facilities served as havens for wounded insurgents. Bitterly, we wondered how much of the humanitarian aid money we were giving Pakistan went to creating and maintaining those places. What an odd situation—our wounded enemy recovering in our erstwhile "ally's" medical system. What would folks have thought if the German wounded had recovered in London hospitals in 1944, only to return to the battlefield to fight later?

The world had changed a lot since my grandfather's day.

As we documented the area around Bermel, we developed information on every cave network we could find. The caves served as primary staging points for the enemy, but the known complexes were not even noted on our maps. Fixing this deficiency proved to be a Herculean task, as the wadis, mountains, and ridges around Bermel were honeycombed with thousands of them. I made Sabatke our designated cave-clearance expert, a job he embraced. Time after time, I watched him plunge through a cave entrance, M4 at the ready, and wondered how he could descend into those dark and confined spaces with such fearlessness. Thank God he never encountered the enemy down there. Instead of sparking hellish firefights, his subterranean investigations revealed supply caches and gleaned bits of valuable intel.

In the flatlands below the cave systems, we became intimately familiar with how the war had ravaged the borderland villages.

Only a few communities still existed around Bermel. Most of the others had been abandoned by the Waziri tribal inhabitants, who had fled to Pakistan to escape the conflict. Their qalats and businesses had fallen first into ruin, then into enemy hands. On our patrols, we would dismount in these ghost towns to find telltale signs that the insurgents were using them as staging points: torn wrappers, empty ammo boxes, abandoned gear. In some cases, we found weapons caches stashed among the ruins.

We could not leave the dwellings for the enemy, but how do you destroy buildings made of mud? We settled on burning their wood and thatch roofs. The walls would remain unharmed, but at least the buildings would not afford the enemy shelter from the elements or, more important, our air assets.

Wheat, our whittling sniper, turned out to be a talented firebug. He seemed to always know when I was about to order a dwelling to be torched. Before the words even left my mouth, he would appear at my shoulder, his best friend, Corporal Colten Wallace, in tow, and ask, "Y'all need somethin' burned down, sir?"

All grins, he and Wallace would set to work. I'd watch and vow that someday, I'd visit them on the Fourth of July. Their fireworks displays would be epic.

Wallace and Wheat were two sides of the same coin. Both were southern cowboys who loved horses, the outdoors, and anything rugged. Wheat was the polished, tip-your-hat-and-say-"ma'am" sort of gentleman, religious and devoted to his wife and family. Wallace was the rough one, a cow-punching brawler type prone to smashing chairs over dudes' heads in a good old-fashioned barroom dustup. Tall and lean, naturally muscular, he could drink a twelve-pack a night and never gain weight. He smoked two packs of cigarettes a day but could run a six-minute mile without even warming up. Women and mayhem made him happy. If they'd both been alive in the 1880s,

Wheat would have been a homesteader; Wallace would have been the guy playing poker with Wyatt Earp.

When Wallace and Wheat weren't exercising their inner arsonists, we were out doing our best to help the few civilians still clinging to their lives in this tortured border region. Most were noncommittal when we approached. They'd seen U.S. units come and go, but the enemy always lurked around. The insurgents had terrorized these impoverished but hardy people, whose loyalty centered on their families and tribal affiliations. Their understanding of a broader Afghan nation simply did not exist, and we were just another passing group of interlopers as far as they were concerned. Like the British and Soviets before us, we would leave at some point too. And then what? The enemy would still be out there, sharpening their knives for the reckoning sure to be delivered to anyone who had assisted us.

Through these long and often boring days, our patrols yielded tidbits of information about the enemy we faced. To my surprise, we were not fighting the Taliban alone. The papers back home made our enemy in Afghanistan out to be a monolithic force. We had made the same mistake during the Cold War, assuming that all Communist countries formed a monolithic, anti-Western bloc. That simply was not the case.

Same thing in Afghanistan. The Taliban was the main group aligned against us, but its influence on the border was much less substantial than that of another shadowy organization, one that the CIA knew well. Known as the Haqqani Network, it had first taken shape during the Afghan-Soviet War in the 1980s, thanks to the acumen of its leader, Mawlawi Jalaluddin Haqqani. Charismatic, moderate in his religious views, and a capable diplomat and organizer, Haqqani led a band of warriors in southeast Afghanistan that destroyed hundreds of Russian tanks and shot down dozens of aircraft while playing a key role in the defeat of the Red Army.

Jalaluddin's moderate views and proximity to the Pakistani border made him a natural fit with the CIA and Representative Charlie Wilson's campaign to support the Afghan insurgency. Before the end of the war, the Haqqani Network owed its funding, its weapons, and some of its training to the United States.

After the Russians withdrew, the Haqqani Network formed a loose partnership with the Taliban. In 1996, Haqqani fighters helped the Taliban throw the Northern Alliance out of Kabul, a battle that established Mullah Omar, the leader of the Taliban, as the most powerful man in Afghanistan. Jalaluddin, though a respected warlord in his own right, did not have the strength to challenge the Taliban for supreme control of Afghanistan. So they remained uneasy partners, sometimes feuding, sometimes working together if it served their own interests.

By the time my platoon arrived on the border, Jalaluddin's sons had taken over the day-to-day operations. They were well suited for the task, as their father had groomed them for specific roles. One had become a fund-raiser in the Middle East. Another had become the military commander. A third son, Sirajuddin, had been named Jalaluddin's successor.

Beneath the Haqqani family's leadership, the network was managed by a core of loyalists who had fought with Jalaluddin against the Soviets and in the subsequent civil war. Below their ranks were the young Turks, rising leaders within the network who earned their reputation while fighting Americans along the border.

The network recruited its foot soldiers mainly from Pakistan, though there were plenty of Afghans in the rank and file as well. Over the years, young men inspired by their mullahs to fight infidels had become the key source of manpower for the network, and under Siraj, it had been trending toward a radical Islamic organization. Those devoted men, most barely out of their teens, had died in large numbers since 9/11, but there were always ample supplies of idealistic replacements waiting for the chance to leave their madrassas and join the jihad.

It took some time for us to understand how the foreign fighters we had killed on the mountaintop on May 8 fit into this equation. Eventually, we unraveled it. The Haqqani Network maintained a loose association with Al Qaida, which supplied it with talented jihadists from all over the globe. These experienced men, many of whom had fought in Iraq, Somalia, or Chechnya, formed the insurgents' version of an NCO corps. They had become the backbone around which the indoctrinated, if inexperienced, sons of Pakistan coalesced. In combat, the foreigners served as small-unit leaders. When on the other side of the border, they functioned as the training cadre, preparing each new wave of jihadist canon fodder for the crucible ahead.

Thanks to our signals intelligence section, we'd come to know a little about Galang, the man who led the jihadists into battle against us. We'd established that he was one of the midlevel leaders in the Haqqani Network's structure. He must have been in his late forties or early fifties, as we were told he had been a fierce warrior in the fight against the Soviets two decades before our arrival. His effective fighting force consisted of about three hundred well-armed fighters built around a core of veteran foreign jihadists. Those numbers came as a shock: Galang outnumbered us almost two to one.

If we had any lingering doubts as to Galang's skill on the battlefield, they were shattered on May 17, when he and his men ambushed our Second Platoon behind Rakhah Ridge. Lieutenant Taylor was home on leave when it happened, which had left the platoon under the command of Sergeant First Class Burley, a loud, brash NCO who was not well liked within the company. He had a short temper and was quick to bully if he thought it would get him his way.

On the seventeenth, Sergeant Burley and his platoon ran straight into a sophisticated, L-shaped ambush established by Galang's men. Using armor-piercing bullets in their machine guns, they raked Burley's vehicles, still aiming for the turrets but also the tires. Trapped in restricted terrain, under severe direct-fire attack, Burley ordered his men to break contact and withdraw from the fight. As they fled, Galang's men hit them again with a secondary ambush.

Second Platoon limped home with one man, Private First Class Follansbee, wounded and in need of medical evacuation. Several other men suffered shrapnel wounds. I watched them come through the gate that day. They parked on the concrete pad in front of the operations center, their rigs bullet-scarred and badly damaged. The men dismounted and began to talk about the engagement in hushed, dispirited tones. One sergeant came up to me and said, "That was fuckin' horrible. I can't go through anything like that again."

I watched them and realized I'd never seen a more shaken group of U.S. soldiers. The ambush had been brutal: May 7 on steroids. I later found out that Follansbee had been shot in the ankle and foot by a bullet that had passed through the rubber weather stripping between the armored door and the frame of his Humvee. It was a fluke shot made possible only by the sheer volume of fire poured on them. After seeing Follansbee carried away by our medics, I wondered again how we had made it through our ambush without anyone getting hurt.

For all the intensity of these first two encounters with Galang's men, it seemed to me that they were not throwing their full weight on us. In each ambush, we faced a platoon-sized force of insurgents. Where were the hundreds that Galang had available? Why ambush us while we were on the move? We dismounted all the time. Why not hit us when our men were not protected by armor plating?

Perhaps Galang was using our platoons as sort of a finishing school for his new men. After a winter of training in Pakistan, they had come into our area to gain combat experience and test their weapons, men, and tactics. If that was the case, the two engagements were little more than warm-ups for something much bigger. Exactly what that was kept me awake that night.

We needed to be ready for whatever Galang's next move would be. That night, I replayed everything that had happened since May 7. What could I learn? What could we apply to our future operations? In my mind, I examined every incident, searching for anything that might help us in the next fight.

Second Platoon had taken a beating. We had too on May 7, but their return to the FOB was totally different from ours. Why? It was all perception. Defeat comes in many forms, both physical and psychological. Second Platoon had arrived home a defeated force. Though we hadn't destroyed the entire enemy force on May 7 and our counterattack had hit thin air as Galang's men broke contact with us, we had still inflicted a lot of damage on them. More important, we had stayed in the fight. That had given us a vital moral victory that Second Platoon hadn't experienced. Breaking contact on May 17 had been the right call, given the tactical circumstances, but the psychological effect it had had on Burley's men was all too obvious. Their morale and confidence had taken significant hits.

I could not let that happen to my guys. Ever.

To further foster our platoon's cohesion, I wanted us to have our own unit emblem on the sides of our bullet-scarred Humvees. Just after the May 7 firefight, Emerick had finished his design at last. During a break in our patrol schedule, he painted his green skull design on each of our vehicles. As he worked, men from the platoon gathered around and watched in quiet awe of his artistic prowess. It was an important moment for all of us; it set the platoon apart and showed everyone that we had our own unique identity. I couldn't wait to take those rigs into another fight and build our brand with the enemy. They would learn that the green skull platoon was not one to trifle with.

The next morning, I met with Greeson and my squad leaders. "Guys, listen. We're facing an enemy that is the best light infantry in the world."

My sergeants nodded in agreement.

"They've been doing this all their lives. When I was playing ice hockey in school, these guys were fieldstripping their AKs. When I was going to prom, they were laying ambushes. Our privates have been in the army for less than two years. They've got guys who've been fighting since Reaganomics."

That didn't sit well. We Americans hate to admit that anyone has an edge over us. But I wanted to be straight. I had to be; there were a lot of lives at stake.

"They have firepower. They don't have the indirect assets we do, but they've got plenty of RPGs and machine guns. They are not weak there."

"Where d'ya think they're weak, sir?" Campbell asked.

Greeson chimed in and grunted, "Grit. That's what we've got and they don't. We went toe-to-toe with them, and they broke first. They ran. We stayed. That's a huge moral victory. Look at how it affected our platoon. The men have been on a tear ever since."

I had been going to say the same exact thing.

Again my leaders nodded. "That's true," Baldwin mused, thinking it over.

I continued, "So here's what we're going to do. We will always stay and finish the fight. Got it? We're never going to break contact. We will never cede the battlefield to the enemy, and we're never going to give them a moral victory."

I let that sink in. Everyone around me had seen Second Platoon's return. They'd seen the splintered blast shields, shattered windows, bloody floorboards, and shredded tires.

I looked around the room and asked, "Agreed?"

Solemnly, each man agreed.

"Okay," I said with finality, "we will stand and fight."

PART III

THE SUMMER OF DISCONTENT

★ ★ ★

TEN

THE GATES OF MORDOR

★ ★ ★

June 9, 2006
East of FOB Bermel
Outlaw country

SOMETHIN' AIN'T RIGHT, SIR."

I looked over at Sabatke. "I know. I feel it too, but I can't put my finger on it."

The road ahead was dark and empty. We stood in the middle of it, our trucks behind us, and stared into the moonlit night.

"Listen to that, sir. Not even an insect," Sabatke said. We cocked our ears and strained to hear anything above our own breathing. Usually on nights like these crickets chirped, goat bells clanged in the distance, and jingle trucks rolled down this road at irregular intervals. I checked my watch. Twenty hundred—eight o'clock. Even at this time, we'd seen lots of traffic before on this road. So far tonight, not even a farmer with a donkey cart had approached us. This was the main road into Pakistan in our area, and it should never be this deserted.

Sabatke shuddered. When he looked back toward our Humvees, I caught sight of the pentagram tattooed on the back of his neck. The sight made me grin despite my uneasiness.

"Tree fucker," I whispered, even though that was Baldwin's pet nickname for Sabo. Baldwin frequently accused Sabo of being a Wiccan, earth-worshipping Druid. Sabo always growled at that characterization.

"Satanist," he shot back with a harsh whisper.

Greg Greeson, my platoon sergeant, materialized out of the darkness. "Call yourself whatever you want, Sabatke. You're still a goddamned Wiccan in my book."

"I prefer Satanist," Sabatke growled a little defensively.

"What do you think?" I asked Greeson.

"Something's not right," he replied.

"That's what we said," Sabo noted.

"How long have we been here?" I asked.

Greeson and Sabo checked their watches. "Couple of hours," they said in unison.

I thought this over. We'd been out for days already, moving from road to road, setting up these snap vehicle checkpoints in order to deny the enemy freedom to maneuver through the province. Usually we stayed in place for only two or three hours. After that, we'd mount up and go find another spot to do it all over again. The constant motion made it difficult for the enemy to figure out which roads were usable and did not give them the opportunity to mount an attack on us while we sat in a static location.

I looked east toward Pakistan. Towering mountains capped by jagged peaks formed ominous black shapes on either side of the road. A cloud moved across the nearly full moon, which caused shadows to ripple across the nearby ridges.

"Looks like we're at the gates of Mordor out here," I said, half to myself.

"Why's it always a fucking *Lord of the Rings* thing with you, sir?" Sabatke growled.

Greeson chortled at that. "Better than that Harry Potter shit you're always trying to get us to read, sir."

I ignored them both, though I was going to say that the cloud-borne shadows moving across the trees looked like Dementors. But I figured if I did say it out loud, I'd get teased mercilessly, and I couldn't make it too easy on my NCOs.

Instead, I said, "It is too quiet. Here's what we're going to do: Sergeant Greeson, you stay here while I take some of our dismounts forward and set up an ambush on one of the slopes overlooking the road."

"Roger that, sir," Greeson said.

"If they're up to something, maybe we can catch them by surprise."

Greeson responded with a long, slow "Uhhuuuuh."

"Jesus, you sound like that guy from *Sling Blade*," I quipped. Sabatke thought that was quite funny. He did his best Billy Bob Thornton: "I don't reckon I'll be killin' no one no more, uhh-huhhh."

"Fucking Wiccan."

"Satanist, goddammit."

I refocused us. "You got my back on this, right?" I said to Greeson.

His eyes met mine. "Sir, I always have your back. Even when you don't know it."

Two years ago, I'd have been drinking with my college buddies on a night like this. Now I've got Sling Blade telling me he's got my six in the middle of a *Lord of the Rings* moment on the other side of the planet. Part of me wanted to hug Greeson. Part of me wanted to just shake my head at how surreal my life had become.

"Okay, I'll take Baldwin's squad. Let's move." The three of us dispersed. I grabbed Pinholt, and together we went to find Baldwin, who was standing by our rigs with the rest of his men.

I briefed him on the plan. He offered a few suggestions, then formed his squad into a wedge. Down the road we went, keeping silent, moving swiftly in the moonlight. We pushed east until an inviting slope appeared off to one side of the road. Halfway up, we found good cover and set up our ambush. While the men spread out to find good fighting positions, Baldwin, Pinholt, and I stayed together in the middle of the squad's line. Baldwin scanned the road with a new thermal imaging scope that looked a little like an old-fashioned spyglass. With the moon up, our night-vision goggles functioned very well, so I felt confident that if anyone came down the road, we'd be able to see them long before they saw us.

The men grew still, straining their senses in order to detect the enemy's presence. Once again, we didn't hear so much as an insect.

Baldwin, who lay on his stomach on the other side of Pinholt, muttered, "This is really weird, sir."

Pinholt agreed. All of us had our hackles up. That sort of silence just didn't happen in Afghanistan. It was becoming oppressive.

A few more minutes passed. I struggled to stay alert. We'd been out four days, working day and night. All of us were smoked, filthy, and reeking.

Pinholt chose that moment to say, "This is fucking creepy."

"Pinholt, that may be the first time I've heard you swear," I said.

"You're a bad influence, sir."

"Finally I have some influence." Now, if I could only get him to drink coffee . . .

We grew quiet again. Sleep threatened to overtake us.

"Something is definitely up," I muttered, thinking about Galang and his inscrutable intentions.

In the darkness, I heard Baldwin whisper, "Good, goddammit."
Pinholt asked, "Why good?"

Baldwin said, "Maybe these fuckers will attack with Bin Laden
in command so I can bring his head back to the States on a platter."

Exhaustion mingled with tension created the perfect stage for a
laughing fit. Pinholt succumbed first. He was always quick to laugh
anyway and tended to spool up to near-hysterical proportions on
a normal day. He tried to conceal it, but his efforts only infected
me. Soon the three of us were alternately giggling and shushing one
another, like brothers on a camping trip.

This was an ambush line, and we were professionals. The
moment ended swiftly, and we reset our game faces. We settled
down to wait in silence.

An hour passed, and we didn't hear a thing. Finally I'd had
enough. I keyed the radio and called Greeson. "We've got nothing.
You?"

His voice had returned to its normal sleepy Sam Elliott. "Nothing, sir."

"Moving back to you, then."

"Roger."

I pulled in my flank security, and we set off back to our makeshift checkpoint. When we reached the rest of the platoon, Greeson
and I talked the situation over.

"Anything?" he asked.

"No. Not even heat signatures from any of the villages around
here. No cooking fires. Nothing." I replied.

He glanced around. "Sir, I feel like we're being watched."

Sabatke joined us and agreed. "You and me both."

"Let's get out of the low ground, sir, and establish an OP somewhere we can tuck in tight for the night."

"Okay," I said. "Let's take a look at the map." Ten minutes
later, we'd found a hilltop a few kilometers behind us that was a

good location for the platoon. It overlooked the road. In the morning, should the enemy start using the road, we'd be able to hit them from the high ground for a change. As an added benefit, the slopes appeared steep enough to protect us should we get probed during the night.

We mounted and set off to find the hill. A few kilometers down the road, we turned onto a narrow goat trail that wound its way up the north side of the hilltop. I dismounted and walked the trail with Baldwin's squad in the lead, our Humvees inching along behind us. The trail was rugged and dotted with razor-sharp chunks of shale. Several times I slipped and fell, catching myself with one hand. Baldwin's men struggled along as well. A few went down hard, suffering cuts and scrapes on the jagged edges of shale that jutted out of the soft earth. We maintained noise and light discipline, saying nothing while relying on our night vision to guide us. That soon failed us, as our eyepieces fogged over. We flipped them up and kept going by the light of the moon.

Halfway up, our lungs burned from the exertion with ninety pounds of gear on our backs. We were up around ten thousand feet, and some of the men began to suffer from altitude sickness. A few threw up. Sweat poured off me. My lungs felt like a four-alarm fire. With each step, I willed myself not to fall out. I couldn't do that, not in front of my men. They had to see their platoon leader as bulletproof and unflappable, able to endure far more than anyone else in the unit. Even after May 7, I could not be seen any other way.

When we finally reached the top, I took a knee and gasped for breath. Head down, rifle on my knee, I sucked wind in the darkness. Thirty seconds of that, and I looked up to see if anyone was watching me. Sure enough, I could make out the shadowy forms of Sabatke, Baldwin, and Campbell walking toward me. Sergeant Waites trailed behind them, looking tense.

No weakness. Never show it. I tried to control my breathing to make it appear normal. I rose off my knee to greet them standing erect.

They weren't having any of my pretensions. Campbell reached me first, a big grin on his face. "Hey, sir. Can't you hack it?"

"Why don't you play a game of hide and go fuck yourself, Campbell," I whispered.

Campbell elbowed Sabatke in the ribs. "Check it out. LT here's having trouble handling a little hill!"

"Hey, I'm here with ya, aren't I? And I didn't see either of you walkin'!" I retorted.

"Everyone shut the fuck up." That was Greeson. He'd come up behind my squad leaders and looked angry, tired, and impatient. We'd run out of near beer. I was worried about him.

"Sir, please put out the priorities of work. I'm fuckin' tired."

I thought it over briefly. "Security, weapons, rest cycle, and food."

Greeson nodded. "Roger, sir."

"Anything for the squad leaders?" I asked him.

He regarded Sabatke, Campbell, and Baldwin. "Yeah. Tell your guys that if I catch anyone sleeping in the turret, the hajjis won't have to kill them. I will."

My squad leaders exchanged nervous looks as Greeson walked away. I heard Baldwin mutter, "That man is in desperate need of a cigarette."

"Sergeant Greeson, can we make sure the men get some rest tonight?"

"Sir, quit being a Joe hugger. We got this."

"Roger." I felt a little stung by that. I cared about the men; it was part of my job. Part of my job was also to recognize when exhaustion and hunger made everyone crusty and not let that affect us. I think Greeson saw the effect his words had on me. It had not been intentional. He slapped my shoulder and said, "Sir, you got other things to worry about. I got this, okay?"

I chuckled and shook my head, thinking that it was simply Greeson's way of saying "Let me handle my business."

"Roger that, Sergeant Greeson."

Bowlegged, he headed off to make sure the men were squared away. I took a long pull from my CamelBak. The water felt glorious on my parched throat. Slowly my heartbeat returned to normal. My breathing became steady and even. Around me, my squad leaders went to work establishing a 360-degree perimeter with our five trucks. The gunners received their sectors and fields of fire. Each Humvee would kick out a couple of dismounts to help buttress our perimeter. Should we be probed tonight, we would be able to meet any attack from any direction.

I walked the line, talking with the men. Over the months, I'd come to know a lot about them—their hometowns, their friends and families. The great thing about small-unit leadership is the enormous bond so easily shared between the leader and his young warriors. It is a great strength, and in a fight I'd come to count on every one of them. At the same time, I knew there would come a point when I might have to order one or more of them into certain death. And I wasn't sure I could do that. That's the crux of the role of a lieutenant. The mission must transcend the bond. But for me, sometimes the familiarity was hard to overcome.

I reached the first Humvee. Bray stood watch behind his heavy machine gun. A blue-eyed, blond-haired hulk of a kid from Louisiana, he was two hundred and ten pounds of sculpted southerner. He spent every second off duty in the gym. He also had the soul of a warrior, something he had proved on May 7.

"How ya doin', Bray?" I asked. I noticed he was drinking a GNC protein shake. He sucked those down like most of us drank water.

"Good, sir, you?"

Never show weakness. I was smoked and sore, my feet blistered and crotch chapped from all the walking. "Livin' the dream, Bray," I said.

I wandered to the next truck in the perimeter. This one was my own, and Chris Brown manned the turret's machine gun.

"Hey, Brown, what's up?"

"Just waitin' for my next copy of *King* magazine, sir," he replied with his Memphis accent. Chris loved to be in the mix with the rest of the men, but his soft eyes revealed a huge heart to anyone who looked close enough. At times I worried about him. He tried hard to be a warrior, and he was, but it didn't come to him naturally, as it did Sabo or Bray. At times I thought he cared too much, and that made him vulnerable.

I kept it light. "What is it with you and that rag?"

"Those chicks are hot, sir!"

I shook my head and laughed. "Okay, Brown, you gonna be able to stay awake?"

"Hell, yeah. I'm good to go, sir." He sounded surprised that I'd even asked.

I gave him the thumbs-up sign and continued walking the perimeter. When I encountered Emerick, I couldn't help but ask him about his latest creation.

He was eating an MRE next to his rig, but he reached inside and showed me another variant of "demon orgy."

"You know, Emerick, you're on to something there. There are a few more in this version," I noted.

"Thanks, sir. Wanted to get the facial expressions just right," he added. "I'll probably redo it," he mused.

"You're gonna be famous someday, Emerick. And I'll get to say, 'I knew him when.'"

"You think demon sex'll sell?" he asked.

"You'll be able to print your own money with this stuff."

We chatted a little while longer. He had everything well in hand. After a moment I moved on to the next rig.

Greeson and my squad leaders had established a tight ring on the top of the hill. We had plenty of cover and concealment, as conifer trees blanketed the slopes and the crest, interspersed with sharp-edged boulders that looked like something out of *Land of the Lost*. Sabatke's Humvee anchored the north side of the line. In the middle, facing east, was Baldwin's rig, whose turret held the fearsome M2. Come morning, if we saw any enemy movement on the road below us, his vehicle would be the tip of the platoon's spear. Beyond it about fifteen meters to the south was Sergeant Waites's vehicle.

Waites had continued to be a challenge for me during our first five months in country. Once, when his rig had been on point during a patrol, we took a wrong turn and I had tried to contact him on the radio. He hadn't answered my repeated calls. Finally, I'd had to dismount and run forward to stop him. When I'd pounded on his door and asked him why he wasn't responding over the radio, he'd answered, "Sir, I don't need no radio. Ain't nothin' gonna happen out here."

I'd lost it right there in the middle of that patrol. It was bad enough he hadn't taken training seriously, but to be so utterly careless in combat was flat inexcusable. After that, I'd made sure that either I or Greeson kept a hawk's eye on him. That radio stunt could have gotten men killed.

Because of my trust issues with him, I gave Waites our right flank. Given the ground, I gauged it to be the side least likely to be attacked.

To cover the west, or rear, side of our perimeter, Brown's machine gun and my vehicle had been stationed about thirty meters behind Baldwin's. Greeson's Humvee completed the perimeter, covering the goat trail on the north side just off from Sabatke's rig.

Five Humvees, three .50-caliber heavy machine guns, a Mark 19 grenade launcher, two M240 Bravo medium machine guns, and twenty-four men. That's what we had to protect our hilltop redoubt.

When I finished walking the line, I noticed that Waites was off to one side, observing the group of squad leaders Greeson had gathered in the center of the perimeter. I walked over to them just in time to hear Sabatke say, "You guys think you have it rough? If I cheated on Carla, she'd cut my balls off. Hell, she knows how to shoot!"

"Isn't she some sort of high priestess in your Wiccan cult?" asked Campbell.

"Satanist, goddammit," Sabatke growled. "And yes. That's why when we're at the mall together, I just keep my eyes down. Keep 'em down. Always down."

Greeson let out another Sling Blade laugh.

Campbell noted, "Sabatke, you've got a badass wife in Carla. Remember how she chewed out Captain Waverly at one of the family readiness meetings? Made him look like a dog whose bone got swiped right outta his mouth."

Our overmatched company commander had not fared well during that exchange. Carla was the only woman I knew who could handle Sabo. They were a match made in Heaven. Or perhaps Hell.

Baldwin's smooth voice cut into the conversation. "You know—I—am—a—firm believer that everything that comes out of my mouth is the truth."

He paused, almost as if he were daring anyone to dispute this. None of us did. "But if my wife were to cheat on me—well, we had a long discussion about that . . ."

Eyes widened all around the circle at the menace in his voice. Baldwin spoke only lovingly of his wife, even when it brought on teasing from the others.

"I told Regina that it may not be six days, or six months—or six years—but one day her brakes would go out and she would die in a fiery car crash." When he finished, he let out a dry laugh that sent chills through me.

"Uh, Baldwin, didn't you meet Regina at a church camp or somethin'?" I asked.

"Yep. I was fifteen. She was thirteen."

"Is your God aware of your plan here, Baldwin?" Sabo asked.

I remembered him at the hospital, his newborn daughter in Regina's arms. He doted on her as only a man hopelessly in love can do.

Greeson let out a long guffaw. "Nah, Baldwin, you got it all wrong."

"Whaddya mean?"

"Look, man, it's all like Jell-O."

We stared at him, uncomprehending.

"Ya see, Baldwin, y'all can pull the Jell-O outta the fridge. Y'all can stick yer finger in it. When ya put it back in, nobody'd ever know."

"What's your point?" Baldwin asked.

"Look man, I been 'round. Seen all there is ta see. If there's one thing I've learned, it's that women're the same. If my wife is cheatin' on me, I'd never know. So there ain't no point in worryin' 'bout it."

"Did you just compare your wife to Jell-O?" asked Campbell.

"Yep."

Baldwin shook his head. Waites looked lost in his own world, divorced from the flow of the conversation. Campbell said, "You must have an interesting relationship."

That prompted Greeson's Sling Blade "Mmmmhmmmm."

Sighing, I said, "I'm glad I'm not married."

The conversation continued. As it did, I realized that there was a subtext here that was never broached. We'd seen enough marriages flame out while in country to know that infidelity was a serious issue. Joking about it made it endurable, especially since none of us could do anything about it while we were in the Hindu Kush. The ribald talk and crude comments were ways infantrymen dealt with emotional issues. It was how we coped. And through it, we bonded in ways we might not ever again.

Campbell and Sabatke debated the point for a few more minutes, until Greeson finally said wearily, "You know, I can't take any more of this."

Shaking his head, he walked off toward his truck, the rest of the NCOs watching him go.

Sabatke departed next. Campbell took his leave, so did Waites, and then it was just Baldwin and I in the middle of our platoon's perimeter. He put a hand on my shoulder. In a big-brother sort of way he said, "Hope you learned something here tonight, sir."

"Yeah, I did, Baldwin. I learned you're all bat-shit crazy."

The laughter felt good. Damn good. But as it drained away, and we were left in silence, the night became suddenly oppressive. As I walked back to my truck, I could not shake a foreboding sense that everything was about to change.

ELEVEN

MORNING ON THE MOUNTAIN

★ ★ ★

June 10, 2006
East of FOB Bermel

ALL ELEMENTS, THIS IS BLACKHAWK THREE-SIX. WE'LL BE starting stand-to in fifteen mikes."

My four other truck commanders acknowledged. We'd spent the night waiting for Galang to make an appearance, but so far he'd been a no-show. My men dozed in shifts and took turns manning our heavy weapons. I'd slept in the front-right seat of my Humvee, still slathered in sweat from the hike up the hill. Now, with the morning chill upon us, I shivered in my filthy clothes.

We made it a standard practice to wake everyone up an hour before dawn while out beyond the FOB like this. Experience had shown that the enemy loved to launch attacks at this time of the morning. Soon all twenty-four of my men were up and in position, waiting to see if the enemy would make a move.

I opened my door and stepped out into the darkness. My mouth was like cotton. My eyes burned, every joint ached, and I felt a stiffness that only a week in a decent bed would solve.

The thin air left us always short of breath. I could feel my body craving oxygen, especially after a night in a cramped Humvee. I inhaled as deeply as my lungs would allow. The fresh air was like a whiff of fine wine.

I walked the line again, checking on my men. The sun crested the ridges to the east, and morning light spilled down into the valley below. I watched it creep toward us, waiting for its warmth to strike my weary body.

I took a second look at the sunrise and stopped cold. Those two ridges on the other side of the valley were taller than our hilltop, a fact concealed by darkness last night when we had arrived. A feeling of dread shivered through me. If the enemy had put a machine gun up there, they'd be able to sweep our entire perimeter with plunging fire.

Beyond the two ridges I could see the mountaintop we'd blasted with bombs and 105s on May 8. We'd found out a few days later that at least twenty of Galang's men had died in our artillery barrages while trying to recover the bodies on the mountaintop. Ever since, we'd kept a close eye on the place, hoping to catch them returning to the cave entrance to dig it out and recover whatever supplies remained inside.

The sunlight stretched up our slope and finally washed over our position. I reveled in it; the heat felt instantly refreshing.

I started on my way again, then paused one more time. Those ridges bothered me. I hadn't realized they were so high or so close. Between them and our position, the valley was narrow, perhaps less than a kilometer and a half wide. I couldn't occupy those ridges, as I didn't have the manpower. But we could plot some target reference points for the artillery at Bermel, just in case we needed it. If we gave them the grid locations of those ridges, they could get on target in a matter of seconds should the shit hit the fan.

I went back to my Humvee and discussed it with our forward observer. As we worked out the grid points on our map, Greeson started passing out MREs and making sure the men had plenty of ammunition. Each rifleman carried seven magazines for his M4. Technically, each mag could hold thirty rounds, but nobody loaded them full. We'd learned that to do so increased the likelihood of a jam. Instead, we made it a policy to carry twenty-eight in each magazine. That way the springs in them still had the tension needed to pop each bullet up into the chamber.

One hundred and ninety six rounds per man. I couldn't imagine blowing through all of that. We were solid there.

The machine gunners carried about a thousand rounds each in hundred-bullet belts. A 240 going cyclic could burn through that in a matter of seconds, but my gunners chose their shots well and fired with controlled, short bursts. We should be good there too.

"Hey, sir, the bad guys are talking." I turned to see Yusef standing with one of our Prophet spooks, Sergeant Dixon.

"What are they saying?" I asked.

Yusef shrugged. "Lots of gibberish, really. But they did say, 'Bring the wood to the place the Americans bombed a few weeks ago.'"

Josiah Reuter, my forward observer, looked up and said, "Hey! That's gotta be the cave site we hit on that mountain over there." He pointed across to the east.

"Right. Let's get some fire on it."

This was going to be tricky. The FOB and our two 105mm artillery pieces were quite a way to the west. To hit the cave site would require a charge eight, rocket-assisted shell, a weapon so powerful that when used, it ran the risk of flipping the cannon onto its back. Last time we had pounded the mountaintop, we'd known for sure that the enemy was there, so taking the chance had been worth it. Now we were just guessing. I wasn't sure Captain Dye would go for it.

"Sir, we have smoke to the north," I heard Brown report from the turret. I stepped away from my Humvee and could see it in the distance near one of the abandoned villages in the area.

I reported the smoke to the FOB. A moment later, Captain Dye, came onto the radio. "Blackhawk three-six! That smoke is us." His voice was strained and irritated, which puzzled me. How was I to know he was out there?

I grabbed a Red Bull and thought about it for a few minutes. Captain Dye was in a bad mood. I needed his permission to use the charge eights and hit the cave site. Did I want to fight this fight and ask him? The request carried a significant tactical risk. If we flipped a gun, our fire support would be severely limited for quite a while.

I THOUGHT ABOUT THE MANY ROCKET ATTACKS WE'D ALREADY taken at FOB Bermel. Chances were that that's what the enemy code meant. They were bringing wood (rockets) to the cave site to fire at our base.

I finished the Red Bull. Okay. It was worth any grief Captain Dye would give me. If those guys were back on the mountaintop, they needed to die.

I called Captain Dye and explained the situation. He listened, asked a few questions, then gave me the green light, adding "Make sure you observe this personally."

No grief. This man is not Captain Waverly at all. Thank God.
"Roger, sir."
I turned to my FO. "Call it up, Reuter."

A few minutes later, the first 105mm artillery shell tore across the sky and exploded on the west slope of the mountain. More shells rained down. Our gunners at Bermel were dead on. Even better, they threw in a mix of ground and air bursts, creating a lethal artillery cocktail. I watched from the edge of our perimeter as the conflagration grew, wondering how anyone could survive such firepower.

"Mission complete, sir," Reuter reported.

I turned and started to walk back to my Humvee. "Ha, ha! Reuter! How about that?" I asked with a smile.

"Happiness is good indirect, sir," he replied. It was a standard refrain our forward observer liked to use. He was right too. Indirect fire gave a platoon like ours an awesome amount of destructive power.

I flicked a glance over my shoulder at the smoke-smothered mountaintop.

Your play, assholes.

I'd walked about halfway back to my rig and was just passing a thick pine tree when I called out to Reuter again, "Let's see what those bastards are saying on their radios now!"

But before he could respond, Reuter and everything in my view disappeared as though a curtain had just dropped before my eyes.

TWELVE

THE ZOMBIE APOCALYPSE

★ ★ ★

. . . Blackness.

. . .

Nothing.

. . .

Where am I?

The morning scene in the Hindu Kush had vanished, replaced by an endless void.

Sean?

That voice . . .

Sean, you need to get up.

Grandpap?

Sean, you have to wake up now.

I struggled to see him. But he stayed cloaked in the velvet darkness. I was left only with the smooth comfort of his voice.

Get up, Sean. You've got to get up. Get up for me.

Something stung my face. I tried to look and see what had just hit me, but I could not penetrate the void.

Am I dreaming?

I tried to shake my head, but I couldn't fire the right neurons. Instead, I floated, captive to whatever moment this was.

Another sting on my face. At least I could feel something. I wanted to move my hand up to touch my cheek and defend against whatever kept hitting me. My hand refused to obey. I felt disembodied, as if somehow my conscious had been separated from my material form.

Sean, get up!

"Grandpap, where are you?" I tried to call out. I had no voice. I just drifted like a derelict ship, lost in time and space.

Something stung my cheek again. This time, a pinpoint of light pierced the nothingness. It grew brighter, wider, until it spread across the blackness like wildfire. It consumed the void, leaving me blinded by blazing white light.

Pain flared. It shifted my consciousness, returned me to my corporal state. My right leg burned. I still couldn't see, but I could feel it.

Shapes moved in the whiteness. For a moment, I thought I could see the sky through a milky film, but it lacked definition and color. A face moved over me, and I wanted to reach up to it but still could not make my limbs obey my brain.

The face came into focus, and dimly I recognized Sergeant Tim Stalter, one of the team leaders from Campbell's squad.

His mouth moved. Why wasn't he saying anything? I tried to read his lips, but couldn't understand. He smacked my cheek with one gloved hand. That explained the stinging. But what the hell?

A telephone buzzed in my ears now. The ringing was all I could hear. Disoriented, I tried to look around and I realized I was flat on my back, perhaps fifteen feet from where I last remembered standing. The tree I'd been passing looked as though a giant had snapped it in half.

Then I saw Sabatke. His face was smeared with blood, his IBA stained crimson with it.

In a sudden rush, my hearing came back. I went from nothing but the telephone to a hurricane of sounds in a heartbeat. The switch blitzed my nervous system. For an instant, I was helpless against the sensory overload, swamped by staccato bursts of fifty cals, explosions, and screams.

"Sir! Sir! You okay?" Stalter shouted at me.

Why wouldn't I be?

He smacked me again. "Sir, you got blown the fuck up!"

My right leg felt afire. Looking down, I saw a piece of shrapnel sizzling on one pant leg. I shook it off, and it snuffed out in the dirt.

Behind Stalter's head, I saw one of the trees that grew along the crest of our hilltop redoubt split apart, splintering in all directions. The top of another vanished in a halo of smoke. Burnt and torn branches tumbled down on my men. Nature was being murdered here.

So are we.

Something else burst overhead. Like a steel cyclone, shrapnel whooshed around us. Stalter covered me with his own body to protect me.

I tried to sit up, but the world tilted sideways and I felt myself slipping back into the soft dirt. Stalter grabbed my IBA and pulled me to him. The world tilted the other way. The hilltop seemed to be rolling in thick ocean swells.

"Sir, you okay?" Stalter asked again.

Where was my grandpap?

Then I remembered he had been dead for six months.

Just then, one of our fifty-cals loosed a deafening volley. Weakly, I turned my head to see what was going on. Greeson lay on his stomach, a tree trunk serving as cover. His weapon was at his shoulder, and when he saw me looking at him, he shouted, "Sir, I'm fucking hit! We're getting slammed!"

The world spun; my head tipped. Stalter caught me from falling over again. My head lolled to the right. My view went sideways. In it I could see Baldwin's rig. Campbell was in the turret, firing the Ma Deuce. That seemed odd.

Then I saw Baldwin.

Father of two.

Regina, his teenage sweetheart, waiting in a base house at Fort Drum for his return.

He lay near Campbell's rig, blood spraying from a gaping leg wound.

"Hang with me, Bennett!" I heard him cry out. Instead of stanching his own bleeding, he was working to save his team leader, Sergeant Garvin. A bullet had torn open his arm, and blood was spewing into the dirt beside them at an alarming rate. Baldwin pulled off his belt and started to fashion a tourniquet.

Baldwin's wound looked bad. I wanted to shout for Doc Pantoja, but my body still refused to obey. Instead of words, I managed only an incoherent gurgle.

Phil.

So much blood.

A swarm of hornets ripped through the nearby trees: incoming machine-gun fire. It had to be originating from those ridges on the other side of the valley.

Get to Baldwin and Garvin, now!

The professional in me knew I had to get artillery onto those ridges.

Your family needs you, Sean. Get up.

My arms were rubber. My head swam. I tried to sit up, only to find myself falling back into Stalter's embrace.

Another explosion overhead severed more treetops and pelted us with cartwheeling branches. Airburst mortars. That was a level of sophistication we'd not seen before.

On the far left of the line, Sabatke stood tall in the middle of the whirlwind, screaming at his men to get behind cover. A mortar round exploded only a few meters from him. He shielded his face with one arm but refused to get down; instead, he stayed exposed and kept shouting at his men, who were hugging the earth around his Humvee. Bullets ricocheted off the rig and kicked up swirls of dirt around his feet. He seemed oblivious to the danger.

In the turret of Sabatke's Humvee, Sergeant Emerick rocked his .50-cal. I could see him snapping off eight to ten rounds at a time, just as we had trained, hammering at the ridgelines on the other side of the valley. *Hold the trigger and say, "Die, motherfucker, die." Ease up, repeat as necessary. That's how you stay on target, don't waste ammo, and minimize a jam.*

Another mortar exploded overhead. Mangled bits of the trees showered Sabatke again. Emerick's head whipsawed backward, a spray of blood filling the air. He dropped out of the turret and vanished.

I was sitting on my ass, my legs out in front of me like a child during reading time, and one of my men just got killed in front of me. I couldn't even react at first; I just stared like a drunk at his empty turret.

Galang just killed my brother.

All at once I was seized by a rage so profound it banished my physical pain.

Emerick. Our platoon artist. Father of a newborn. His wife, Jessica, is a sweet and comforting woman. I visited them at the hospital too, shared their joy for a few brief minutes after their child was born. And I just watched him die.

I rose shakily to my feet. Bullets tore the ground beside Stalter and me as one of Galang's machine gunners traversed our position. I started to fall, but Statler caught me.

"I got ya, sir. I got ya," he said.

PROPPED AGAINST STATLER, I PUSHED MY WAY UPRIGHT.

Get to Baldwin and Garvin. Now.

Campbell howled with rage and burned through the last of a hundred-round belt. Before reloading, he peered down at Baldwin and Garvin.

"Hang in there, man, hang in there!" His voice rose an octave. "Doc! Doc! We need you!"

Help them, Sean! Get your ass over there now.

No. My heart keened. My head cleared. Focus. Be the leader the entire platoon needs.

Right then I felt another part of me die.

The mission or the men you love?

Mission first.

Little by little, the reality of combat stole portions of my humanity.

Clinging to Statler, I made the professional decision I needed to make. In his ear, I shouted, "My truck, let's go!"

Leaning on Statler, we half ran, half staggered to my vehicle. When I got there, I grabbed the radio handset from Reuter.

"FOB Bermel, this is Blackhawk three-six." Was that really my voice?

Something exploded on the east side of the hilltop. Mortar? RPG? The blasts were coming one atop another now. Another airburst mortar detonated to the north, shredding the already splintered trees.

"Blackhawk three-six, this is Blackhawk five, what the hell is going on up there? We can hear it!" That was our company executive officer.

"We're getting hammered. We're outnumbered, and we need help. Send the QRF to my location right now."

A pause as the XO digested this. A bullet bounced off the side of my Humvee. Lead impacting armor makes a distinctive, flat *tunk;* there's nothing in the world that sounds remotely like it.

"Roger! Roger!" his excited voice came back across the static. "We'll get someone to you ASAP."

ASAP? What did that even mean? My men were dying here. The QRF—quick reaction force—was Second Platoon. Ever since it had been ambushed last month, Burley, their platoon sergeant, had displayed a notable reluctance to get into another fight. At times, he'd take his platoon out and sit in a safe position, then radio false location reports back to the FOB so it appeared as if he were moving around as ordered. Having him lead our rescue force? That did not bode well for us.

Reuter, in a voice so detached it could have come from the grave, said to me, "Sir, we've got to get out of here."

So here's what we're going to do. We will always stay and finish the fight. Got it? We're never going to break contact. We will never leave the ground to the enemy, and we're never going to give them a moral victory.

I looked across our perimeter. Baldwin's vehicle looked as if it had been used for target practice at a redneck convention. The hood was spackled with bullet holes, the windows were spiderwebbed with cracks. Campbell was still in his turret, but steam boiled over the nose of his Humvee from a ruptured radiator. Sabatke's rig was in even worse shape—tires flat, engine belching smoke, windows wrecked. And when I studied my own, I could see gouges across the fenders, hood, and doors.

The only thing we have over those guys is grit. But where's the line between fighting for a moral victory and reliving the Alamo?

Then I realized that the point was academic. Escape was not an option.

"Reuter, we can't go anywhere, we've got three trucks down."

"Yeah, but, sir . . . we need to get the fuck out of here."

I put my hand on his shoulder. "Reuter, listen to me. We can't leave. But we can start calling fire on those ridges. And the cave. You got that?"

He nodded in slow motion.

"Way to go, bro. Get those 105s rocking for us." I handed him a radio. He regarded it curiously for a moment, as if his brain wasn't processing. Then it all clicked into place. His eyes focused again. "I got this, sir."

"I know you do, Reuter. You always have our back."

He keyed the mike and went to work.

In my truck's rear left seat sat Specialist Bobby Pilon. He was tall, lanky, and athletic, with a voice that sounded incongruously like Towelie's from *South Park*. He stared at me with uneasy eyes, his face even more pale than usual. The other guys in the platoon called him Powder for his Casper the Friendly Ghost–like complexion.

He'd propped his M249 SAW between his legs, barrel up, box magazine facing the front seat.

"Pilon. Hey, how you doing?"

No response. He stared at me with fearful blue eyes. I had no doubt our expressions were identical.

"Pilon," I said again, "we've got to lay down fire, and I need every man and gun we can get on the line."

His eyes steadied and speared mine.

"I need your SAW over on the eastern flank by Baldwin's truck. Can you reinforce that section of the line?"

He gazed out behind me at the maelstrom of fire sweeping the hilltop. Mortars still rained down. Machine-gun fire stitched the trees, rocks, and vehicles. Baldwin and Garvin lay in a bloodied heap. He would have to run through all of that across open ground to execute my order.

"ROGER, SIR," HE SAID WITHOUT INFLECTION. HE UNBUCKLED his seat belt and slipped out of the Humvee. He looked my way one last time, and I could see that calm resolve had frosted over the fear in his eyes. I had a sickening feeling that I had just ordered this gentle kid from Michigan to his death.

Without a word, Pilon brought his SAW to the low ready and rushed into the inferno engulfing the hilltop. I saw him stumble once, twice, but both times he recovered and kept running. An RPG sizzled overhead. Machine guns raked the ground. He didn't slow down; he never hesitated.

How does a man find such courage?

I needed to be there with him. The eastern flank was the center of the fight, and that's where a platoon leader had to be. I should have gone with Pilon.

"Blackhawk three-six, this is Blackhawk six." Captain Dye's call broke my concentration. I grabbed the radio handset and replied, "Blackhawk three-six, we're taking a shellacking here, sir."

"We can see the airbursts. You guys are in some serious shit." He said.

"We're not going to last," I said flatly.

"Hang on, brother, we're coming to you."

I breathed a sigh of relief. He was only a few kilometers to the north with Delta's heavily armed Humvees. We wouldn't have to depend on Burley's Second Platoon for our salvation after all.

Captain Dye would not let us down.

I cradled the handset and turned back toward the fight. Pilon had made it to the eastern hillcrest. With a single fluid motion, he dropped in the prone and popped his bipod open, just as Sabo had taught him back at Fort Drum. A moment later, his weapon was spewing lead.

Time to get on the line with the rest of the men. I steeled myself. The volume of fire sweeping the hilltop made May 7 look like a warm-up exercise.

I moved to the Humvee's fender, ready to make a run for it.

There's only one way to handle a moment like this one. Courage is a fleeting commodity and can be crushed effortlessly by a single fond memory of home. A backyard barbecue, a fragmented flashback to a moonlit dance with a beautiful girl—those are psychological bullets in combat. One glimpse of what has been makes a soldier yearn for what can be again. That yearning can be as caustic as acid. It burns away the resolve you need to get the job done.

One stray thought can paralyze just as effectively as a bullet in the spine.

Give yourself to the moment, Sean.

My legs began to move. Still dizzy from the mortar blast, I ran like a drunk across the open space, hearing the whip crack of bullets all around me. Something knocked me off balance, and I almost went down. At the last second, I stutter-stepped, righted myself, and kept running. Later, I found a bullet hole in my assault pack.

More RPGs arced and whizzed into the perimeter. One exploded off to my right on the crest of our hill. Another sailed overhead and detonated behind me. The machine guns chattered. My men screamed obscenities. I ran on.

Finally I threw myself down behind a tree not far from Pilon. From there I had a bird's-eye view of the battlefield. The enemy had emplaced three machine guns on each ridge on the other side of the valley. They'd positioned them in such a way that their fields of fire interlocked directly across our hilltop. It had taken someone with a keen tactical eye to set that up, and I wondered if Galang himself was out there directing this fight.

They had hit us with mortars to pin us down while they moved their machine guns onto the ridges. Once emplaced, they had unleashed hell upon us. We were facing a very capable force. How many times had a U.S. platoon faced such overwhelming firepower? Six heavy machine guns plus mortars—there was no way we could withstand this much longer.

To my left, Baldwin secured the tourniquet to Garvin's arm. Baldwin's leg looked bad, and the dirt around him was soaked with his blood.

Go to him.

The man I used to be bucked against the leader I had to be in combat.

"Pantoja! We need you over here!" I might as well have been whispering in a hurricane.

Focus.

What was their next move? In training, we learned to conduct assaults by using one squad to lay down a "base of fire" on the enemy before maneuvering on him. By blanketing his positions with lead, we could pin him into place so our other squads could strike the enemy's flank. We called the element doing all the shooting the "support-by-fire" position.

That's exactly what the enemy had done on the far ridge— they'd set up two support-by-fire positions.

They're going to maneuver on you, Sean.

This was no May 7 hit-and-run. Galang was coming after us for sure. And it wouldn't be long.

Two support-by-fire positions. What does that mean?

A pair of RPGs exploded among my men. I could hear them screaming, their voices full of rage.

Two support positions. Two pronged attack. That's what I would do if I had a full company to maneuver.

I sat up sharply, feeling a bolt of terror. The enemy had seized the initiative; it held fire superiority and the high ground. The tactical situation had tilted drastically in its favor. We were in trouble.

"Prepare for an assault! They're gonna be coming over those hills!"

Sabatke hollered back, "Sir! We're red going on black on ammo! We've got almost nothing left!"

All across my line, I saw nothing but wounded men. Garvin, Baldwin, Greeson, Sabatke—all bleeding and battered. Emerick's turret remained empty. I squashed the image of him getting hit.

I realized we needed a man on that gun.

Campbell checked his ammo situation. "Same here, sir. Going black."

Behind me, I heard Greeson's growl. "Conserve your goddamned ammo! Don't shoot unless you can see 'em. Got that? Shoot at only what you can see!"

I looked over my shoulder and saw him standing bowlegged, his shoulder wounded, unflappable even in the midst of this crisis. I felt a surge of love for the man.

"Sir, we gotta get the casualties out of here." He was right. Garvin and Baldwin would be smack in the path of any enemy assault, helpless to react. We needed to clear them away from the eastern flank and get them to Doc Pantoja, our medic, back by my Humvee.

"Roger that."

The volume of incoming suddenly spiked. Rocket-propelled grenades, mortars, and machine-gun fire hammered our hilltop. All we could do was stay low, but with the cross fire they had us in, we had no safe place.

I peered around the tree trunk and watched the muzzle flashes flaring from the two ridges. I wondered how Reuter was doing with the artillery support.

Come on, Reuter, we need those big guns to speak.

The enemy didn't give us the time. Howling like banshees, they poured over the tops of the eastern ridges and down the tree-covered slopes toward the valley floor. Two groups, scores of men, raced for us in a dead sprint that reminded me of the zombie apocalypse movies filmed back in my hometown in Pennsylvania. *Dawn of the Dead* meets Afghanistan. They were already less than a kilometer away, and I realized that they would be on us in a matter of minutes. Clearly, that was the point. If they could cross the valley before we could get indirect onto them, we didn't stand a chance.

Down they went into the valley. They flowed around rocks and trees, never slowing or wavering. They angled for our northeast and southeast flanks, sweeping wide as they ran and forming two prongs of a giant pincer with us in the middle.

Most of the enemy carried AK-47s at the low ready, but others shouldered RPGs or light machine guns. Wicked knives, perhaps eight inches or longer, sat in leather sheaths attached to their belts.

I thought of a captured Taliban video we'd seen. In it, the enemy had decapitated a helpless Afghan soldier with one of those wicked long knives. They had done it slowly, just to maximize the pain and horror. The dying man had gurgled and cried as he bled out, finally going limp in his tormentor's arms as his neck was completely severed.

They're coming for our heads.

I reached for my portable radio, only to discover it had been blown off of my chest rig at the start of the engagement. I had no choice now; I had to get back to my Humvee, get on the radio, and then organize a rescue for Baldwin and Garvin.

I stood up and ran back through the sheets of fire, staying low as I went. When I reached my Humvee, I found Doc Pantoja working on my dismounted M240 machine gunner, Specialist Howard. Howard sat on his knees with his arms outstretched and shaking. His hands were burned and blackened. His face was covered with blood, chunks of skin, and tendons. I could see flecks of red flesh and white pieces of bone in his hair.

"RPG exploded in front of me, sir." He explained that the stuff all over his face and hair had come from Garvin. Howie had been standing behind Bennett when he'd been shot.

His voice was calm. "Don't worry about me. I'll still be able to kill these assholes."

Greeson broke cover to streak for Garvin and Baldwin. His movement drew a firestorm from the two enemy positions. He flung himself prone as bullets laced the ground around him.

I turned to Pantoja and Howie. "Guys, we've gotta get Garvin and Baldwin."

Both men nodded. They were game for anything. Pantoja glanced over at them. Garvin lay against a tree, Baldwin's belt wrapped as a tourniquet just below his shoulder. He looked wan and weak.

Next to him, Baldwin lay in the reddish dirt, blood coursing from a hole in his boot at shin level.

"We need to get over there now," Pantoja said as he finished wrapping and taping Howard's hands with gauze.

"Howie, can you put that 240 between them while we pull them out of there?"

"Yes, sir."

"Go now."

Hands bandaged, Howie cradled his machine gun and sprinted through the fire. He hadn't taken more than a dozen steps when a mortar round buried itself in the dirt not fifteen meters to his right. He was fortunate. The shrapnel sprayed away from him. A second later, the concussion wave struck Howie and he went down on one knee as a fresh fusillade of machine-gun fire flayed the hilltop. He got right back up—no hesitation at all—and ran on until he reached the edge of the perimeter. He deployed his 240 and joined the fight.

Do I watch and stay by the radios? Do I get back into the fight?

Or do I do the only thing that will save my conscience?

Sometimes, being the leader I was supposed to be meant retaining elements of the man I already was, even if it meant putting the greater good at stake.

I turned to Pantoja. "Doc, We gotta do this too. You coming?"

"With you, sir. Always."

"Ready? One . . . two . . . three!"

We broke cover from behind the Humvee and charged flat out for Baldwin. A bullet cracked right past my ear. Another round tore into my assault pack again. One chewed up the ground where I was about to plant my next step.

Doc Pantoja stayed right with me, a few meters to one side.

Something exploded to my left. The concussions slammed into me, blowing me off my feet just as a furnace of heat struck my side and back. I hit the ground and tumbled side over side until dirt, sky, trees, and rocks all vanished in that terrible dark void once again.

THIRTEEN

DESOLATION WALK

★ ★ ★

THERE WAS A RUSH OF WHITE NOISE IN MY EAR, AS IF I'D fallen asleep in front of a TV whose station had gone off the air.

Forcing one eye open, I found myself lying on my right side about ten meters from Baldwin and Garvin. Doc Pantoja had reached them. A Mexican national who had joined the army to gain U.S. citizenship and pay for college, Pantoja took care of his wounded with such devotion that he'd long since been known as one of the best medics in the battalion.

He drew a syringe from his aid bag and stuck Garvin with it. Morphine, no doubt. Then he went to work trying to get a better tourniquet onto his arm. Garvin's head fell to one side, and I saw anguish on his face.

Baldwin ignored his wound. He was on the rim of our hilltop now, his M4 at his shoulder, picking targets. He knew the score.

Every rifle was needed for this fight, but as the blood kept bubbling out of that hole above his boot, I knew that he could not stay on the line much longer. If we didn't get him out, he was going to die.

On the far north of the line, an RPG exploded next to Greeson's rig. Bray was in the turret, manning the Mark 19 grenade launcher. The blast sprayed the side of the Humvee and knocked the weapon out. Bray frantically tried to restore it to action.

To Greeson's right, Private Lewis climbed into Sabo's turret and began picking targets with the fifty-cal. Lewis was new to the platoon and was so quiet, I'd hardly gotten to know him. Now bullets spanged off his turret's armored shield, but he paid them no attention. This was his first patrol with Outlaw Platoon. So much for easing into a combat deployment.

The white noise in my ears diminished. As if somebody had turned down a stereo's volume, I began to hear the sounds of battle again.

Garvin let out a crazy laugh. His head lolled; a smile broke the clutch of pain on his face. The morphine was kicking in. I wanted to move, to get to them both, but I couldn't gain control of my body. All I could do was lie there, a spectator to the suffering of my brothers.

Something oozed from my ears. It slid down my neck like Jell-O. With a supreme effort, I brought up a trembling hand and swiped it off my skin. Was I hit? Was it blood? I focused on my fingers. No. Whatever this was looked clear with a little bit of pink. I'd never seen anything like this come out of a human being before. It smelled vaguely like bananas.

Fuck it. It isn't blood. No need to worry about it.

A monarch butterfly flitted past my face. It alighted on a small weed growing out of the dirt a few inches from my head. I couldn't take my eyes off the fragile creature. A thick black band outlined its gold wings while its tips were spotted white. Such beauty.

Beyond its perch on the weed, I could see Baldwin's leg still bleeding into the dirt. Garvin's disembodied laughter rose over the sounds of battle while Doc Pantoja struggled to stanch his arm wound.

Violence and pastoral serenity. To which world did I belong? Who was the insignificant creature here? The tiny butterfly or the broken man lying nearby watching it? In the grand scheme of things, did either of us matter?

The butterfly leapt into the air.

I hope you make it through this, little guy.

Garvin's voice cut through the din of gunfire. "Hey, you fuckers!!" he shouted. "I got my Purple Heart! I got my Purple Heart!"

Baldwin looked over his shoulder at our medic. "Get Garvin out of here!"

Another mortar exploded on the crest of our hill. Doc Pantoja jumped across Garvin's body, shielding him from the shrapnel whirring past.

Enough was enough, I had to get up.

That was easier said than done. I rolled onto my stomach and tried to push myself up onto one knee. The effort seemed extraordinary. My head rocked and rolled. A wave of nausea struck me.

Get the knee up. Good. Push up, come on. Come on.

I felt my boots meet moondust. Swaying, the world spinning, I stumbled over to Garvin and Pantoja. Just as I reached them, Doc lifted himself off Garvin's body. As his head came up, he suddenly jerked sideways and spun into the dirt.

"Doc! Doc!"

He lay motionless. I reached for him, calling his name repeatedly. Garvin, high on morphine, lay on his back mumbling about his Purple Heart.

Finally Pantoja moved. He rolled over, his face a mass of blood. He'd been shot in the cheek. A wedge of white fat hung limply from the wound.

Forward Operating Base (FOB) Bermel's Hesco bag wall. FOB Bermel was our first home in Afghanistan, dominated by Rakhah Ridge to the east, which the enemy used nearly every day as a perfect launching point for rocket attacks against us. *Author collection*

On the border during a mounted checkpoint, I'm looking into the distance at oncoming traffic from Pakistan, a country that played a vital role for our enemies during their spring offensive in 2006. *Author collection*

This photo of Outlaw Platoon (officially Third Platoon) was taken during our first month in country at FOB Bermel. We trained together for nearly two years before deploying, but nothing would fully prepare us for the terrifying reality of combat in Afghanistan. *Front row, left to right:* Bobby Pilon, Luis Perez, Colten Wallace, Alexsandr Nosov, Mitchell Ayers, Jonathan Dugin, Dennis Leiphart, Jose Vega. *Second row, left to right:* Richard Haggerty, Zachary Gotass, Charles Byerly, Joseph Connor, Keith Lewis, Bennett Garvin, Philip Baldwin, Josiah Reuter. *Third row, left to right:* Sean Parnell, Gordon Campbell, John Saint Jean, Brian Bray, Chris Brown, Jason Sabatke, Marcel Rowley, Ryan Wheat, Tim Stalter, Robert Pinholt, Marty Belanger. *Fourth row, left to right:* Travis Roberts, David McLeod, Erwin Echavez, Khanh Nguyen, Mark Howard, Anthony Kienlen. (Not pictured: Greg Greeson, Jose Pantoja, Jeff Hall, Jeremiah Cole.) *Author collection*

At an early patrol to the Bermel bazaar, the company command group met with village elders to discuss the needs of their tribes. *Left to right:* First Lieutenant Dave Taylor, Captain Jason Dye, and me. *Courtesy Jason Dye*

Outlaw Platoon's Green Skull insignia was designed to strike fear in the hearts of our enemies. Later in the deployment, that's exactly what happened. *Courtesy Robert Pinholt*

Chris Cowan (*far right*) and me standing with our "allies" during a border security meeting. The other men were part of the Pakmil Frontier Corps of the Pakistani military, who routinely gave insurgents the freedom to conduct cross-border attacks on us. Later in our deployment, Pakmil Frontier troops began to attack coalition forces directly and even embedded with Haqqani Network fighters as they launched cross-border raids. *Courtesy Josiah Reuter*

One of the strongest enemy engagements hit us on May 7, 2006. Here, I'm moving through the kill zone to the top of the knoll. The gunner behind me was traversing to bring his weapon to bear on the enemy, who had the high ground again, to the left. At the top of the photo, one of the insurgents can be seen moving through the trees along the ridge. *Courtesy Travis Roberts*

In the aftermath of the May 7, 2006, battle, the expressions on the faces of the Afghan National Army soldiers say everything about what happened. *Courtesy Travis Roberts*

Payback is a bitch. The enemy wasn't the only one laying ambushes, and this time Alexsandr Nosov holds the high ground. *Courtesy Richard Haggerty*

Ryan Wheat, obviously thrilled with his fire-building accomplishments. *Courtesy Bobby Pilon*

Sergeant First Class Greg Greeson being awarded his second Purple Heart by Colonel (now Major General) John W. Nicholson Jr. Like many of my men, Greeson chose to stay with the Outlaws even though his head wound was serious enough to merit evacuation. *Courtesy Travis Roberts*

Greeson's first brief with Outlaw Platoon. The men wondered what kind of leader they had inherited, but he would soon put all doubts to rest. *Left to right, on the trucks:* me, Greeson, Campbell, and Đugin. *Courtesy Travis Roberts*

Back inside the wire after a battle on June 10, 2006, I stood in front of Philip Baldwin's shot-up Humvee, mentally and physically exhausted, my head throbbing. Still, I had to try to project strength for my wounded and weary soldiers. *Courtesy Josiah Reuter*

"Roads? Where we're going, we don't need roads." We tried to make our own way through our patrol area, and wadis were a natural avenue for us. The few actual roads were often laced with IEDs and ambushes, so we stayed off them whenever we could. *Courtesy Robert Pinholt*

Staff Sergeant Gordon Campbell and Specialist Richard Haggerty investigate the enemy camp we uncovered on May 8, 2006. In the bag were the personal effects of an enemy fighter, including a snapshot of him with his children. We also found prescription bottles from Pakistani hospitals and a handwritten notebook full of American telephone numbers. *Courtesy Travis Roberts*

Sniper Sergeant Ryan Wheat (*right*) and Campbell (*left*) burning down an enemy hide site. Whenever we could, we tried to deny the enemy any source of concealment. *Courtesy Travis Roberts*

During World War II, our battalion advanced into the Italian Alps, fighting America's enemies on the snowy battlefields of Europe. Two generations later, we carried on the legacy of the 10th Mountain Division as the grandsons of the original Catamounts, fighting our own pitched battles in the Hindu Kush. *Courtesy Travis Roberts*

Corporal Colten Wallace lets loose with a cathartic battle cry in the wake of an ambush. After we killed or drove off the insurgents, we found this long-abandoned compound that the enemy had been using as a base of operations and burned it to the ground. *Courtesy Robert Pinholt*

Second Platoon's defining moment came during Operation Catamount Blitz on November 7, 2006. Here, Staff Sergeant Jeff Hall (*front*) and Lieutenant Courtney Carnegie (*left rear*) lead the assault up the mountainside to find and rescue a dying marine. This photo was taken seconds before they charged straight into the enemy's flank, fought their way forward, and found him. *Courtesy Travis Roberts*

Abdul, the best "'terp" (interpreter) we had, standing on the road to his hometown. He was the only 'terp allowed to carry a weapon, and our lives became inextricably linked as a result of the 9/11 attacks. *Courtesy Josiah Reuter*

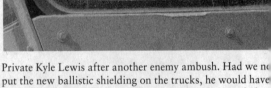

Private Kyle Lewis after another enemy ambush. Had we not put the new ballistic shielding on the trucks, he would have been shot in the head . . . again. *Courtesy Robert Pinholt*

Brian Bray getting ready to roll. *Courtesy Travis Roberts*

Private First Class Jeremiah Cole retrieving a supply drop about one hundred meters outside of FOB Bermel on May 16, 2006. This photo was taken two months to the day before his first enemy engagement. *Courtesy Marcel Rowley*

Staff Sergeant Philip Baldwin sitting in a truck before a patrol. His tactical acumen and life experience set the tone for the platoon's overall success in combat. *Courtesy Josiah Reuter*

Corporal Robert Pinholt (*left*) was my young, highly intelligent, opinionated driver and Sergeant Michael Emerick (*right*) was our platoon's artist. *Courtesy Robert Pinholt*

Doc Jose Pantoja contemplating the enemy's "long, dark reach" prior to leaving the wire on a mission to aid one of our own on a terribly difficult day. *Courtesy Travis Roberts*

Wallace snapping out shots at the enemy in the mid of a kill zone righ on the Pakistani border. The enem had the high ground that day. *Courtesy Robert Pinholt*

The emaciated children of the Afghan border region. This photo was taken a few kilometers from what we came to call the Village of the Damned. *Courtesy Robert Pinholt*

Sergeant Keith Lewis giving the Afghan girls coloring books. We quickly learned that if we didn't separate the boys from the girls and try to spread the gifts around, the boys would beat the girls raw and take what we'd given them after we left. *Courtesy Travis Roberts*

Wallace standing shocked just moments after his truck ran over an anti-tank mine. We had been betrayed by a spy in our midst, and this would become the platoon's worst day. *Courtesy Travis Roberts*

Chris Brown performing his legendary "Thriller" dance on top of his Humvee before a mission. *Courtesy Robert Pinholt*

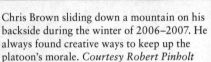

Chris Brown sliding down a mountain on his backside during the winter of 2006–2007. He always found creative ways to keep up the platoon's morale. *Courtesy Robert Pinholt*

Chris Cowan, better known as "the Constrictor," putting his trademark headlock on Chris Brown. *Courtesy Travis Roberts*

"You're a member of this platoon now. Don't fuck it up." This was my initiation into the platoon at the Joint Readiness Training Center (JRTC) in Fort Polk, Louisiana. For days, I walked around the entire brigade with remnants of the word "cherry" written on my forehead. *Courtesy Marcel Rowley*

Michael Emerick entertaining both the platoon and some locals outside of Malakshay during a lighter moment on patrol. *Courtesy Robert Pinholt*

Specialist John Saint Jean, our "Haitian Hammer," in the turret before he was wounded in action. *Courtesy Travis Roberts*

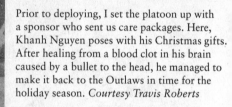

Prior to deploying, I set the platoon up with a sponsor who sent us care packages. Here, Khanh Nguyen poses with his Christmas gifts. After healing from a blood clot in his brain caused by a bullet to the head, he managed to make it back to the Outlaws in time for the holiday season. *Courtesy Travis Roberts*

Marcel Rowley, our platoon prankster, pulls security with his squad automatic weapon. This iconic image represents well our generation's commitment to country . . . with attitude. *Courtesy Josiah Reuter*

"Sir, you okay?" he asked me. Before I could respond, he crawled over to me and started looking over my head.

"Doc, your face . . ."

"Let me check you out," he insisted.

I turned my head. More of that pinkish fluid, sticky and thick, leached from my nose and both ears.

"I'm good, I'm good," I said to my medic. "It isn't blood. Get Garvin out of here."

Ignoring the blood flowing down his ruined face, Doc clawed his way over to Garvin. "Hey, Doc! I'm getting a Purple Heart! How about that?" Pantoja grabbed him by his body armor and pulled him upright. Standing now, he slipped Garvin's good arm around his neck. He called me over to help, and I reached for Garvin's wounded arm to keep it above the level of his heart. Together we staggered through the fire toward my Humvee.

Now it was Baldwin's turn. He'd been shooting his M4 down at the onrushing enemy horde, but now he began to inch his way back toward the center of our perimeter. He was about thirty feet away from me, scrabbling through the dirt by pushing himself along with his one good leg. As he clutched the ground to pull himself forward, a bullet smacked the dirt an inch from his outstretched hand. The bullet missed his body but scored a direct hit on his psyche. It seemed to flip a switch inside him. Perhaps for the first time, he thought of Regina and the kids. The full weight of his situation hit him.

He rolled onto his back, his helmet rolling forgotten from his head.

"Baldwin!" I shouted.

His head turned, as if in slow motion, to regard me. His eyes were flat and desolate. He had given up.

No way. This isn't going to happen. Not to this man.

"Doc! I need help!"

I lumbered to my feet and drunk-ran toward Baldwin. When I

reached him and grabbed the handle on the back of his body armor, the look of abject surrender vanished, replaced by pure relief.

Baldwin was a huge load to move. Six-four, two-twenty. With one leg disabled and so much blood lost, he was too weak and immobile to get to his feet. I grabbed his IBA and tugged him forward. He moved only a foot or so. He had me by at least thirty pounds. Once more I pulled him forward, and I felt him kicking with his good leg, trying to help me with what leverage he could offer.

And then Doc was by my side. His facial wound ran from his jawline across the bridge of his nose. He looked as though he had lost a knife fight. He reached down and seized Baldwin's arm.

"Let's go," he said.

Together we dragged Baldwin back to my Humvee. Safely concealed behind the rig, Baldwin was at last out of the direct line of fire. Silently Pantoja went to work on him, cutting open his saturated pant leg to dress the wound in his shin.

"Stay here. We got this," I said.

But Baldwin had no interest in staying put. "Sir, you need every rifle out there."

"Stay here!" I ordered again. Before he could respond, Greeson sprinted by, carrying ammunition from one position to another. I was amazed at how fast he could move, especially given his shoulder wound. He was five foot six, bowlegged, and forty years old, but he possessed the speed and agility of a twentysomething track athlete.

"Sir, Campbell's been hit. Lewis is down, too. Shot in the head," he reported as he went past.

Pinholt appeared beside me. "Sir, we're about to be overrun. We need to Z out our radios."

"No way," I said instinctively. In worst-case scenarios, we were trained to erase the frequencies on our communication systems so the enemy could not listen to our chatter. By doing so, we would lose all ability to call for more fire support or troops.

"Sir, we need to do it," Pinholt insisted.

"No. We cannot lose our link to the FOB."

Both enemy assault elements had cleared their own slopes now and were pouring across the valley floor, a hundred men at least. How many did we have left? A dozen? Maybe Pinholt was right.

We lose our radio link, we all die.

"Reuter!" I shouted, turning to my forward observer, who was sitting in my Humvee with the radio handset to his mouth.

"Sir?"

"Call in everything you can. Work the fire missions. Danger close, got it?"

"Yes, sir."

He keyed the handset and began barking coordinates.

I looked at my RTO. "Do not Z out these radios. They go down, we all go down, got it?"

"Yes, sir."

"Good. Grab a radio and come with me," I told him.

It was time to walk the line. I looked left and saw Bray at the far north, his gym-sculpted figure still in Greeson's turret trying to get the Mark 19 grenade launcher into action. Next in line was Sabo's ruined rig. Nobody was in the turret. Lewis must have been shot out of it just as Emerick had been. Sabo grabbed a can of .50-caliber ammunition out of his rig and ran through the fire to Baldwin's rig. He passed the can up to Campbell, who quickly loaded a fresh belt into his Ma Deuce. Sabo had always been paranoid about ammunition, an effect of his last deployment's firefights, and he always jammed extra cans into his truck. I was grateful for that now.

On the far right, Private Dugin, our platoon head case, manned Waites's turret. We had an extra fifty-cal that day, and Dugin was not as familiar with it as Campbell, Bray, or Emerick. I could see him fiddling with it, trying to get it to fire more than a few shots at a time. The Ma Deuce is a tricky weapon and requires finesse to get the head space and timing just right so that the weapon will fire full auto without jamming. Incorrectly set, the fifty becomes a big bolt-action rifle.

Dugin worked on it, his hands shaking. He was a young kid who'd only wanted to fit in with the rest of the platoon, but instead of being himself, he had tried to ingratiate his way into the inner circle with transparent and outrageous lies. He'd claimed to have played Big Ten football, said he owned the most popular bar in Watertown, and once told the men that he had played in a well-known rock band.

Dugin racked the fifty's bolt and tried to trigger off a burst. No joy. The weapon fired once and jammed. He went back to tinkering with it.

Next to Waites's truck, Wheat lay prone with his scope to his eye, scanning for targets. I couldn't see Waites. Wheat coolly took a shot. His M4 bucked, and he adjusted his aim. Above him, Dugin tried to fire his machine gun again. It barked once, then jammed.

Wheat pulled his eye away from the scope and said, "Dugin, what the fuck?"

"I don't know what's wrong, Sergeant!"

As Wheat gave him advice, I started across the hilltop for him. I hadn't taken more than a dozen steps when a spout of gray-black smoke entwined with fountains of dirt erupted between me and Waites's truck. Shrapnel splashed away from us and tore limbs off a nearby tree. The blast wave struck before I could react, driving me sideways onto my knees. It felt as if someone had just hit my head with a baseball bat.

"Hey, sir, you okay?" Pinholt asked, pulling up beside me.

The world was spinning. I had vertigo. "Yeah, I'm good."

Weakly, I struggled to my feet as another barrage of RPGs struck our hilltop. More plumes of dirt and smoke peppered the scene. A mortar exploded on the far side of the perimeter. The enemy machine gunners continued their merciless work.

Pinholt and I reached Waites's truck and took cover. Dugin tried to fire the fifty again. This time he unleashed a long burst that chewed through most of his hundred-round belt. Then an RPG exploded near the Humvee, sending shrapnel pinging off its armored hide. The concussion hit Dugin and threw him against one side of the turret. When he recovered and tried to fire the fifty, it jammed again. He went to work on it with his Gerber.

"How you doing, Wheat?" I asked.

"Goin' good here, sir, but we're about to have company."

He pointed down the hill. Perhaps twenty enemy fighters had broken off from Galang's southern attack force and were moving laterally around the base of the hill.

"They're tryin' to get aroun' behind us, sir," Wheat noted casually.

Dugin's fifty plus the four men assigned to Waites's truck were all that stood between us getting overrun by this new threat.

I said to Wheat, "Okay, get ready."

Wheat nodded. "Don't y'all worry now, sir. We'll handle 'em."

I wish I had Wheat's calm.

"Dugin!" he shouted. "Hold up! Fire on my mark, got it?"

"Yes, Sergeant."

Dugin waited. Wheat lay down again and stuck his eye into his scope, watching patiently. He wanted to pick his moment for absolute maximum shock value. Finally the flanking enemy reached an open stretch of ground perhaps a hundred and fifty meters away.

"Fire! Fire! Fire!"

Dugin mashed his thumbs down on his butterfly triggers. The Ma Deuce bellowed once, then jammed. He racked the bolt and fired one more shot. I wondered if the RPG had damaged the weapon.

"Dugin, what's wrong?" Wheat asked.

"Dunno. Dunno."

He racked the bolt. A shell casing flew out of the chamber.

Before he pulled the trigger, he threw his Gerber into the dirt beside the Humvee.

What the hell?

Another pull on the trigger, and the weapon jammed again. This time Dugin had no tool to fix it. He jumped out of the turret, slid off the hood, and grabbed the Gerber. Wheat's calm demeanor cracked. Face red, he said through clenched teeth, "Dugin, what the fuck are you doing?"

Dugin climbed back into the turret. He tweaked the head space and timing again, then tossed the Gerber overboard a second time. Incredulous, we stared at him as he jumped out of the turret to retrieve it. When it happened a third time, Wheat scooped the Gerber up and climbed onto the Humvee. He made a few quick adjustments on the Ma Deuce, test fired it, and swung it back into Dugin's waiting hands.

"Good to go!" he yelled and slapped Dugin on the shoulder. He leapt back to the ground and landed beside Pinholt. He looked at my driver and asked, "You ready?"

"Roger that!"

"Wait a tick. Let 'em get a little closer," he said. Pinholt nodded once, his eyes a bit wider. How close did Wheat want them? In our laps?

Galang's men were less than a hundred meters away now, still sliding around our southern flank. Another few minutes, and they'd be behind us.

Dugin blasted off a long burst. The fifty's deafening roar had never sounded more comforting. The enemy dived for cover as the heavy bullets tore through bushes and trees, shattering rock formations and men with impunity.

"I'm about ready to get on this shit," said Wheat.

He spotted movement and placed his eye to his scope. "Ah, there ya are," he mumbled. His M4 snapped twice. Double tap.

Down the hill, his bullets knocked a man off his feet. He flopped to the ground, two red stains center mass, his rifle falling beside him.

Pinholt joined in. Dugin's fifty hammered away. Wheat triggered off another pair of bullets. Another man dropped.

They stopped moving laterally now and began to assault up the hill. Wheat killed another man with two more shots. That made them cautious. Some went to ground and began to shoot back. Others crept forward using the available cover.

Dugin's fifty thrashed them. Wheat's precision sniping claimed another victim. The attack was breaking down.

Waites appeared out of nowhere, standing beside the back-left fender of his Humvee. His weapon was at his side, barrel down. He looked disengaged.

"Waites!" I shouted to him. He didn't reply.

His head swiveled from side to side.

"What the fuck is he doing?" Pinholt asked Wheat.

"No idea."

Head still on a swivel, eyes the picture of desolation, Waites walked right between us and started down the slope into the teeth of the enemy force. Fully exposed, rifle still at his side, his sudden move surprised the enemy. There was a pause in the firing. Quickly enough, they recovered, and a flurry of AKs unleashed in full auto at him. The air cracked and whipped with bullets. The ground around him churned. He kept walking toward the enemy.

Pinholt screamed, "Sergeant Waites, they're trying to kill you!"

My black-sheep squad leader didn't respond.

Wheat and Pinholt exchanged glances. In that instant, they knew what had to be done. Wheat covered Waites with quick, well-aimed shots. Pinholt rose into the firestorm and charged down the hill. He caught Waites by his IBA and stopped his momentum. Two men exposed sparked an AK feeding frenzy. Dugin's fifty answered, but the fusillade continued.

Through it, Pinholt single-handedly dragged Waites back up the hill. He set him down next to Wheat's fighting position. Waites offered no resistance.

I crawled over to him. "Waites?"

No response. His head had stopped moving. He looked catatonic.

The terror and strain of combat affect every man differently. It had made Dugin momentarily lose his senses and throw his Gerber into the dirt. For others, such as Sabo, it arouses rage and adrenaline. With Wheat it had the opposite effect; he went cold and calculating.

Here I was confronted by a new response. Waites was no coward, not by a long shot. His psyche just could not process in these conditions. He'd shut down completely. All his lackadaisical behavior these past months came into focus. He had refused to consider combat a possibility. It could not happen, this moment could not come. Deep down he knew his mind would not be able to function in battle. Denial had become his defense.

"Waites?" I said again.

Reality has a bad habit of making denial irrelevant.

"Wheat?"

"Yeah, sir?"

"Your squad now," I said.

"I got it, sir." Silently he stripped Waites of his magazines and handed a few to Pinholt. Waites didn't resist or say a word. He just gazed out into space with a thousand-yard stare.

"They're coming again!" Pinholt shouted. Wheat's rifle cracked twice. Another insurgent died. Dugin's fifty boomed. He was spot-on this time, handling the huge weapon like a steely-eyed veteran. He'd found his battle legs.

Three men against twenty, and they were holding their own.

To the north, though, a crisis brewed. I heard Chris Brown's 240 rip through a belt. Had they gotten behind us after all? I got up and ran back to my rig. Brown had traversed north and was shooting at targets to the left of Greeson's Humvee. Baldwin had refused to stay out the fight. Using my door as cover, he stood on one leg, blazing away at the enemy to the north.

Greeson appeared. He'd been bolting from one position to another, handing out ammunition to the men. He stuck a finger out at Baldwin and said, "You. Sit."

"We need everyone in this fight," he protested.

"Stay here and get treated," I ordered. He looked pissed.

I checked with Reuter. "Any birds en route?"

"Negative, sir. All the air assets are tied up elsewhere."

"Keep trying."

I huddled up with Greeson. A good dynamic existed between the two of us. I was always the hot one. He ran cold and kept me grounded. We'd become so close that we could finish each other's thoughts. Throughout the fight, we didn't even have to communicate much, but all along we functioned smoothly as a team.

"Greeson?"

"Yeah, sir?" he growled through dirt-crusted lips.

"What's our next play?"

Somebody screamed, "They're comin' again!" The sound of gunfire grew fast and desperate. The tempo of the fight was changing, building. I looked at Greeson and saw relentless determination etched on his face. But I also saw a touch of fear.

"Fuck, I dunno, sir. Shoot back."

Has it come to that?

He grabbed a handful of M4 mags and dashed across the perimeter. I checked my own situation. Five mags. I'd given two to Wheat.

A platoon leader should never be directly in the fight. The radios are his best weapon. But there are moments imposed upon us by the enemy when there is no other option. Briefly, I thought of Major General William Dean, whose division had been overrun in the summer of 1950 during the Korean War. As his men had broken under the weight of a tank assault, he had grabbed a bazooka and fought street by street in the city of Taejon.

Greeson was right. This was one of those moments. So I did what he suggested and ran after him to the east edge of the perimeter. Campbell was still in the turret of Baldwin's rig, his hands and arms burned and studded with pieces of shrapnel. But he was working the fifty like a gruesome artist. The enemy cleared the road and reached the base of our hill. They were only a couple hundred meters away now. One more rush, and they'd be on us.

They paused, and I could see them forming up into fire teams. In groups of three or four, they began bounding uphill toward us, each squad working to cover the other's movements.

That's exactly how we'd do it.

Sabatke started to run for me. A jagged chunk of shrapnel had cut open his forehead. Blood was trailing down both sides of his face and across the bridge of his nose. It made him look hellish.

"Sir! They're coming up the hill! They're coming up the hill!" A fusillade of enemy fire sent him diving for cover. The volume of incoming swelled again as we started taking AK fire from those below us. Bullets bounced and whirred off Campbell's armored shield. He seemed oblivious to the danger.

From below arose a hundred war cries, intermingling into one terrifying undulating sound. "Li-li-li-li-li!"

My men began shouting back, "Motherfuckers! Come and get some!"

Campbell tracked a target and unleashed a burst. "Eat that, fuckers!" he screamed.

"Allahu akbar!"

"Li-li-li-li!"

"Suck my dick!"

Galang's squad and fire team leaders barked out orders. The firing grew climactic as the fighting narrowed to point-blank range.

We don't have the ammo for this.

Below me, I saw a fire team dash from one stand of trees to another. Less than a hundred meters away now, they moved with practiced speed, howling as they went. They wore man jams, olive drab pants, and old-style green field jackets. Some of them had chest racks bulging with extra AK-47 magazines. I saw a few wearing black ski masks.

All of them carried those eight-inch knives on their hips.

Another fire team broke cover and surged toward us. This time, Campbell caught them cold. He triggered his fifty, and its stream of bullets ripped them apart with appalling violence. Their gory remains decorated the slope and festooned the trees. The trailing enemy fire team froze at the horrific sight.

Right then, the first 105mm artillery rounds from the guns at FOB Bermel struck the base of the hill. The ground bucked and shook. Flames and smoke jetted skyward. I watched one shell vaporize three men. But more came on, sprinting even faster, driven by the realization that their only hope now rested on getting to the top of the hill, where we could not call in artillery without killing ourselves. It was the one way they could mitigate our firepower advantage.

About thirty meters away, I spotted an enemy fighter partially concealed behind a tree. He was yelling something to four other men advancing ahead of him. As I took aim, my eyes had trouble focusing and he ducked behind the trunk. Which side of the tree would he peer around next? I had a fifty-fifty chance, so I picked left.

Sure enough, he exposed his chest and head for just an instant. A slight adjustment, and my sight was on him, center mass. My rifle cracked. A jet of blood erupted from his neck, and he spun away from the tree to collapse in the dirt.

★ ★ ★

I FELT NOTHING. NO TIME TO THINK ABOUT THAT NOW.

Campbell's machine gun made a metallic *click* sound. He'd burned through the last rounds on that belt. A quick check of his Humvee revealed that it was the last of the fifty-cal ammo. He let out a long string of obscenities as he reached for his M4. Soon he was blazing away next to his empty machine gun, still in the fight.

One by one, our heavy weapons ran out of ammunition. Brown's 240 went silent. So did Private Dugin's fifty that was mounted on Waites's rig. Nobody was in Sabo's turret now that both Emerick and Lewis had gone down with head shots. Despite every effort, Bray's Mark 19 refused to fire. Our best weapons were all but useless. Desperate, the gunners drew their 9mm pistols, racked the slides, and fired into the onrushing waves of enemy. It was a measure of last resort I'd never thought I'd see.

Another fire team sped forward. They attracted a rash of fire from my men, but none of them went down. Ten meters away, they went to ground behind rocks and trees to spray us with their AKs. Behind them, another squad swept uphill as soon as the lead squad began suppressing us.

What next, Sean? What next?

I thought of the 20th Maine Volunteer Infantry Regiment on day two of the Battle of Gettysburg. All afternoon those Union men had repelled wave after wave of Confederate attackers. Finally, with more than half the regiment down, their commander, Colonel Joshua Lawrence Chamberlain, ordered a final, desperate bayonet charge into the teeth of the attacking force.

We were at that point. Only we didn't have any bayonets.

FOURTEEN

BLOOD BROTHERS

★ ★ ★

CHRIS BROWN'S PISTOL CRACKED. CAMPBELL'S RIFLE bucked. Wheat double-tapped another insurgent. Pilon's SAW chattered. Sabatke ducked into his Humvee and snatched a pair of M18 Claymore mines. Withering AK fire be damned, he planted one next to each front fender, facing down the hill.

Galang's men squeezed closer. They had us, and they knew it.

A head appeared in Sabo's turret. No helmet, just filthy hair caked with blood. Our artist lived. A rush of relief flooded through me.

He pulled himself up to the fifty and quickly checked it over. It still had a few rounds left. He swung the weapon down and soon found a target. He triggered a burst. Then another. A fifty-cal at point-blank range creates an indescribable mess out of human beings. For those nearby who somehow escape its wrath, the carnage it wreaks inflicts paralyzing terror.

Emerick was holding his own.

To the north, a sudden swell of gunfire rose above the din of our own battle. I could hear AKs and enemy machine guns hammering furiously at some new target. Fifty-cals, 240s, and a Mark 19 answered back.

Captain Dye and Delta Platoon had joined the fight. They were coming in across the enemy's right flank and would have to shoot their way through the insurgents assaulting Sabo and Greeson's section of the line. If we didn't coordinate with them, we ran the risk of accidentally shooting at each other while aiming at the enemy in between. I'd have to make sure that did not happen.

I backed off the crest, rose to my feet, and ran for Greeson, who was picking his shots from behind a tree.

The enemy made a rush at Sabo. He killed them with a Claymore. Those mines are like shotguns on steroids or Civil War cannons loaded with grapeshot. They spray a kill zone with hundreds of tiny steel balls that shred anything unarmored in their path. Their optimum range is twenty to thirty meters. In a defensive fight, they form the last line of defense before hand-to-hand combat.

Screams and shrieks of pain filled the air. Sabo detonated the other Claymore. Emerick's fifty went dry.

I reached Greeson and took a knee next to him. From his vantage point on the northern edge of the line, we could see Delta's Humvees in the valley below us. They'd stumbled into Galang's flank security element, which had sparked a vicious secondary firefight that had distracted the enemy and stalled their attack.

Mortar rounds rained down on the hilltop again. A fresh stream of RPGs joined in as Galang's support-by-fire element risked hitting its own men in the hope of finishing us off before Delta could fight its way to us.

The linkup between our battered platoon and Delta had to go flawlessly. There was no margin for error here. After all we'd been through, I could not stomach the idea of one of my men getting hit by friendly fire. I broke cover and started running downhill. Greeson shouted something and came after me, but I ignored him.

Delta's rigs reached the base of the hill, and I recognized Sergeant Chris Cowan standing tall in Captain Dye's turret, going cyclic with his 240.

Captain Dye's remaining rigs blew through Galang's flank security and struck the northern assault element from the rear and flank. The enemy fighters recoiled away from the Humvees as they rumbled up the hill.

If Wheat's element can hold out, we may pull this off.

I waved at the lead rig's driver and directed him into place. Greeson helped guide the rigs as they got closer to our lines. One by one, the Delta trucks rolled to our perimeter and took station on the east side.

Captain Dye dismounted into machine-gun, mortar, and RPG fire. "What the hell is happening here?" he exclaimed as we met up just behind his rig. Around us my men fought on, bloodied and wounded, most down to their final rounds. Greeson started cross loading ammo from Delta's trucks so our men could stay in the fight.

Captain Dye had arrived in the nick of time.

Sergeant James Newton, a big redhead known to be an excellent shot, stepped out of one of the Delta rigs, hefting a Vietnam-era M14 rifle. He joined us as I briefed Captain Dye.

"Half my men are down, sir. They're attacking in two elements. Two platoons plus. We're out of ammo and need to get our seriously wounded out of here."

"Where do you want me?" Newton asked.

Just as he did, Emerick stumbled out of Sabo's truck. He and Newton were friends, and the big redhead marveled at our artist's head wound and the burns on his neck and face.

"What the hell happened to you?" he asked.

"Check this out," Emerick said as he held up his helmet. There was a splintered hole in the front and a bigger hole in the back side. The chin strap had been severed.

"I got shot in the head, Sergeant Newton! Can you believe this? It knocked me out cold," Emerick let out a peal of crazy laughter. The bullet had grazed his left side, exited the back of his helmet at a downward angle, and gone through part of his vest to ricochet around inside the truck.

"Unbefuckinleavable," Newton exclaimed. Before Emerick could reply, bullets shredded a nearby tree.

"Emerick, get down!" Newton shouted.

Emerick didn't bother to duck.

The enemy re-formed and came at us again. The range narrowed to mere meters. It astonished me that they would try again despite the addition of Delta's heavy weapons on our perimeter. One by one, our fifties rejoined the fight as Greeson delivered fresh ammo to our gunners.

Newton ran over to support Campbell and protect Baldwin's crippled truck. He'd mounted a beautiful Leupold scope on his M14, not that he needed it at such close quarters. As the fresh enemy assault closed in, he prepared to fire. Campbell, who had just finished loading a belt that Greeson had given him, triggered his Ma Deuce. His bullets walked through an advancing team and tore three men apart.

"You fucker, those were mine, I had them in my sights!" Newton shouted at Campbell.

The enemy wouldn't quit. The fight grew even more intense. Delta's platoon anchored us, or we would have gone down for sure. Still, we couldn't hold the enemy off indefinitely. We needed more firepower and more men.

Where was Second Platoon? Back at my rig, I checked in with

the FOB. Our company executive officer was on the net now, and he told me he was still working to get us some air assets. Sergeant Burley had taken up a supporting position with Second Platoon several kilometers to our rear.

I paused to think this over. Why was Burley not coming to join us?

On a hill a few hundred meters to our northwest, a head appeared over the crest. Then another. Soon a dozen figures flowed over the hilltop and down the slope facing us.

They were carrying AKs.

More followed. A dozen. Two. The lead element opened fire on the run, shooting from the hip like something straight out of a movie.

I had one mag left. I'd given all my others away. Even with Delta's trucks, we couldn't stop this fresh threat. Unconsciously, I clutched my Gerber knife.

I can't believe it has come to this.

More men poured over the crest. And then I saw a marine in their ranks.

"They're ANA," I said to myself.

Combat whipsaws your emotions in an extreme way that nothing else can. I'd gone from despair to euphoria in a matter of seconds.

The Afghan troops sprinted into our perimeter and counter-assaulted the enemy through our firing line. Galang's men reeled from the blow and fell back pell-mell to the base of the hill. Several more marine Humvees and ANA Toyotas joined us from the northwest. We'd gone from having five trucks, three of which had been rendered immobile by damage, to having fourteen.

Captain Dye's call for help had brought us two hundred Afghan soldiers. FOB Bermel was virtually stripped of soldiers. Yet Second Platoon had not joined the fight.

The battle raged below us. The Afghans were on a tear today, hoping to exact revenge for May 7. They pushed Galang's force back across the road on the valley floor. The enemy's machine guns caught some of the ANA in the open. The Afghan troops fell back or went to ground. The counterattack stalled, but the enemy did not break contact. A stalemate ensued.

Greeson caught up to First Sergeant Grigsby and asked, "Hey, can we use your trucks to get our wounded out of here?"

"Roger that! Load 'em up in those two," Grigsby replied, pointing at two Humvees on the northwest side of our hill. They were out of the main enemy fields of fire, which made them perfect for this mission of mercy.

"Sir, let's get Garvin and Baldwin out of here," said Greeson. We returned to my Humvee to find Garvin semiconscious. He'd lost a lot of blood. Baldwin had somehow crawled back into the fight. We could see him shooting into the valley while lying prone just behind the crest of the hill. The bandage on his leg was soaked; Pantoja had not been able to stanch his blood loss.

Sergeant Stalter grabbed Garvin and hoisted him off his feet. Greeson and I ran to go get Baldwin. But as we reached him, he shouted at us, "Get the fuck away from me! Take care of Garvin first!"

Stalter called out, "We got him, don't worry."

Baldwin had lost so much blood he couldn't stand anymore. The fact that he was still in the action was a testament to his lion heart. Now he was starting to fade. Greeson and I tried to lift him, but he was almost deadweight.

He mumbled something. His eyes had lost their luster. He'd given all he had to give. And then some.

SEEING US STRUGGLE, SABO AND OUR PROPHET spook, SERGEANT Dixon, rushed over to help us. Each of us grabbed one of Baldwin's limbs, and we carried him back toward the marine Humvees.

That was a terrible mistake.

Somewhere on the far ridge, an enemy machine gunner saw five Americans clustered together. The target we presented was too great to resist.

Dixon went down first, a bullet in the arm. He dropped his hold on Baldwin, and the sudden shift of weight caused all of us to slip and fall atop one another. We lost our grip on Baldwin, who flopped motionless to the ground.

Dixon turned, mouth agape at the sight of his own blood squirting over Baldwin. The bullet had severed an artery in his arm; with every heartbeat his life force fountained from his body.

Pantoja appeared beside us. He pulled Dixon to a knee, secured a tourniquet on his arm, and dressed the wound in a matter of seconds. The blood flow slowed to a trickle.

Baldwin stirred; he tried to raise his head, but the effort proved too much. He looked petrified.

"We gotta get them to the trucks," Greeson ordered. Dixon, now sheet white from blood loss, lifted Baldwin's wounded leg with his unwounded arm. The rest of us picked him up as well. Staying low, we moved as fast as we could off the lip of the hill, down the northwest slope to the waiting Humvees.

Before we could slide him inside the truck, Baldwin cried, "Sir, sir?"

The terror in his voice made us freeze.

"I'm fucked up."

Mouth open, shallow, rapid breathing. He was going into shock. I could see Afghan dirt ground into his teeth.

"You're gonna be okay, bro," I said.

"I'm shot in the back."

What?

When we all went down, Baldwin took a round at the base of his spine. We'd had no idea until that moment.

"I can't feel my legs."

He seized my hand with his, and as he stared at me with saucer eyes, he squeezed it hard. As weak as he had been, the fear assailing him now evoked one last burst of strength.

No words came. I held my brother's hand until they pulled me from him. Door closed, driver gunning the engine, the Humvee lumbered off for FOB Bermel. The second one, carrying Garvin and Dixon, soon followed. I watched them go, Greeson and Sabo standing beside me, the blood of our brothers drying on our hands and arms.

FIFTEEN

THE PLACE BEYOND DEVOTION

★ ★ ★

Two Apache gunships stormed over our battle-torn hilltop just as we reconvened at my Humvee. They arrowed into a steep climb until, hundreds of feet above us, they leveled off and plunged down into a gunnery pass. Their 30mm guns belched flame. Rockets spewed from pylon pods. A Hellfire missile went down range. Below us, the enemy side of the valley turned into a typhoon of steel and smoke.

The sight of those gunships riding to our rescue energized our weary men. They rose as one, arms high, cheering as the choppers dealt death to our tormentors.

As the Apaches strafed, I found Captain Dye. "We've got fixed wing coming in. Couple of A-10s."

Whatever aviation spigot had been shut off earlier was now open wide. I grinned and gave him a thumbs-up.

Then he added, "And a B-1, too."

The B-1 Lancer had been built as the last of the Cold War strategic bombers. Designed to carry nukes into the heart of Soviet Russia, each one could now carry dozens of satellite-guided bombs. For us, having one in the air was like an infantry platoon on Iwo Jima having a B-29 squadron on call.

"Wrath of God," I said.

"We need to get the ANA back here," Captain Dye said. He started to run after them, but I grabbed his shoulder. "Sir, I got this. You're working the radios. If you go down, we all go down."

He stopped and thought it over. "You're right. Go ahead."

"I'm on it," I replied.

The Apaches made another gunnery run. The enemy fire slackened, but we were still receiving occasional bursts from the ridges. I found one of the marine NCOs and told him what we needed. It took about twenty minutes for him to round up the Afghan troops—it was like herding cats—but soon everyone was tucked behind our hilltop perimeter.

Or so we thought.

The Apaches pulled off in preparation for the A-10s' arrival. They choppered east to pick off any of Galang's men trying to escape into Pakistan.

Over the radio, we heard the Warthog drivers roll into their attack runs. The peculiar sound of their engines rose in the distance.

"Hold it! Hold it! We've got men on the ridge!" First Sergeant Grigsby warned.

Somehow a squad of exceptionally aggressive Afghan troops had fought their way forward, across the valley, and halfway up one of the ridges. In the process, they'd lost contact with the rest of the ANA force.

Through our binos, we could see them skirmishing with one of the support-by-fire positions. Captain Dye told Reuter to call off the A-10s, whose pilots pulled up and went into orbit a few miles away. It took another half hour to get those hard chargers to cease their assault and return to us.

Once they did, hell visited Galang's men.

The Warthogs whistled in first, flaying the ridges with their tank-busting cannons before unleashing six satellite-guided bombs. We watched the concussion waves roll off the ridges toward us. A moment later, the ground shook as though a volcano had just blown its top.

Somehow the enemy managed to stay in the game. The remaining machine-gun positions continued to lash at us. Our rigs took hits. The men stayed hunkered down. It was time for the wrath of God.

"Pound those assholes," Captain Dye said to Reuter. Our forward observer keyed his mike and talked to the Lancer crew. "I don't care if they have high heels and miniskirts. Drop everything you have on that ridge!"

We heard the air force pilot chuckle through his confirmation.

Miles overhead, the B-1 Lancer reached its release point. The bomb bay doors flung open, and the crew disgorged its deadly load.

Seconds passed. The weapons fell with precision, their fins making minute corrections to their flight path based on the data stream flowing to their electronic brains from a satellite in orbit above us.

The ridges simply exploded. Eleven bombs struck in precise succession, each one overlapping the other until it looked as though a giant's fist had punched upward through the earth's crust, splintering rock and trees in all directions. In the holocaust of smoke and flames, men disintegrated. Weapons melted. Dugouts vanished.

Peals of thunder rolled through the valley. Our hilltop trembled and quaked. In seconds, smoke engulfed the stricken ridges and all we could see was debris raining down for hundreds of meters in all directions.

When it was over, the silence was almost unbearable. Galang's force had been pulverized.

The fighting had lasted for almost six hours. Exhausted, we hooked up our three disabled rigs and towed them off our hilltop for home. Our long column traveled west with barely a word shared among us. Empty shell casings littered our Humvee's floorboards, and as we bounced along the rugged Afghan roads, they jingled like sleigh bells.

When we reached Bermel, the homebodies turned out in force. The divide between combat troops and the men who work behind the wire grows wider in moments such as those. Band of brothers? No. Battle sifts those relationships like nothing else.

We called them POGs (Personnel Other than Grunts) or FOB-BITS. They smiled and laughed and took photos of our battered trucks as we parked out on the maintenance pad. They had spent the fight safe inside the base, uniforms clean, body armor stowed under their bunks. Now they behaved like the picnicking civilians who had turned out to watch the Battle of Bull Run during the Civil War. Combat tourists. What was worse, the POGs failed to notice how their ball game–like reception affected us. My men endured it, but just barely. Engines off now, the men dismounted to lean against tires, smoke in silence, or just stare into space.

I wasn't normally a smoker, but I was that evening.

My head throbbed. That weird pinkish fluid still dribbled from my ears and nose. Each time I took a step, the world tilted. Staying on my feet was an effort, but I refused to sit down. I didn't want the men to think I was weak.

"Woah, lookit that," a POG with a camera marveled as he studied the bullet holes all over Sabo's Humvee. He started snapping pictures as his buddies laughed and smiled.

I wanted to punch the son of a bitch.

Rowley came up to me. He'd been stuck on the FOB with one of our fire teams, forced to pull security on the base perimeter.

"Sir, I'm sorry I couldn't get out to you," he said, looking ready to burst.

"Don't worry about it, Rowley." I took a drag on the smoke I'd been given and tried not to gag.

"No, sir, you don't understand. We all tried to go out with Second Platoon when they left to go get to you."

"You did?" I asked, surprised.

"Yeah, but Sergeant Burley told us 'no fucking way' he was taking us out with him. He ordered us back to the barracks."

That was not good.

"Why not?"

"He didn't say."

The platoon will think it is because he never intended to reach us. If he'd taken Rowley and the rest of our team with him, they would have raised all manner of hell for not coming to our rescue.

That was going to cause a rupture between the platoons.

Yusef walked by, looking wide-eyed and weary. I asked, "How you doing?"

"Long day, Commander Sean, eh?" He forced a smile. He looked like a loan shark when he did that.

I hadn't seen him once during the entire fight. I suspect he stayed in one of the Humvees. Just before we'd pulled off the hilltop, he'd appeared and stood around, watching the men hook up towlines to our crippled rigs.

I missed Abdul.

Meanwhile, we had twelve wounded men. Three had already been evacuated. The others needed medical attention. I walked to Greeson and saw that he already had the men moving to get treatment.

Quietly, they lined up at the aid station's door. We'd recently lost our doc, who had been a family practitioner back home. When the FOB's gate had been hit by a suicide bomber a few months back, he had frozen in the middle of the crisis as horrifically maimed

Afghan soldiers had been carried into the aid station. A few days later, he had been transferred to FOB Salerno and we'd never seen him again.

He'd been replaced by a scowling Asian American female physician's assistant who was one of the few women on our FOB.

I stayed outside, smoking and staying within myself. I knew I needed to get checked too, but I didn't want to do it until the men were all treated first. Sunset approached. The sky warmed to a yellow-orange glow and made the few clouds look gilded in gold. I finished the cigarette and cast the butt into the dirt.

OVER AT THE AID STATION, MY MEN WERE WALKING AWAY IN groups of two or three. Something was up.

I went inside just in time to hear the female PA patronizing Campbell. "Hey, you can handle this stuff, right? You're an infantryman."

Campbell's expression transformed from exhausted to indignant. He walked out without a word, despite the fact that slivers of shrapnel were still embedded in his arms.

"Next," she called.

Reluctantly, another one of my men stepped forward. She glanced over him. "You're gonna be fine. Next."

My rage boiled over. Storming over to her, I barked, "What are you doing? Do you have any idea the hell these guys just went through?"

"Hey, LT, you don't speak to a captain that way. I wonder what your commander will think about this."

"Treat my men with respect," I said in a low, irritated voice.

She ignored me and in a bored tone said, "Next."

She barely even examined the rest of my men. As soon as the

last one left and I went out with them, she called Captain Dye and complained that I had treated her with disrespect. He asked me to meet him at the aide station.

Walking back in, I saw her pleading her case. When Captain Dye asked me what had happened, I explained everything I saw. His face reddened.

"Listen to me," he said, his voice measured but freighted with anger, "when my soldiers come in here, I expect you to provide them the best possible care. Do you understand me? I know that you're a captain too, but this is my FOB and these are my men. You treat them with respect."

Her bravado wilted.

"Bring your wounded back in, Sean. Have them looked at again."

Wearily, the men lined back up. She offered cursory exams again, but this time she stowed the attitude. When she got to me, she looked at the pinkish fluid draining from my ears and said sarcastically, "You're fine. You just need to clean your ears a bit better."

Back outside, Greeson sent the men to chow. Everyone was looking forward to a bite to eat and a long night's sleep after the day we had.

Walking back to my hooch, I found Captain Dye waiting for me.

"Hey, sir. Thanks for having my back at the aid station earlier."

Without warning, he gave me a man hug.

With reluctance, he said, "Sean, get your guys together. You're going back out tonight."

My head swam. I thought my ears had played a trick on me.

"Set up a checkpoint at the mouth of Route Trans Am."

Trans Am intersected with one of the north–south roads in our area. It was a major road into Pakistan and a very dangerous place.

He wanted us to go park out there, set up a roadblock, and see what came at us.

"Sir?" was all I could manage.

"Take Second Platoon's trucks. Cross load your ammo and gear."

"Sir, half my men are wounded, and they need to rest," I finally said.

"I know, Sean. Just do it," he replied, putting one hand on my shoulder.

When I explained all this to Greeson, his normally cool demeanor melted in the face of solar rage. I felt the same way, but we both knew we couldn't refuse the order. After taking a moment to compose ourselves, we went off to tell the men. They were too tired to even complain.

In the darkness, we gathered at our vehicles. Second Platoon pulled theirs up alongside ours. In their clean ACUs, they worked alongside my men to move our ammo, food, and water into their Humvees. Bandaged, burned, and bloodied, my men worked like automatons. But the stark difference between how they looked and how Second Platoon did was not lost on anyone there that night. Sergeant Burley did his best to ignore it, preferring instead to hurl invectives at anyone who crossed his path. His behavior made our teeth grind.

Second Platoon went to bed. In their undamaged trucks, we drove out into Indian country, cold fury keeping us awake. Whatever chance we'd had of keeping some semblance of a bond between the platoons evaporated that night. The chasm between us was complete.

SIXTEEN

CHICKENSHIT SQUARED

★ ★ ★

THE FIGHT ON JUNE 10 COST OUTLAW PLATOON DEARLY. Garvin, Baldwin, and Dixon had all been severely wounded and were evacuated from theater to undergo months of medical treatment back in the States. Nine other members of the platoon had suffered wounds as well. Almost half of the men on the hilltop had earned Purple Hearts in one day of combat.

Galang did not survive unscathed. Our intel section learned that he'd been critically wounded during the final stages of the assault. Carried out of the fight by his surviving men, he'd made it back to the Pakistani hospital that was supplying his fighters with prescription drugs. Doctors there had amputated one of his legs. Though we hadn't killed him, we had at least knocked him out of the fight for a while. I hoped that whoever took over for him would lack his tactical savvy. Brigade told us that they'd never seen such a sophisticated assault by the enemy, and I was tired of us being the test dummies for their new tactics.

Galang's attack cost his forces at least sixty-five men on the ridges and around our hilltop perimeter. Another thirty men died at the cave complex we hit with 105s at the start of the morning. Almost a hundred men killed in one engagement. Battalion told us that it was the largest battle on the frontier in years and the biggest victory since 2002.

It didn't feel like a victory, not with Baldwin, Garvin, and Dixon gone. Killing off Galang's entire network would not have balanced out the loss of those three men. Besides, we all knew the score: had it not been for Captain Dye and Delta's platoon, the Outlaws would have died to the last man.

The fight had cost us two squad leaders. Waites's zombie walk toward the enemy on June 10 had destroyed his squad's confidence in his leadership. We had to move him out of the platoon. Unlike Captain Waverly, who had vanished from the battalion after he was relieved, Waites stayed at Bermel to become an instrumental part of our civil affairs operations until he was later wounded during a surprise rocket attack. Even then he returned to Bermel as soon as he was well enough to execute his duties. His devotion drove him to serve in any capacity his mind would allow. There was honor in that effort.

Our southern sniper, Sergeant Wheat, took over Waites's squad. During our hilltop stand, the men had responded to his calm leadership. He exuded confidence, and the men told stories of his sniping with a measure of awe in their voices. First Squad would be just fine.

On the other hand, Baldwin's experience and insight could not be replaced. He'd been our point man, the NCO whose sixth sense had steered us out of trouble on many occasions. Along with Greeson and Sabo, Baldwin had played a key role in our mission planning. To the younger men in his squad, he had been a steadying presence, a voice of reason, and a guiding presence. He wasn't a yeller; he didn't berate the men to get them to do what he wanted. Instead, a few soft-spoken words was all it took to get them to respond. The life that Baldwin had sacrificed at home to be out with us made his motives beyond question. At times, soldiers will grumble about an NCO making a decision that is not in their best interests but made to advance that sergeant's career. Nobody ever thought that about Baldwin. Few NCOs commanded more respect.

Losing Garvin was a double tap to the squad's morale. He was beloved as a team leader. Compassionate and understanding, he connected with his soldiers in ways other young NCOs could only hope to do. He treated them with great respect. In return, they drove through walls for him. He motivated and inspired. On the battlefield, he always led by example.

Greeson and I decided to promote Colt Wallace into Garvin's role. Though he didn't have Bennett's experience, he was self-assured and respected and possessed a natural charisma that Greeson felt would make him a fine young leader. Wheat was his best friend and could help mentor him along too.

We reached outside the platoon to replace Baldwin. Sergeant Chris Cowan, who had been Captain Dye's radio operator, took over Second Squad. Initially, the men weren't sure what to think of him. He possessed a very dry and sarcastic sense of humor, which left some of the men confused as to when he was joking around and when he was being serious. Whereas Baldwin had held his squad to high standards but led with a tempered hand, Cowan was tough and exacting. Chris was a phenomenal NCO, but Greeson and I knew it would take time for the cohesion that had existed in the squad to develop again.

Three days after the June 10 fight, Lieutenant Colonel Toner ordered us back to battalion headquarters at FOB Orgun-E. He'd heard about what happened at the aid station with the physician's assistant and wanted all of us to be thoroughly checked over by the battalion's medical staff. In the meantime, the physician's assistant disappeared from Bermel, never to be seen again.

The chance to get back to a larger base with better chow and more supplies appealed to the platoon. Despite the clear threat Galang's force posed to us around Bermel, getting ammunition had become a serious headache. Fortunately, battalion kept on hand ample quantities of everything we needed. Of course, the paperwork maze to get it seemed insurmountable, so Greeson used all means available to "scrounge" every round he could find. While the men went through their medical checks, he crammed our Humvees full of machine-gun belts, drums of 40mm grenades, and crates of .556 rifle ammunition. Forget the unit basic load-out we'd been trained to carry; we planned to double it. Fourteen mags per rifle, two thousand rounds for the machine guns, and eighty grenades for the Mark 19. That's what we would roll with in the future so that next time we wouldn't run out of ways to kill the enemy.

The medical staff did what they could for the men. Every one of our walking wounded needed better care than was available at Orgun-E. The docs told them they would be sent to Bagram for further treatment. To a man, they refused. They would not leave their brothers, even if it meant living with pain in the weeks to come.

Campbell's arms were full of shrapnel, but the wounds had started to heal over. The doc picked out what pieces he could reach, but the rest would need surgery. "Forget it, Doc," he said. "I'm staying here."

Sabo said the same thing when his turn came, as did Greeson when the doc looked over his shoulder wound.

I stood off to one side, listening to the medical staff try to reason with my men. Their devotion to the platoon put a lump in my throat.

After the last man had been treated, Greeson came over to me. "Sir, you need to get looked at. Don't give me any shit, just go do it. Now. That's an order."

"What are you, my mother?"

"Somebody's gotta look out for you, 'cause you won't do it."

Under his watchful gaze, I went to have my turn with the doc. Since June 10, I'd had a nearly constant migraine headache, bouts of vertigo, and blurred vision. I wasn't about to tell the doc any of that.

He looked me over, noted the fluid that had dried and turned to a spongy mass in my ears, and told me I had to go to Bagram and get an MRI.

"I'm not leaving," I said.

He regarded me and said, "You've got postconcussive syndrome. Your brain could be bleeding or swelling. You need to be evaluated at a better facility."

The men set the example for their leader that day. My brains could have been leaching out my ears, and I would not have left them. When I refused evacuation again, the doctor threw up his hands and muttered, "You're all crazy."

As we left, I caught Greeson smiling at me.

Our moment at the battalion aid station at Orgun-E solidified the platoon as a family. Everyone hurt. Everyone would have traded a limb to get out of theater and see home again. But they would do it only as a platoon. They would not let their family carry on the fight without them.

Back at Bermel, the long patrol cycles continued. We would spend three to six days out beyond the wire, then come back for a few days to rest up and carry out duties at the base. Cole was there waiting for us every time we rolled through the gate, eager to do anything he could to help the platoon. He'd lost more weight, and I'd run into him at the base's makeshift gym many times. He'd pat his shrinking stomach and would say something like "Sir, it is only a matter of time before I'm out there with y'all."

In the meantime, he happily did as much of the mundane scut work as the rest of the platoon would let him do after we finished a patrol. He would unload gear, help service the trucks, and clean weapons, and he'd just light up as he worked. Being around the men had that effect on him. He missed us, and it was obvious to everyone in the platoon that he hated being left behind.

Those mini-reunions with Cole became part of our end-of-patrol ritual. I found myself looking forward to seeing him, as his levity always picked me up in spite of the exhaustion and soreness I felt after those long sorties.

After the rigs were taken care of and our gear was squared away, the men would hit the chow hall for a hot meal. Greeson and I usually met with the squad leaders to go over any lessons learned from the last mission. We'd take those lessons and push them out to the rest of the platoon after everyone had a chance to eat. As a platoon, we developed new tactics, rehearsed them on base, and devised countermeasures for the enemy's latest ambush techniques. It was a constant evolution. One slip and we'd fall behind, and that could be catastrophic. The enemy forced us to think and adapt constantly.

We decided we would move around in the battle space more. That way, the enemy would be hard pressed to set up another June 10–style assault on one of our nocturnal perimeters. Stay fluid, keep the enemy guessing, and never let them get the drop on us again. In the future, all potential ambush sites would be shot up with our fifties or the Mark 19 before we drove through them, a tactic called "reconnaissance by fire." If an enemy force did lurk in the area, firing at it would almost certainly trigger a response and get it to reveal its positions to us.

When we analyzed the attack the enemy had initiated against us on May 7, plus the one that had rattled Second Platoon, we concluded that the best way to handle such an ambush would be to drive through it to a preplotted rally point and circle the wagons. From there, we'd dismount, call in air and artillery, then counterattack.

Every day on the FOB, we took time to rehearse our new tactics and plan for every possible contingency. The enemy had learned lessons from May 7 and made changes to how it did business. Now we did the same. Whose new game plan would be better remained to be seen. One thing was for sure: we'd get the opportunity to find out. Contrary to its behavior in years past, the enemy did not melt away and lick their wounds in Pakistan. The Prophet spooks heard them chattering on their radios every day as they observed us from concealed positions. For the moment, though, they turned cagey and elusive. Try as we might, we could not bring them into battle again.

WHILE ON PATROL ONE DAY IN MID-JUNE, PROPHET SPOOKS called from Bermel and reported that an enemy force was nearby. An enemy scout had just radioed, "We've got five camels approaching. Get ready."

Camel was the enemy's code name for our Humvees. They were watching us from a concealed ambush position somewhere ahead. We braced ourselves for the coming attack, went over how we would handle it, and pushed forward.

Nothing happened. A few minutes later, the Prophet spooks checked in to tell us that the enemy had said, "Do not attack! Do not attack! It is the Green Skulls!"

THEY'D SEEN EMERICK'S OUTLAW INSIGNIA ON THE SIDE OF OUR Humvees. Thanks to June 10, we had a reputation among our enemy now. On that day, they wanted an easier target.

We came off our patrol cycle the next morning and transitioned into FOB duty. As stressful as our missions outside the wire were, we at least possessed a sense of freedom and independence. Nobody messed with us. Back at the FOB, a host of brewing conflicts existed that our status as veterans exacerbated. After June 10, the line between those of us doing the fighting and those doing the supporting on the bases had never been more clearly defined. Our tolerance level for the petty rules and politics we faced on base diminished, even as they seemed to grow more acute and offensive. Chickenshit squared. We internalized every slight, noticed every inequity between us and the Fobbits, and fumed with resentment over the lack of respect we thought they telegraphed. The platoon withdrew into itself, the men building a protective wall around those they trusted. Everyone else was viewed with quiet suspicion.

It started with little things related to men living practically on top of one another. Sergeant R. Kelly, Delta's platoon sergeant, continued to sing with headphones on at all hours of the night and morning, despite being told early and often to be quiet. After days of sleep deprivation out in the field, all we wanted was a decent night's sleep. Next door was an NCO who was conspicuously absent every time Delta rolled outside the wire, who also lacked the grace to respect that need for sleep. Earlier in the spring, I'd just tried to ignore it. But after all we'd been through without seeing this sergeant shoulder his responsibilities and help lead his platoon in combat, I burned with indignation.

R. Kelly did not belong to our company. He was part of our battalion's Delta Company. The platoon from Delta that had served with us at Bermel was not part of our administrative chain of command. This meant that for R. Kelly's platoon, all matters of pay, awards, promotions, discipline, and mail went through Delta Company, not through Captain Dye. Dye had only tactical control of R. Kelly and his platoon. He could not discipline or initiate investigations and did not have the ability to take care of issues within the Delta Platoon in a swift manner. Basically, R. Kelly fell through an administrative crack, a glitch that he exploited. Until Delta Company could send its first sergeant down to check on the platoon at Bermel, R. Kelly was safe from any punitive action.

Meanwhile, his daily patterns fell under our company's scrutiny. Instead of patrolling with his men, he seemed to be following a female mail carrier around the brigade's area of operations. That particular mail carrier was detested by our platoon. She was rude and officious and handled our care packages like Ace Ventura. The men called her "the Mail Bitch."

One of the few joys the platoon found at Bermel was the small cadre of dogs we'd inherited from the 173rd Airborne guys we had relieved in February. Though it was against regulations to keep pets on base, Captain Dye recognized their morale value to the men and looked the other way. Doc Pantoja and the other medics had vaccinated them, so they posed no health threat. The platoon built kennels for them and taught them tricks.

The Mail Bitch did not like the dogs. Whenever she came on post, she complained loudly about them, even though she never had any actual contact with them. She was just the kind to make trouble at higher headquarters about them for the sake of making trouble. Not that we didn't have other, more important things to worry about—such as staying alive in the face of a cunning enemy. A Fobbit like her was so removed from the tip of the spear that she cared nothing for such things. Instead, the rules and regulations served as her refuge from the obvious disgust the combat troops held for her. We'd seen her wield them as weapons against those she didn't like, which added to everyone's stress and made the men protective of the dogs when we were back at base after a patrol cycle.

Calling home while at Bermel turned into another festering issue. We knew that our time on base would be limited to a short forty-eight- or seventy-two-hour cycle before we had to get back out into the field. That gave us only a small window to call our loved ones back home. The Fobbits monopolized the phones available at the MWR (morale, welfare, and recreation) hooch. My men would show up there, eager to touch base with their wives, girlfriends, or parents and tell them they were safe, only to find they had to wait for hours to get a chance to make a ten-minute phone call.

To compensate for that inequity, we let the men use a couple of the company satellite phones, which could be checked out for short periods at the operations center. That worked well at first, but there were times the men forgot to sign out the phones or return them. I ended up having to track them down.

One night, I combed the barracks looking for a missing sat phone. None of the soldiers had it, and I grew testy with frustration. I had shit to do and did not need to be running around trying to find a phone.

As I checked around for it, somebody mentioned that the 'terps occasionally used them. That surprised me, and I felt a fleeting sense of disquiet over the discovery. A sat phone can be used to call anywhere on the planet. A local national on our base using one could be seen as a breach in operational security.

I hustled over to the 'terp hooch, where I found Yusef curled up on his cot, talking quietly into the missing sat phone. He was alone; Bruce Lee and Shaw were out on duty. When he saw me enter, he hung up and said sheepishly, "Just talking to my family, Commander Sean."

He handed me the phone. For a second, I had my doubts as Captain Canady's and Abdul's warnings came back to me.

What the hell. He hasn't seen his family in months, just like us.

"Come to me or Captain Dye in the future, okay?"

"Sure, sure, Commander Sean."

I took the phone and carried it to the operations center. I had to be there anyway to start a shift as the company's night-battle captain. When I arrived, I found Pinholt manning the radios. We greeted each other warmly as I racked the sat phone and checked it back in.

We were in for a long night. Battle captain duty involves mainly hanging out in the operations center to handle any incoming calls from units on patrol or from the perimeter. If something serious came up, we'd have to wake Captain Dye—or drag him away from another Halo 2 tournament on the Xboxes floating around the FOB. Since saving us on June 10, he'd retreated within himself a little. Of course, we all had, but the fact that we were not seeing him out and about as much had not gone unnoticed by the men.

The first hours of the night shift passed slowly. With nothing going on, Pinholt and I ended up in another series of unusual conversations. We jumped from topic to topic—he was still reading *Atlas Shrugged*—until we ended up talking about day trading. He had been learning the ropes from Khanh before he'd gone down to Helmand Province. Khanh was so good at it that he'd already cleared several thousand dollars just working the Net whenever he had access here at the FOB.

The outside door opened, and Lieutenant Taylor stepped in. He'd just come back from leave, and I was happy to see him. By that time, we were the only lieutenants at Bermel, which meant that the two of us constituted our peer group. He was the one person on the FOB I could share friendship with and not have it limited by the distinction of rank. Beyond that, his return meant that Sergeant Burley would be less of a thorn in everyone's side. Perhaps the damage caused between the two platoons could be healed. I knew that my men didn't hold anyone but Burley responsible for what had happened that day, so I had hope.

"Hey, man, what the hell happened out there on June 10?" Taylor asked.

His blast of anger caught me off guard. I had no response to it.

"I heard what you did on that hill. Do you even care about your men?"

I went from surprised to enraged in seconds. I stood up as he continued to rant at me. Where was this coming from? His words cut to the quick. I wondered if Burley had filled his ear with bullshit.

Finally I could take it no more. "You weren't there. You don't know what the hell you're talking about!"

"I thought you'd be a leader, Sean. But you're being reckless!"

"Don't talk about things you know nothing about, man!"

He looked stunned by that response. He'd been on leave when Second Platoon had been hit in May. So far, Taylor had yet to experience a significant firefight. Throwing that in his face laid bare the divide between us.

He turned and stormed out of the operations center. Yet another relationship had frayed in the aftermath of combat.

When I came off duty that morning, I returned to my hooch to find Sergeant R. Kelly already singing. I sat down at my rough-hewn plywood desk and booted up my computer. I needed to vent.

As I waited for Windows to load, I stared at the screen and thought about Taylor's words. He was my only peer at Bermel. I couldn't vent to my men; that would have been a total breach of my responsibilities as a leader. I couldn't go to Captain Dye; we just didn't have that kind of relationship. Behind closed doors, I probably would have talked to Baldwin about it.

Right then I missed his guidance with a crushing sense of loss. He'd been like a big brother to me. And now I didn't even know where he was.

I logged in to my e-mail. Greeson had just gone home on his midtour leave. I wrote him a note to tell him what happened.

Home. In moments like this one, I'd find comfort in my family's company. I reached for the St. Christopher medal. The silver had lost its luster again, and I didn't have the energy to clean it. Besides, nothing stayed clean out here on the frontier.

I palmed it and thought about my grandmother's words: "Take this. It will keep you safe."

It had saved me twice.

My family's always been my refuge.

I'd been writing to my dad every chance I had. Most soldiers tell their families none of what happens in combat; they fear how they will react to the details. I hadn't been doing that. My dad had asked, and I had never been anything but totally honest with him. In the past months, the bond between us had grown even deeper as we exchanged e-mails between patrols. By nature, leaders live a lonely life. As close as we can be to our men and NCOs, there is still an invisible wall that cannot ever be broken down, lest a lieutenant grow too familiar with his men. Familiarity can breed contempt. In a fight, that could lead to a hesitation to follow orders. Plus, a lieutenant who is too emotionally invested in his men might make the wrong decisions in combat. In trying to spare their lives, he could actually make the mistakes that end up getting them killed.

My dad's e-mails and our few phone conversations had balmed some of the sense of isolation I'd been feeling.

I pulled up his e-mail address. I wouldn't write about Lieutenant Taylor and what he had said. That sort of company business needed to stay within the company, at least for now.

RIGHT THEN, A BOLT OF HOMESICKNESS LEFT ME ALMOST BREATHless.

The words began pouring out.

Dad,

The enemy meant business, and did not stop coming. It was like the Russian horde. Eventually, we were going to run out of ammo, and they were going to overrun us. I'm a damn Platoon Leader, and I had 1 magazine left when our QRF (Quick Reaction Force) arrived. We killed tons of them, and they just kept coming wave after wave. Half of my platoon will get Purple Hearts. My shrapnel wounds are healing fast, my headache is going away, but I still can't hear out of my right ear and the ringing is annoying as hell.

I paused and reread the words. As a soldier and a leader, I cannot complain or show weakness to anyone. Such a revelation here would destroy my ability to command in battle and ruin the hard-won respect I'd earned from the men. Leadership exists on a knife edge. Any sign of hesitation, doubt, or inability to hack it would have pushed me out of the platoon's inner circle.

I could deal with getting shot at. I could deal with the threat of capture and beheading while my empty M4 lay at my side. I could deal with the pain in my head, the vertigo, the sleepless nights where the buzzing in my ears kept me company. The one thing I could not deal with was being pushed out.

Sean the leader had to be tough. Sean the man needed to unburden himself. As I started typing again, I realized that just by reading my words, my father was performing a noble and selfless service for me. Somewhere on the other side of the world, somebody I loved knew what I was going through. And he was standing strong for me.

SEVENTEEN

SKELETON CREW

★ ★ ★

June 26, 2006
Checkpoint outside Malakshay

THE SPECIAL FORCES LIEUTENANT COLONEL REGARDED ME
with skepticism. Behind us, the rest of his team huddled
around a laptop, silencers on their weapons, cool-guy gear dangling from their chest rigs. Before we had left Bermel, I wanted to
tell them that all that stuff would just slow them down where we
were going. No matter how fit a soldier is, at 10,000 feet the only
thing you can afford to carry is water, ammo, and your weapon.
Everything else just drags you down.

"So that was the May 7 fight," I concluded. I'd been instructed
to give the Special Forces team a brief on the combat my platoon
had experienced. I started to explain June 10, and the lieutenant
colonel's look of disbelief solidified.

I concealed my frustration and continued the brief. The special operators had been pushed down to Bermel to get a better feel for the amount of enemy activity. Captain Dye had asked me to take them out on patrol with us for the next few cycles, something I was not looking forward to doing. We'd had some friction with other Special Forces teams in our area, and as a result my men did not hold them in high regard. There were attitude differences between us regular line infantrymen and the SF guys, and I'd come to regard any liaison effort with them as a ponderous and difficult task. The ones we had encountered seemed to have all the elite attitude without the tactical acumen needed to keep them alive while on patrol. Rather than focusing on the enemy, they seemed to us to be preoccupied with frivolous and extraneous details, such as what color they should paint their weapons. We also didn't think much of them and their refusal to wear protective gear such as helmets. Most of the time they walked around nonchalantly in baseball caps. After what we'd gone through, that sort of theatrical stuff came across as sheer stupidity.

Having the lieutenant colonel and his men with us ran the risk of compromising our patrols. We did things very differently from each other, and I feared that dichotomy would cause issues on the battlefield. With the enemy all around, we didn't need issues. We needed smooth and seamless. Just thinking about the mission ahead made me tense.

After we had departed Bermel, we drove south to establish a traffic checkpoint outside Malakshay, the village we had passed through on May 7.

When we arrived at our designated point, we dismounted and set up concertina wire obstacles across the road. The trucks took up overwatch positions, and the NCOs posted sentries to provide security for us.

From our vantage point outside town, we couldn't detect a

single sign of life. Malakshay looked abandoned, and I wondered if the last holdouts had finally fled to Pakistan.

Or maybe they were lying low because they knew something was going to happen again.

While the men stopped the few vehicles that approached our checkpoint, the Special Forces lieutenant colonel asked me a few questions. The nature of the questions convinced me that he knew a lot about counterinsurgency operations. As I talked with him and felt him out, I noticed he possessed a hard-bitten aura about him, as though he'd spent his life in places none of the folks back home could ever imagine. His salt-and-pepper hair, close cropped, made me guess that he was perhaps fifty years old. His leathery face was tempered bronze by years of life outdoors.

Shortly before noon, the radio squawked, "Blackhawk three-six, this is FOB Bermel."

I stepped away from my guest, leaned into my Humvee, and picked up the handset.

"This is three-six. Go ahead."

"You're being watched, three-six."

I glanced around. We had set up our checkpoint on the straight stretch of road east of the village so we had good fields of fire in all directions. A few kilometers away rose Gangikheyl Hill. We'd climbed to its peak on a patrol sometime after May 7 and poked around in the hope of finding anything of intelligence value that could fill in more about the force that had hit us that day. Up along the summit, Wheat had discovered the snipers' hide. Now I wondered if the enemy was up there again.

"What are they saying?" I asked.

"We heard 'I can see camels. Five of them.'"

We had five rigs out with us. Nobody else was patrolling. They had their eyes on us.

Captain Dye came over the radio to tell me that the enemy was massing for an ambush behind Rakhah Ridge. Their radio chatter was more undisciplined than usual.

"Delta's coming your way. Link up with them, and head east behind Rakhah Ridge. Movement to contact. Let me know what you need. Six out."

It would take Delta Platoon at least thirty minutes to reach us.

I briefed the platoon, or what we had left of it at the moment. We had rolled with a skeleton crew that morning. Besides having to leave a squad behind to help guard Bermel, a number of the men were on leave, which had trimmed our numbers to the bone. Greeson had just departed for his fourteen days stateside, which had left Sabo as acting platoon sergeant. Baldwin was gone; Cowan was on leave too. So was Pinholt. Pantoja was off taking his citizenship exam, bandaged face and all. The rest of the men were weary and still carried the bruises and half-healed wounds from our hilltop fight.

After I finished outlining the situation for the platoon, the men checked their weapons and climbed into their Humvees to wait for Delta to arrive. Meanwhile I got together with Reuter to plan a series of artillery missions and target reference points. If we were going to drive into an ambush, I wanted to soften them up first. The Special Forces lieutenant colonel stayed close and observed our preparations.

By that point, we knew the ground behind Rakhah Ridge very well. We knew the best ambush points, the enemy's infil and exfil routes. Reuter and I worked together and picked out the most likely spots the enemy would use today. Then we gave our 105 gunners those coordinates with specific target reference numbers. That way, once in the fight, we could just call for fire on a predesignated spot. It would save us time.

When we finished, I trooped the line. The men held no illusions about what we faced. We would be in battle again soon, and the anticipation of it weighed on them. They smoked in silence, eyes opaque. They'd put on their game faces.

On my way back to my Humvee, I encountered Yusef. He was leaning against Campbell's rig, drinking green tea. Technically, he was Captain Dye's 'terp, but he still patrolled with us a lot. I appreciated that since Bruce Lee had turned out to be a disaster and Shaw usually went out with Delta. I'd once asked Yusef why he made a point of rolling with us. " 'Cause I like you Outlaws, Commander Sean." He said that in a sincere tone. True enough, he spent a lot of time with the men. I'd even found him shooting the breeze outside the barracks with them between missions. I'd meant to talk to the squad leaders about it so they could put an end to that level of fraternization, but something more pressing always came up.

"How you doing, Yusef?"

"Fine, fine, Commander Sean." He beamed at me, cup in hand.

"Be ready today, okay?"

"Okay, Commander Sean."

I started to walk away, but he said, "Commander Sean, whaddya get when you cross female deer with big green pickle?"

I turned around. "What?"

"A dildo!"

"Dude, do you even get that joke?"

He gave me his best used-car-salesman grin and made a lewd gesture to confirm that he did.

Nearby, Colt Wallace turned to the Special Forces colonel and drawled in his southern accent, "That Yusef's as funny as a wet joint."

I returned to my Humvee. Ayers sat behind the wheel. He was a good driver, and I was glad to have him. But I'd grown accustomed to seeing Pinholt there. His calm was always a comfort. I sat down to settle into the wait, door open, one leg dangling outside. Overhead, I heard Chris Brown busy in his turret. I looked up to see him rack his 240's bolt back. He checked to make sure that his ammo was properly loaded, then slapped the feed tray cover closed with just his left middle and index fingers. The best gunners learned to do it that way so that in combat, their right hand can stay tight on the weapon's pistol grip and the left hand doesn't have to move more than absolutely necessary. Attention to such tiny details means the difference between a good gunner and a great one.

I checked my watch. Delta Platoon was twenty minutes out.

What are the chances Sergeant R. Kelly's bringing 'em out?

No need to be bitter.

That wasn't me, and the sudden rush of it seemed out of character.

I was in a mood. My head still throbbed, I couldn't hear out of my right ear, and I still had that pinkish crap leaching out of my ears and nose. Having the Special Forces guys with us didn't help, either. No doubt the ones with us today were comparing their own firefights with what I'd told them about ours, feeling quite superior to us regular infantry, thank you very much.

I'd had enough of feeling inferior over the years.

Third grade. I sat in class, struggling to read aloud for our teacher, Miss McKewin. She was a bloated woman with craggy teeth and a skin condition. We feared her.

"Whatsamatter?" she asked, laughing at me as I got stuck on a word. "Can't you read?"

The class erupted in laughter.

What the fuck dredged that memory up? I was supposed to keep all thoughts of home locked away, especially in moments like these.

I snatched a cigarette and started smoking, doing my best to conceal how I was feeling from the other guys in the truck.

When my mom heard what the teacher had said that day, she went down to the school. I found out later that Miss McKewin had said to her, "Your son . . . hmm . . . let's just say he's not going to be an engineer like his daddy."

My mom is the most loving and open human being I've ever

known. But cross her or come after her family, and it is on. In front of the principal, she tore that teacher apart. By the time she finished, Miss McKewin was sobbing, the sleeves of her cardigan sweater shielding her face.

My mother waited until she poked her head back up. When she could see Miss McKewin's eyes again, her voice went arctic. "You listen to me. My son may be quiet, but he's going to be a leader someday."

I took another drag on the smoke and looked over at the Special Forces colonel. He looked cucumber cool, a slight smirk on his face as if he was eager to see just how fucked up we were compared to his guys.

People intimating I'm not good enough has been a theme in my life. Miss McKewin was just the first of many to follow. And now a new one was sitting in my Humvee, passing silent judgment on things he could not ever understand.

I checked my watch again. Would this wait never end? I hated getting inside my own head, especially given what we were about to do. Now that we'd been through it, we had no illusions. The mystique of combat had been stripped away. None of us longed to be tested by it anymore. By now we knew the measure of ourselves.

I thought through the plan. It seemed sound. I finished the smoke and flicked the butt into the dirt as I war-gamed every possible response we might encounter from the enemy.

This is my platoon. My men. I've got this.

Delta Platoon's four Humvees and eighteen soldiers arrived, prompting Chris Brown to say, "Gee, not Second Platoon. There's a surprise."

Staff Sergeant James Newton—"Big Red"—stepped out of his truck. Huge, fair-skinned, and hot-blooded, Big Red inspired equal amounts of fear and affection. His men loved him, even when he jumped on them. All others, including officers, had to play by his rules or suffer his wrath. He didn't care about rank or convention; he just cared about what he thought was the right thing to do. Morally absolute, devoted to his platoon, Newton was all business and kick ass. He was an NCO I couldn't help but admire. But I was always careful not to piss him off.

Though Delta's platoon was technically commanded by Captain Herrera, he'd been a navy supply officer before joining the army and had virtually no experience with motorized infantry operations. When he went out with the platoon, he was smart enough to let Newton run the show, at least until he learned the ropes.

Normally, the platoon sergeant would lead the men in that sort of situation, but with R. Kelly flying around theater "squaring away our mail," the de facto leadership of Delta had long since passed to Big Red. After June 10, Greeson and I had had a closed-door meeting with him to discuss the realities outside the wire. We promised that no matter what happened, we'd always come to each other's aid should one of our platoons end up in trouble again. That moment sealed a bond of trust between us that helped mitigate Second Platoon's behavior and set our minds at ease. Neither platoon would ever have to rely on Sergeant Burley again. In a scrap, I knew we could count on Big Red.

"Where's Captain Dye?" I asked, surprised not to see him.

"Operations center," Newton replied.

I took it as a sign of trust that he'd given me a company minus to maneuver with today.

I sketched the plan for Newton: "We'll drop artillery to soften them up. As soon as the last shell lands, we hit the objective area. They'll have no time to react before we arrive. Got it?"

"Roger, sir."

"We'll advance to contact. If we get ambushed, get to your nearest rally point, establish a perimeter, and counterattack if you can."

Newton grinned. "I like that."

Our new Prophet spook, Sergeant Eric Murray, reported,

"Lieutenant, the enemy just reported Delta's arrival. Said, 'Four more camels just showed up. They'll be coming for us soon.'"

"Okay. Reuter, let's pound 'em with artillery."

In seconds, the first 105 shells left the guns back at Bermel some fifteen kilometers away. They whistled overhead to impact on the far side of Rakhah Ridge.

"Mount up," I ordered. Thoughts of home vanished. I existed in the moment, without a past, with no confidence that there'd be a future beyond this next fight. It was a cold and rootless place, but it was where I needed to be. Only the men and my bond with them anchored me to the here and now.

The Prophet spooks reported, "Okay, we're on target. One just said, 'They're hitting us with artillery.'"

I smiled at that.

A moment later, we got another update: "One of them just reported that the shells are impacting close.'"

The smile widened. We'd picked the right area to hammer.

I radioed the platoon: "Okay, guys, be ready. They're waiting for us."

Bermel called in: "Their commander just told them, 'Stay in your positions, and the artillery won't hurt you.'"

"Did any of his subordinates reply?" I asked.

"Yeah. They said, 'Allahu akbar.'"

Fuck. Doesn't sound like they're going to break and run.

"Let's go," I ordered. Outlaws leading the way, Campbell on point, our nine Humvees churned through the dust toward the back side of Rakhah Ridge.

"Okay, three-six, they see you. 'Here they come. Be ready.'"

Time to see how Special Forces guys fight.

We hadn't gone far when the Prophet spooks called in one final enemy message: "Remember, aim for their gunner's heads."

EIGHTEEN

ARRIVAL MOMENT

★ ★ ★

THE 105S WENT SILENT. WE ROLLED AROUND GANGIKHEYL Hill, passed the May 7 ambush site, and reached an intersection behind Rakhah Ridge. Delta Platoon swung right. We swung left. We'd hunt the enemy down and reinforce whichever element made contact.

Campbell's rig reached a large, sweeping turn in the road, forcing us to slow down. Ridges and hills dotted the landscape around us. The enemy could be hiding on any one of a number of pieces of high ground. The hackles on the back of my neck stood at attention.

We're about to be hit.

I reached for my handset to warn the platoon.

The enemy volley fired almost a dozen RPGs at us simultaneously. Campbell's rig took a direct hit. The explosion slammed McLeod against the side of his turret, breaking his forearm. He slipped and nearly fell into the turret. But through the swirl of smoke and flame, I saw him hanging on with his one good hand. He wasn't going down.

Another rocket slammed into our truck right between the doors. Shrapnel and sheets of flame jetted upward, burning Chris Brown in a dozen places.

"What the fuck?" he screamed. "How many goddamned RPGs do they have?"

Behind us, the opening volley hit two more Humvees. Shrapnel wounded four of our five gunners. Dugin took a nasty face wound that sent blood pouring over his IBA and splattered his turret. Howie, his hands still recovering from the burns he had received on June 10, was studded with RPG shrapnel across his arms.

Miraculously, none of the rigs went down. As accurate as their volley had been, the enemy had failed to score a catastrophic kill.

The radio squawked, "We're getting hit! We're getting hit!" It was Captain Herrera. Several kilometers away, Delta Platoon had been ambushed simultaneously. Both elements had their hands full. We would not be coming to each other's rescue. The enemy had changed tactics on us again.

Machine-gun fire whipsawed across our column. A second volley of RPGs followed the first. The turret blast shields sparked and clanged as bullets and whirring steel splinters ricocheted off them.

All five of my gunners clicked their safeties off and went cyclic. The Mark 19 boomed. Brown's 240 spewed fire. The fifty-cals chugged. In seconds, we created a halo of lead and explosives around us that sent at least some of the enemy diving for cover.

I keyed my radio. Out of the corner of my eye, I saw Chris Brown get thrashed around in the turret from another RPG. "We're in their kill zone, keep moving. Don't stop. Rally at checkpoint Bandar Two. We'll circle the wagons and counterattack." Over the company net, I heard Delta Platoon doing the same thing, using a building we called Hotel California as its rally point. It was three kilometers south from us.

Campbell's rig sped up. I saw McCleod handling his hundred-pound Ma Deuce virtually one-handed. He hammered the enemy fighting positions, some of which were less than a hundred and fifty meters away.

More RPGs lanced across the road, exploding on either side of our rigs. The gunners poured it on.

"Doin' great, guys, keep it up."

We rounded the corner, and the road opened up into a narrow valley. I expected we'd be out of the kill zone at that point, but even as we hit a straight stretch and picked up more speed, the enemy continued to deliver withering volleys on us.

Their kill zone on May 7 was only a couple hundred meters wide.

The ridges on either side of us looked alive with fireflies. Muzzle flashes, and lots of them.

The road rose out of the valley and passed an abandoned village perched atop a plateau. That was our rally point. It was almost two kilometers away.

"Reuter?"

"Yeah, LT?"

"Start calling fire on our target reference points along these ridges."

"Roger that."

He went to work. As we sped through the valley, towering mushroom clouds formed and billowed on either side of us as the 105s barraged the enemy. Our column split the space between barrages, dealing out death as we rolled for the rally point. Not an unnecessary word was shared. Nobody screamed. There were no obscenities hurled at the enemy, just lead and explosives.

We'd become cold professionals.

We hit the high ground, still taking fire. A tire shredded. Rockets sizzled past. We had ammo to burn this time around, and nobody held back. If our machine-gun barrels warped, so be it. We'd replace them during a lull.

We reached our rally point, guns still blazing. The edge of the enemy's ambush line was now about 600 meters away, primarily across the road on the east side of the valley. Their muzzle flashes winked on even as our drivers formed a perimeter.

The rally point would be a perfect defensive position. Years ago, a village had thrived there. It was a ghost town now, the compounds long abandoned and gone to ruin. The outer walls of nearly every qalat had partially collapsed, which actually served us well. We used the breaks like giant firing slits for our Humvees. The rigs nosed up to them, and our dismounts bailed out and formed up into fire teams. With a few quick orders, they swarmed into the nearby buildings to ensure that no enemies lurked within.

Our temporary medic, Doc Pham, ran up to me and asked, "Lieutenant, where should I set up the casualty collection point?"

Pantoja would never have asked me that. He'd have had it handled.

"Work that out with Sergeant Sabatke," I replied.

"Sir, we have more indirect coming. No air available due to the weather," Reuter reported. Gray clouds overhead darkened the landscape, and dust in the air mingled with the clouds to constrict visibility for our aviators.

I called Bermel and gave Captain Dye an update.

"We're sending help to you," he told me.

I didn't think we needed it, but better always to error on the side of caution.

Sergeant Murray, our new Prophet spook who had replaced Dixon after he'd gotten wounded, stacked up with one of our fire teams. They flowed past a crumbled wall and into a courtyard, ready to enter and clear a squat one-story dwelling. On the far side of the valley, a machine gun went cyclic. Bullets chewed the outer wall, blowing clouds of dust and bits of dried mud into the air. The gunner adjusted fire and raked the courtyard. Sergeant Murray was shot off his feet, a bullet in his ankle. Doc Pham rushed to his aid.

Sergeant "Bear" Ferguson appeared at my side. He and Tony Garrett had come out with us, and I was grateful to have their mortar available. I pointed at the nearest enemy muzzle flashes, and they went to work.

Dugin, his face a mask of blood, climbed out of his turret and dropped beside me. His helmet was askew, and his chin strap had been unclipped.

"Dugin, how you doing?" I asked.

Wild-eyed, he froze like a hunting dog and made a sweeping gesture with one arm. He looked as though he were moving in slow motion. "There's the enemy! There's the enemy!" he shouted melodramatically.

Chris Brown saw it and checked fire for a moment. "Dugin!" he screamed. "Shut up and shoot!"

Dugin wiped a fresh trail of blood off the side of his face and remained next to the vehicle, rifle in one hand. "Sir," he called to the Special Forces colonel, "I'm sorry I've let you down. I'm sorry."

The colonel looked confused, unsure why my gunner was talking to him.

"Dugin, either shoot back or get to the casualty collection point," I ordered.

"I'm sorry. I've let you all down," he blurted again. Mumbling, he went to go get treated by Doc Pham.

The other Special Forces guys dismounted with us. In the middle of the fight, they huddled up behind one of our trucks and popped their laptop open. One of them set up a miniature satellite array.

Soon another was banging away on the keyboard. This particular team reported straight to Special Operations Command, and they were doing just that in real time with some form of secure instant messaging.

Technology. Gotta love it.

The men finished clearing the abandoned dwellings. Campbell, Wheat, and Sabo barked orders. The men fanned out to form a perimeter among the ruins. Soon the entire platoon, except for the gunners and drivers, lay prone, using the half-fallen walls as cover from the considerable incoming that raked across the village.

The Special Forces colonel dashed past me and dived onto his belly beside a chunk of fallen wall. Rifle to his shoulder, he triggered off a string of controlled shots. I swear I saw him grinning.

Howie, Brown, and McCleod stayed in the fight despite their wounds. McCleod's forearm was already swelling, and he couldn't use his hand at all now. I marveled at those young men.

THE MARK 19 BELCHED GRENADES. THE FIFTIES FLAYED AND ripped. Brown's 240 went cyclic again.

The ridge on the far side of the valley was soon blanketed in smoke.

The enemy fought on but did not maneuver on us. Perhaps with Galang down, they'd lost their taste for close-quarters combat. We were gaining fire superiority, and the time was growing ripe for a counterattack.

It would not be easy. We would have to cross a lot of ground to get to them. But no way were we going to just sit here. I wanted to punish them, deal them a decisive blow that would wipe this cell out once and for all.

I checked in with Big Red. Delta Platoon had its hands full. It had circled the wagons at Hotel California, but one of its Humvees had suffered a catastrophic RPG strike. The men were dishing it out, but since they rolled lean, they didn't have the dismounts to kick out into the fight that we had. For now, though, they were holding their own.

The Special Forces team slapped their laptop closed and joined the fight, their silenced weapons making dull *tunk-tunk-tunk* sounds.

The quick reaction force arrived. Once again, the marines with their Afghan protégés had come out to reinforce us. As their pick-ups and Humvees bounced into our perimeter, I heard somebody say, "Why the fuck is Second Platoon always MIA?"

That's on Burley, not the men.

With the reinforcements, I had well over a company of troops—120 men—that I could maneuver. I called back to Bermel to talk to Captain Dye and let him know I intended to counterattack.

We held fire superiority now. We kept up the volume of fire, mowing through our available rounds. Even though we'd brought twice the usual ammo load, Sabo was taking no chances. He worked furiously to transfer ammo from the Afghan trucks to ours until we had more than enough bullets to burn.

I called a leaders' meeting in one of the ruined compounds. My squad leaders gathered quickly. The Special Forces colonel joined our circle. His face glistened with sweat. "This is like the Wild West!" he exclaimed. "I haven't been in a fight like this since Colombia in the eighties!"

"Listen up," I said. "We're going to counterattack that ridge."

The colonel lit up. "What?"

"We've got a good base of fire. Sabo, you stay with the gunners. Campbell, Wheat, get your men and come with me."

"We're counterattacking?" the colonel asked.

"Yes."

"Right the fuck on. Let's go get 'em!" he blurted out, a wicked grin on his face. My squad leaders burst out laughing. Coming from an old gray-haired warrior, the words seemed incongruous.

Right then, the bond between the colonel and the rest of us became complete. "We'll move in five. Go get ready." Everyone scrambled to assemble for the attack.

I returned to my truck one last time to check in with Delta before we moved. It had lost a second truck to an RPG, but another element of Afghan troops had arrived with their marine embeds, so they had the situation in hand. I told Big Red what we were about to do, then wished him luck.

Just before I gave the order to advance, the enemy struck.

Eight men wearing man jams, field jackets, and chest rigs full of AK mags boiled out of a wadi that ran along the flank and rear of our plateau. We'd just finished reposturing for our counterassault, and now we had to pivot in place to deal with this new threat.

A hundred meters away, they made a rush for my truck, screaming and firing from the hip as they ran. My gunners spun their turrets around and hammered at them, but we'd been caught by surprise and our accuracy suffered.

They went to ground and started sniping at us. Ferguson direct-fired his mortar at them. Our machine guns scythed back and forth. Our dismounts repositioned themselves to add their weapons to the fusillade.

An insurgent jumped to his feet and jackrabbited for the wadi. Our machine guns chased him all the way until he vanished behind the wadi's lip. A second later, two more broke cover and fell back. The others stole away. Within minutes, the enemy squad had vanished.

What the hell was that?

When I returned my attention to the ridge on the far side of the valley, I understood exactly what had just happened. We'd just been juked right out of our jocks. Silently, I cursed myself for not anticipating it.

That eight-man team had been a feint. They had hooked behind us, lain in wait for the perfect moment, then made a show of assaulting us right as we were about to jump off with our own attack. Their move had derailed ours and forced us to react. With our attention diverted, the main enemy force had broken contact. They had slipped over the ridge to the east and disappeared toward Pakistan.

The din of battle died away. On the north side of the valley, the enemy disengaged from Delta Platoon as well. Soon silence graced the late afternoon. We stood alert, fingers on our triggers, coldly awaiting their next move. But they had gone, and once again we held the battlefield.

The Special Forces colonel pulled me aside. "Lieutenant, you guys deal with this every day?"

"Just about every time we leave the wire, sir."

"Nobody knows how intense things are out here. I want you to know I'm going to personally tell Major General Freakley about it."

"Thank you, sir. We're pretty shorthanded. Could use more troops."

"I'll pass that along."

"Thanks." I needed a cigarette. Then I remembered that I didn't smoke.

"You ever think about going Special Forces?"

Not really. But I didn't want to offend the colonel. "Sometimes, sir."

"You get in touch with me if you ever decide that's what you want." He put a hand on my shoulder and smiled. Looking around at the men busy at their tasks, he lowered his voice and said, "You know, these soldiers respect your decisions."

Without thinking, I said, "I love these men, sir."

I'd never said that out loud before.

Perhaps there are no heroes, just men who are not afraid to love.

I thought of Brown, Howie, and McCleod. I thought of Dixon picking up Baldwin even after he'd been shot and was going into shock. I thought of Pantoja ignoring the ragged hole in his face as he treated everyone around him.

Love cements selflessness.

If Dugin was the exception, he also proved the rule. His bullshit lies and puppy-dog devotion didn't play within the platoon. But what was he really doing? He was trying to be validated; he wanted to belong. But he always went about it the wrong way, and he couldn't connect. He couldn't fit. He couldn't love or be loved. He just didn't know how. Ultimately, that disconnect made the difference between returning to the turret to stay in the fight and heading to the casualty collection point. Dugin was no coward; June 10 had proved that. But without that bond, without that love the rest of us felt for one another, he was never going to give himself selflessly in battle. That limitation was good to know.

Outlaw Platoon had bonded in a way that made us fierce in battle. Our selflessness was our secret weapon. In the months to come, my job would be to keep our chemistry intact. It would be tested by internal tensions as well as external ones. I had no doubt of that. No matter what, it needed to be nourished and protected.

Sabo found me lost in thought. He moved alongside me and asked, "We going to head home, sir?"

I shook my head. Through clenched teeth, I replied, "No way are we giving the ground to the enemy. We stay here tonight." They might have thwarted my counterattack—again—but we would secure the moral victory and dare them to take it from us.

Sabo offered a broad smile. "Fuck, yeah, sir."

Word was passed. The men made preparations to stay the night. The perimeter was reinforced, battle positions improved, MREs passed around.

The self-doubts were gone. The second-guessing and the over-analyzing of my leadership style—those were weaknesses we could no longer afford. I silently shed those weights; I had experience leading men in battle now.

This fight had transformed us, furthered our becoming. Gone was the euphoria we had felt in May, replaced by steel and icy professionalism. The adrenaline rush combat produced didn't last as long this time, either. Nor was it as intense. Our bodies were growing used to that chemical surge, and its effects were diminishing with every injection.

We were reaching a peak. Almost halfway through the deployment, we knew our jobs and ourselves. Combat had become a known quantity. There were no more surprises save the ones the enemy schemed to spring on us. Perhaps we'd have a few surprises for it in the weeks ahead. This battle had been our arrival moment.

At dusk, I stood beside a crumbled qalat wall and gazed across at the ridge on the far side of the valley. Here and there, smoke still coiled up from fires sparked by our 105s. Broken trees and blackened shell holes dotted the scene. The enemy had fled. We'd outgritted them yet again. I wanted to throw my head back and let out a victory cry. But such a thing does not become a leader. I kept it tight.

After dark, the Special Forces colonel came to me with a crucial piece of intel we'd been lacking since the start of the spring offensive. His team had the same signal intercept capabilities that our Prophet spooks possessed, with some extra (classified) features thrown in for good measure. He briefed me on what they'd learned. When he finished, I rounded up Sabo, Campbell, and Wheat to tell them the news.

"We know the enemy's intentions now," I said. That got everyone's attention.

"They are seeking a decisive victory over an American platoon. They want to pin us in a kill zone by disabling our vehicles, then overrun us and kill us to the last man. They plan to behead anyone they capture. If they catch us in an observation point again, they will try a direct assault, just like June 10."

Sabo growled, "Guess we'll ratchet things up."

The other men nodded. I saw grim determination on every face.

We discussed this news for several minutes, developing more plays for our book should the enemy return tonight. When we finished, I said, "Every time they come at us, we'll be ready. We'll slaughter them, just as we've been doing. Intel intercepted some enemy radio transmissions that confirmed we took out another twenty of the bastards—at least. Good job. Keep it up."

Nods all around. For an impulsive second, I wanted to add something else. I swallowed the words before they reached my lips. Men do not do well when tender emotions exist between them. They can be there. They can even be tangentially recognized. But to acknowledge them directly would have violated the structure of our relationships and turned the moment awkward. I went quiet rather than run that risk. But I suspected everyone in the leaders' huddle that night was thinking the same thing. Forget firepower and ammunition, forget grit, forget numbers and access to indirect. All those things had been available to other units overrun in other wars and battles.

As the meeting broke up and my NCOs returned to their squads, I stood in the ruins and let my mind dwell on the words I hadn't had the heart to utter.

Love's the only thing that will see us through this. If that love fails, or if we let circumstance and friction grind it down, we will surely die.

I was glad I hadn't said that to my squad leaders. Just hearing it in my head sounded gay enough. I'd have never lived it down. No matter. Spoken or not, we all knew it to be our central truth.

NINETEEN

ROCKET'S RED GLARE

★ ★ ★

THE SUN, A MOLTEN CRESCENT PEEPING OVER RAKHAH Ridge, streaked the sky with bands of gold and red. The haze lingering in our valley caught the light and tinted the air the color of dried blood. We could have been campaigning on Mars.

Dawn: our time.

Back home, this moment of spectacular beauty is missed by so many of our friends and family. Here, it was the start of every business day. Dawn served as a trough between restless sleep and the emotional suck of combat, a waiting period in which I could gauge the platoon's mood.

We had lined the rigs up on the gravel next to the operations center in preparation for the morning's mission. Today we would take the Special Forces team to an Afghan checkpoint east of FOB Shkin. We'd be in Abdul's old neighborhood for the first time since he'd been killed.

Chris Brown, all of twenty-one, stood in the turret of my Humvee, arms peppered with shrapnel now buried within cauterized wounds. He wore a floppy booney hat and had thrown a black-and-white-checked Afghan scarf across one shoulder. Its tassels dangled on his chest. He flipped up the booney hat's brim, revealing a tuft of brown hair on his forehead. He looked ready for a GQ photo shoot. *Accessorize your ACUs on an Afghan budget.*

Ayers was by the Humvee's door, looking up at Brown as Brown regaled a small audience with some goofy tale. He had deepened his voice and put a Philly street accent into it, which made him sound like Rocky Balboa.

"So I says to the kid, I says, 'Yo kid, yous ain't got nothin'. Nothin'.'"

I walked past, shaking my head. Brown was from a middle-class Memphis family and was about as street as I was.

"Hey, Brown," somebody interrupted.

"Yo, homey! What's you wan'?" he replied, striking another ridiculous pose that prompted cheers from the platoon.

"'Thriller'!"

He made a show of considering the request.

Sabo, who'd been by his own rig talking to Rowley, sauntered over, trying to look cool and uninterested. A few more of the men gathered while others smoked next to their trucks, attentive to the spectacle.

Brown popped out of the turret and stood on the Humvee's back deck, his pistol snug in a holster strapped to his belt. That back deck had served as his makeshift dance platform many times in the past. He had the platoon's full attention now.

"Check it!" he shouted. He strutted forward and onto the spare tire stowed like an old-style continental kit on the Humvee's rear. Hands on his hips now, he thrust his pelvis, spun, and landed with catlike grace on the back deck. His audience cheered.

Head twitch left. Claws right, claws left, two stutter steps, and then a moonwalk into a pivot turn. I wondered how many times Brown had watched that old Michael Jackson video to get the moves down so perfectly.

He slid left, head shaking, then crouched, hands on his thighs, and did a miniature version of the monster stomp laterally across the deck.

Sabo actually cracked a grin. He'd been ultraserious recently, so that was good to see. He had a Mossberg 500 shotgun strapped across his back and a pair of sunglasses on.

"Fucking whack job," I heard him mutter.

The catcalls continued. Brown hammed it up, and I stood at the edge of the scene, content to take the platoon's pulse. Despite everything we'd experienced these past months, the men were lighthearted and at ease. If an outsider were to stumble upon this scene without context or location, he'd never guess we were about to drive into battle.

THE SILLINESS CONTINUED UNTIL THE SPECIAL FORCES TEAM showed up. The colonel greeted me, and we discussed the plan for the morning.

"Showtime," I said.

The platoon transitioned quickly into steely combat mode. Brown strapped on his body armor and slid back into his turret. The rest of the men geared up. Within minutes, we were in full battle rattle, ready to roll, with our weapons loaded, safeties on.

The men were looking forward to the day's mission. Though we might encounter the enemy, we'd be able to stop at FOB Shkin for a while to grab a bite to eat. Its chow hall had much better grub than ours. The thought of something other than corn flakes for breakfast appealed to me.

First, we had to drop the Special Forces guys off at the Alamo, our nickname for a remote Afghan checkpoint directly opposite the Pakistani border.

Our Humvees carried the scars of our firefights, just as our bodies did. Paint chipped, their armored skins pockmarked with bullet divots, they were the mounts of battle-hardened men.

We plunged south into the Afghan morning, once again that tiny bubble of Americans in a hostile landscape. An hour and a half later, we arrived at our destination. The Afghan troops manning the Alamo opened the front gate, and we motored past bullet-scarred walls, pitted Texas barriers, and sandbagged guard towers to park not far from the outer wall, which was composed of a single row of dilapidated Hesco bags. Just as our rigs telegraphed our status, so too did this remote and battered outpost. This place had taken a beating.

The Alamo had been the original site of FOB Shkin. It overlooked a gated border crossing directly in front of a Pakistani town called Angoor Ada. Sharp-peaked mountains dominated both sides of the town, and our Pakistani allies had deployed a company of regular army troops on their slopes, well supported with quad ZSU-4 antiaircraft machine guns positioned in concrete bunkers. They were the old Soviet-era versions of our fifty-cals and could penetrate thirty-two millimeters of hardened armor at five hundred meters.

We dismounted to stretch our legs and say good-bye to the Special Forces team. Sabo came over to me. "Check that out," he said, looking pissed off as he pointed toward Pakistan.

Over the Hesco-bag wall, I could see Angoor Ada. It was a typical ramshackle little town with mud-walled qalats and tin-roofed structures forming a commercial district. Above downtown Angoor Ada, a Taliban flag fluttered in the midmorning breeze.

"Allies, eh?" he remarked sarcastically.

Something flared on the right-hand slope beside the town.

A second later, a 107mm rocket hummed overhead. It slammed into one of the guard towers, blowing sandbags and bits of wood through the air.

"Take cover!" somebody screamed. The platoon dived behind the Hesco-bag wall just as another rocket hammered the outpost. The ground shook. The men hugged the Hesco-bag walls. A dazed Afghan soldier picked his way out of the guard tower's wreckage. His head and shoulders were smoking. When he saw us staring at him, he gave a weak thumbs-up.

"Garrett!" I shouted to my honky gangsta mortar man.

"Sir?"

"Start hitting those launch sites."

"Sir, them beeches might be too far."

"Give it a go anyway. Maybe we can get them to stop firing!"

Garrett hefted his weapon and moved away from the protection of the Hesco-bag wall. He and Ferguson planted the mortar in the dirt, took careful aim, and popped a round into the tube.

Not even close. The range was too great. A third rocket streaked right over us to impact only a few dozen meters away.

"Holy shit, that was fucking close!" Garrett shouted. The shock of the near miss knocked the gangsta affectation out of his voice. I realized that it was the first time I'd heard the real Garrett.

"Fuck it, get back over here," I called to him and Bear.

We heard another one cook off from its launch site. The red glare of its fiery engine stood stark against the morning's blue sky. An instant later, it gouged a crater near our Humvees.

"SABO, WE'VE GOT TO MOVE THE TRUCKS TO BETTER COVER. GET 'em up against the Hesco wall."

"Roger, sir." Sabo turned and passed the order along. Another rocket landed, this one a little farther away than the last two. My drivers broke cover and ran to their Humvees. Yet another rocket exploded, this one less than twenty-five meters from us. As they started the trucks and moved them behind the wall, I stood up to take a look at the enemy.

They were firing at us from just below the concrete bunkers that housed the PakMil antiaircraft guns.

I moved to my truck and called Captain Dye to request indirect. "Negative, three-six," came his answer. "That's Pakistani territory."

Another rocket skittered past, low and fast. Everyone molded himself against the Hesco-bag wall as it spewed shrapnel and flame across the outpost. The explosion sent peals of terror through us.

We can't shoot back?

"Jesus Christ, these things are close," Garrett groaned as he made himself as small as possible beside me.

We lay against the wall, chain-smoking in silence, each blast like a wrecking ball to the platoon's spirits. Soon all that remained inside us was a sense of helplessness and cold fury. As the barrage continued, even the fury gave way to naked terror.

Rockets are mind-fuck weapons. Where they land is beyond our ability to judge, and their fall is so random as to seemingly require an act of God to kill anyone. "You buy it that way, it was your time, dude" was a common response to the attacks at Bermel.

This time was different. The bastards on the other side of the border had us cold in their sights. With their aim unhindered, they took their time and sent each rocket straight into the Alamo with deadly accuracy. Between salvos, our nerves sang like overstretched guitar strings as we waited for the sound of the next launch. When it came, the ensuing seconds reduced us to silence, begging God for it to land long. Then, even though we knew the detonation was coming, the sudden flat *BOOM* rolling at us always came as a shock. With rockets, even the expected blast is unexpected. You never know the exact moment it will hit, and that switch from tense expectation to reacting to it sends the nervous system into convulsions. We jumped and started so many times our bodies began to shake uncontrollably.

We huddled together as each one exploded dangerously close. A few landed less than thirty meters away. Dirt pelted us until we resembled albinos and our mouths were gritty and foul. With each blast, our sinuses burned from the stench of cordite. A metallic taste lingered on the tips of our tongues. We could smell our own fear—a sourness laced with panicky sweat and body odor.

Each launch made us second-guess where we had taken cover. Could this be where the next one hits? What if we took cover further down the wall? Would that be a safer spot? Our minds tormented us, unsure whether some decision we made would freakishly put us into a rocket's path. It was a dreadful head game that left our confidence completely shattered.

During World War I, the soldiers of the western front had learned to crater jump to avoid such mind games. They'd believed that the chance of another shell impacting atop a previous hit was mathematically improbable, so once the shrapnel passed and the smoke cleared, they'd seek solace in the torn and shattered earth.

Of course, one look at the overlapping craters at places such as Verdun dispelled the reality of such suppositions. Besides, here we could not do that. The rockets didn't leave deep enough craters, and it would have been far too dangerous to move around. All we could do was lie there, captives.

I saw the platoon change. The men's eyes grew hollowed and wide. We'd been through dangerous encounters before, but we had always been able to fight back. That gave us something to do and occupied our minds. Our inability to act now exposed us to terror's fullest effects.

Sabo was the only one to react differently. After a rocket exploded on the other side of our Humvees, showering the rigs with shrapnel that tinked off their armored hides, he sat up and shouted something. His eyes flared, and he flashed a maniacal grin at me, as if this was the place he had been born to be.

As I watched him, a couple of Apaches ventured out to our aid. Between rocket strikes, we could hear the bass roll of their rotors swelling as they approached. Meanwhile, the barrage did not let up.

The Apaches arrived overhead. Their crews detected the launch sites, could see the teams reloading for the next volley. But they could not shoot. The Pakistan Army troops on the slope were intermingled with the enemy rocket teams.

Our "ally's" soldiers functioned as our enemy's human shields.

The sight of the Apaches slowed the rate of the incoming at last. The brief lull gave us a narrow window of opportunity to escape. We seized the moment, climbed into our rigs, and sped through the smoke for the front gate. We passed the smoldering guard tower along the way even as the next wave of rockets pummeled the Alamo. The ANA swung the gate open, and we rolled for the safety of the open road.

We didn't slow until we reached FOB Shkin a half hour later. In the chow hall there, the men kept to themselves. Hardly a word passed between us. The different chow we'd so looked forward to had no taste. We ate without relish, then headed on our way.

A platoon's morale is an elastic quality. From its baseline, events affecting the men can cause it to bend in different directions. Mail gives it a boost; so does hot chow after a long day. A small gesture by a first sergeant showing that he has the well-being of the men in mind can also go a long way. A victory in combat can bring euphoria; a defeat will bring despair and doubt. We'd seen or experienced the gamut, and the men had always returned to their baseline laughing, irreverent selves after a while. It was our natural state.

But something had happened under those rockets. We'd never

felt so utterly helpless. Being unable to fight back had stripped us of our aggressive spirit. It had left us feeling impotent, mere observers of the death and destruction thrown our way.

We raged against an enemy we were not allowed to kill, who launched its attacks against us from the bosom of our ally's army. The Alamo had penetrated deep into the platoon's psyche. It tipped us into a downward slide, one in which our emotional state began to lose its elasticity. We were not going to rebound from this as we had from all the other blows we'd absorbed. We were becoming numb, and that worried me.

Late that afternoon, we returned to Bermel through the Afghan National Army side of the base. The ANA soldiers had spent the day inside the wire. We passed knots of them playing dice games and kicking soccer balls. Here and there, others sat in the dirt with vacant eyes, smoking hash. Their polyglot uniforms were ill tended. They were poorly groomed. They looked like a unit that just didn't give a shit.

From my turret, Chris Brown exploded, "You motherfuckers! Fight for your own goddamned country!"

"Brown, knock it off," I said.

"Fuck them! We're out every day getting shit on, and they're in here playing soccer."

"Brown, come on," I repeated. I couldn't be harsh to him. It wasn't the time for that, not with the state of morale the way it was. Besides, part of me felt the same way.

We parked at the maintenance pad and dismounted. The men moved slowly, their eyes hollow. It felt like defeat.

Sabo came to me and asked, "Guidance, sir? Order of priorities?"

"Same as always," I replied.

"Roger." He paused and added, "Happy Independence Day, sir."

"What?"

"Fourth of July today, sir."

I had forgotten.

"Happy Independence Day, Sabo," I managed.

Beside my rig, I thought of fireworks and backyard barbecues, parades and cold beer. A lifetime and half a world away, those had been the trappings of my life. Sparklers, Piccolo Petes, Lady Fingers, and mailboxes blown to fragments in mischievous pranks. Burgers served seared and steaming on buns smeared with ketchup and mustard. Bags of chips arrayed in ranks along picnic tables, flanked by stacks of paper plates and bottles of pop. Kids laughing. Adults jabbering. The soundtrack of a cocooned and contented people.

I lit a cigarette and looked around. The men worked to prep the trucks for the morning's mission. Nobody joked. The talk was all business and sparse at that. A couple of times, tempers flared.

Above the operations center an American flag flew in the evening breeze. We'd returned at sunset. Our day started and ended with these moments of spectacular beauty, and normally the sight of the flag set against the blazing sky instilled a sense of pride in me. Tonight it made me feel bitter.

I realized that my hands were shaking. Afraid the men would notice, I stepped away from the Humvees.

This was Afghanistan's revolution, not ours. We had fought our war for independence. With great leaders like Washington, Adams, and Jefferson, we had thrown off the yoke of terror and oppression and forged a new era. Two hundred plus years ago, they had set those celebratory tables across America upon which now rested our nation's ample bounty.

But who was the Afghan Washington? Hamid Karzai? Give me a break. He was little better than a war lord. There was no one. The closest had been Ahmed Shah Massoud, the leader of the Northern Alliance. We had found his likeness all over the Bermel

Valley on the walls of homes and businesses. Some people even carried wallet-sized pictures of him in their pockets.

Al Qaida had assassinated him just before September 11. It knew that if anyone could unify this fragmented and parochial land, it was he.

The sounds of laughter from the Afghan side of the compound reached our ears. It felt like salt in the psychological wounds we'd suffered this day.

This is your revolution. Yours. Will you give what is needed to have your Independence Day?

"Sean, you all right?"

I turned to see Captain Dye regarding me with concern.

"Yeah, I'm okay. I guess we found out today why they moved FOB Shkin away from the border."

"I guess so. I'm sorry I couldn't give you any indirect."

Thank you, PakMil assholes. Allies, my ass.

"You sure you're okay?" he asked again. "Your hands are shaking."

"I'll be all right, sir," I lied. "It was just rough having to take it for so long and not being able to shoot back."

He put his hand on my shoulder and shook me gently. "If you need anything, let me know."

"Thank you, sir."

Unspoken was, *We're infantry. Handle it.*

After checking in at the operations center, I started to walk over to my hooch. Mountains of paperwork awaited me there, and I was dreading the amount of time it would take to get done tonight. I'd have to forgo chow again.

Along the way, I noticed that a few of the men had pulled our dogs from their wire enclosure. I wished I could see who was out there, but in the night I could make out only their shadows. Part of me longed to join them.

The oldest two dogs, Zeus and Jumper, dashed around them,

eager to stretch their legs. We also had five pups, all roughly four or five months old. They barked and bayed as they danced happily from one soldier to the next. Soon they were squirming in weary arms, the men sharing subdued laughter. Maybe there were still remnants of our old selves after all. We just needed some help recovering it.

Those dogs gave us a small connection to the life we'd had back home. On a night like this, I was grateful that they were there for my men.

I walked back to my hooch and stepped into the hallway. Sergeant R. Kelly was singing away in his creepy falsetto. At least he'd started early tonight. Maybe he'd wear out and give us a break. I shook my head with frustration and went to my door.

It was ajar.

Cautiously, I pushed it open. My room was dark, but I could see a figure standing beside my desk.

"Who's there?" I asked harshly. It was not unknown to have stuff stolen on base. Had I interrupted a thief?

"It's just me, sir."

"Cole?" my voice betrayed my astonishment.

"Yes, sir."

I clicked a light on. He was holding a plate of cold cuts and a mug of coffee.

"You're the one?"

He smiled sheepishly. "Just doing my part, you know, sir?"

My reaction caught him off guard. He retreated to humor. "No worries, sir. I figure the one thing I know is how to eat and serve food. Besides, if I can get the LT as fat as I am, he won't be able to keep me off patrol!"

This selfless kid had been anonymously boosting my morale for months. Now, when I caught him, he just laughed off his gesture.

"Thanks, Cole."

He placed the food and coffee on the desk and slipped past me for the door. "Hey, sir, do me a favor. Don't tell the men. They'll think I'm a kiss-ass."

He vanished before I could reply.

I stood and looked at the open doorway for a long moment before sitting down to eat Cole's meal. If briefly, it lifted my spirits.

Then R. Kelly launched into a new riff, and my struggling mood collapsed. If he kept that up, there'd be no sleep, even with my headphones on. To drown out the buzzing in my ears—and R. Kelly—I'd taken to listening to movie themes and classical music on my iPod. It gave me enough white noise to disengage my brain for a while. I looked forward to that tonight.

First the paperwork. I flipped open my laptop to power it up. The movement sent a little air current flowing through the room. It rustled the paper hanging on the plywood wall to my right. The movement caught my eye. A few months back, I'd received a care package from my family that included a picture my cousin Freddie had drawn for me. I'd laughed when I pulled it out to find what he'd created.

I looked at it now. Green grass along the bottom edge. A sun in one corner with pencil-line rays radiating out. A helicopter hovering in the background. In the middle, he'd drawn me, a rifle-armed stick figure with a helmet, smiling beside an American flag. He'd scrawled across the scene, "Thank you, Sean!"

I THOUGHT OF FREDDIE RUNNING AMOK, A BUNDLE OF ENERGY and excitement, dying to start the family fireworks display. I ached to see that again. I could almost taste the burgers and beer, smell the fireworks, hear the easy banter shared with my blood.

Those are dangerous thoughts.

Hot summer days in T-shirts and shorts, standing at the start of a Pirates game at PNC Park. Americans from all walks of life covered their hearts with their hands as the celebrity du jour belted out "The Star-Spangled Banner." Twenty thousand voices cheering the last line: "And the home of the brave." It was the place of my grandpap, the gathering point for the Parnell family that transcended generations. How many games had we been to together over the years? The fresh-cut grass, the hot dogs and brats, the sun warm on our faces as we cheered our childhood heroes on.

Heroes. I'll never see them that way again. I've seen who real heroes are. And they don't wear cleats on game day.

I'D ALWAYS ASSUMED THE DAY WOULD COME WHEN I WOULD SIT in those stands and share those moments with my own son, my own daughter. I'd feed them junk food and babble in their ear about the infield fly rule, stealing bases, strike zones, and arcane statistics.

The thought of that day never coming filled me with dread.

I did not want to go out tomorrow. Fuck the bullets and rockets and RPGs, mortars and eight-inch knives awaiting our necks. Why risk all we have waiting for a nation whose warriors refuse to give their last full measure in their own defense?

I needed to be home; the separation suddenly felt like an oozing wound.

Get control of yourself.

I could not pull my eyes from Freddie's drawing. Only six, he had carefully sculpted every letter, and I wondered who had helped him with the spelling. Where had he sat as he worked on this for me? Had he decided to do it on his own, or had he been prompted by someone in the family?

The meat sizzling on the grill fills the backyard with blue-gray smoke. The smell is indescribable, a direct line to our inner cave-man. Each lungful feels like home.

I inhaled, but all I smelled was stagnant air made foul by too many men living atop one another.

I couldn't face the paperwork tonight. Somehow I'd find time in the morning to get it done. Instead, I opened my e-mail account and read the few waiting messages. Nothing of note. No word from home tonight.

I started to write my dad, but the words didn't come. How could I describe a day like this one? What phrases did I have that could possibly convey what a rocket barrage does to the human mind?

No. Tonight I would not burden my father, even with words inadequate to the experience.

My eyes returned to the drawing.

I REACHED UP AND PULLED IT OFF THE WALL. WITH ONE LAST look, I folded it in half and placed it out of sight.

"I'm sorry, Freddie," I whispered.

When I climbed into my bunk a few minutes later, I realized that my hands had ceased to shake.

TWENTY

LAST FAIR DEAL GONE DOWN

★ ★ ★

Mid-July 2006

HEYA, LT!" CHRIS COWAN BEAMED AT ME. UNIFORM CLEAN, eyes bright, all chiseled brawn, he looked like he'd just stepped off the set of *300*.

"How was home?" I asked as I went to shake his hand.

"Handshake, my ass!" He wrapped an anaconda-sized arm around my neck and drew me into a headlock.

"Ow! Goddammit, Cowan!"

"Great ta fuckin' see ya, sir," he said as he squeezed my neck. Chris was well known for his steel-trap headlocks. Nobody he liked escaped this treatment, and he'd been nicknamed "the Constrictor" for it. Since coming to the platoon, he'd also ensured that he led the way on every patrol. For Cowan, being on point was a deep source of pride, and the men respected him for his willingness to always take the most dangerous position in our formations.

He let me up and handed me my hat, which had fallen into the dirt. "Home was home. Got drunk a lot. Glad to be back with Michelle. Now I'm glad to be back with the men."

We chatted and walked to the chow hall to grab dinner. Since the rocket barrage at Alamo, the platoon's morale had flatlined. Perhaps Chris's return could revive some of our spirits. It was good to have him back. Before he'd left, he and I had spent a lot of time lifting weights together in our makeshift FOB gym. I'd found him to be highly intelligent and his sense of humor more sophisticated than I first realized.

Soon Pinholt, Pantoja, and Greeson would be back, and the platoon's heart would be intact again. We also expected Echavez, our Mark 19 gunner extraordinaire, and our Russian warrior, Nosov, to rejoin us soon from Helmand Province. While down there, they'd seen considerable combat. Khanh had taken a serious bullet wound to the head in one fight and was in Germany now getting treated. Last we'd heard, blood clots had formed in his brain and the docs were very concerned about his prognosis.

After dinner that evening, I stepped outside to check in at the operations center. We had a mission in the morning, and I needed to go over a few things with Captain Dye. But on my way out of the chow hall, I ran into First Sergeant Christopher, and the two of us paused to talk over some business.

Behind us, the Mail Bitch, back in our area again, exited the chow hall. She'd been hanging around the FOB all day, for what purpose nobody seemed to know. As far as we could see, she hadn't brought any mail with her. But she was an E-6, a staff sergeant, and that rank shielded her from most questioning. At that level, NCOs are supposed to carry themselves with honor and integrity.

A dog started barking; a woman screamed in fear. First Sergeant

Christopher and I spun around to see Zeus challenging the Mail Bitch. He looked sickly, and despite the attention of our medics, his condition had deteriorated until we were all worried about him. The Mail Bitch backed away, wailing "Get it away from me! Get it away!"

Cowan materialized next to the dog, and he stopped barking. Of all the soldiers on post, Cowan had developed the tightest bond with our brood of canines. He spoke softly to Zeus, then led him back to the kennel. Cowan and our executive officer had built the dog pen with wire framing pulled from discarded Hesco bags. It was actually quite ingenious.

"That mongrel attacked me," said the Mail Bitch, her fear gone and replaced by outrage.

Oh shit.

First Sergeant Christopher went over to deal with her. I didn't want anything to do with that scene, and besides, it was out of my jurisdiction, so I beat feet over to the operations center to get an update on our next mission. When I got there, Captain Dye briefed me on the area he wanted Third Platoon to patrol in the morning. Then he gave me the latest intel on what was happening around Bermel. I took notes and was soon so absorbed in planning for the next cycle that I forgot all about the Mail Bitch.

The next morning, we headed out on patrol. We were out for several days again, sleeping in the field. The enemy eluded us this time. It felt as though we were playing a shadow game with Galang's replacement. Ever since the end of June, the enemy had made themselves scarce, though our Prophet spooks still heard them chattering. I couldn't help but think they had gone to ground to study the last fight to learn from it and develop new tactics. It would fit the pattern, that's for sure. Perhaps they were off rehearsing their next operation, just as we did on the rare days we spent on base.

We returned to Bermel exhausted, filthy, and eager to stuff

something other than MREs into our stomachs. The men serviced the trucks, cleaned their weapons, then headed for chow.

Cowan found me, his face crestfallen.

"What's wrong?" I asked.

"The dogs are gone," he said, his voice flat.

"Did they get out again?"

"No."

We locked eyes, and I knew what he was going to say. And I didn't want to hear it.

"The Mail Bitch said Zeus bit her."

"That's bullshit. I saw it happen. He just barked at her and scared her."

Cowan looked stricken. "I know. Somebody killed all of them, sir." For a long moment, he couldn't speak. Then he added, "I could understand Zeus, but why all of them?"

The story came out in pieces over the next few hours. After the Mail Bitch claimed she'd been bitten, our chain of command had had to act. Staff sergeants are taken at their word, and the dogs were an indulgence in direct violation to standing theaterwide orders.

While we were gone on patrol, a medic from battalion had flown in to carry out the job. He had taken them to the aid station and, one by one, injected Zeus, Jumper, and the puppies. The men on base who had seen him do it said the medic seemed to be getting a thrill out of the job. Whether or not he did didn't matter to me. What mattered was the platoon's reaction to that news, and it was not good.

The medic had carried the dogs to the burn pit and thrown their lifeless bodies in with the trash.

It was a good thing he'd left the base soon after he'd finished his work. The men had wanted to pulverize him.

The next day, as we gathered for the morning mission, the

platoon carried with it a mood of profound sadness. I wanted to do something—anything—for them, but there was nothing to be done. It was a fait accompli.

I suppose if we'd had a psychologist out there with us, we would have all been diagnosed with severe depression at that point. The men had been hammered in so many different ways, they'd stopped caring. To do so would only have invited more pain. Instead, they wore their sadness like a defensive shroud.

As we loaded up in our Humvees, Chris Brown stood in my turret, his eyes distant.

"How you doing, bro?" I asked gently as I opened the passenger side door.

His chin sank to his IBA, and he shook his head. "How many times are we going to get kicked in the crotch?" he finally asked, more to himself than to me.

Anger and indignation I could work with. The infantry feeds on such emotions; it motivates and makes us eager to release violence upon our foe. There was no fight in Chris that morning, and he was the barometer of the platoon's morale. I saw his resignation reflected on everyone's faces. Cowan moved like a sleepwalker. Even Sabo appeared affected.

As I watched the platoon struggle that morning, I realized that I had overlooked a reality of Afghanistan. We were facing two enemies, not one. The Haqqani Network's fighters we could handle. Any time they chose to challenge us, we would smite them with firepower and make them pay for the effort. We would not give ground, and I knew we would never know defeat.

But this other enemy was more devious. How does one do battle with FOB politics? At the moment, I was at a complete loss. Without a doubt, we needed to figure out a way to do it, because more blows like this one could tear the platoon apart.

It was with relief that we put Bermel in our rearview mirrors.

The countryside was ours, devoid of politics, stupid rules, and petty slights. It was the one place where most feared to tread. We were among our own kind, depending on men we trusted and loved. And the danger the insurgents presented at every turn seemed a small price to pay for these respites.

While we were gone, wheels began turning around the battalion. The Mail Bitch's presence at Bermel came under scrutiny. Late at night, I had heard her enter R. Kelly's room on several occasions, where they would whisper to each other for hours. She should never have been in our hooch in the first place, as it was in violation of General Order #1. Professionally this was an inappropriate relationship, one that could have cost both NCOs their rank. After their connection was brought to the attention of our chain of command, the Mail Bitch was never seen at Bermel again.

Not long after we departed, Delta's capable and hard-nosed first sergeant got wind of the situation and initiated an investigation into R. Kelly's behavior. The first sergeant discovered that while the men whom R. Kelly was supposed to be leading in combat were out on patrol, their leader would not roll with them. He would disappear for extended periods of time to fly to other bases. The excuse he gave our chain of command—that he was trying to sort out his platoon's snarled mail situation—wore thin. Delta's first sergeant came to Bermel and tore into R. Kelly with a cold fury. Before leaving, the first sergeant gave R. Kelly a direct order: Patrol with your men. Do your job.

Truth be told, his behavior had destroyed any chance of earning a warrior's respect. When he grudgingly began rolling with Delta's platoon, the men tolerated him but did not follow his orders without first looking to Big Red for affirmation. In combat, those who are willing to fight follow only those who are willing to lead, and lead competently. When bullets fly, rank does not matter. R. Kelly became just another body in a Humvee.

As soon as the heat died down and R. Kelly's first sergeant's attention was diverted to other matters, he stopped going out again. He excused it by saying that the logistical demands of a platoon sergeant required his full attention on base.

When I heard that whopper, rage flared up in me.

Tell that to Greg Greeson.

TWENTY-ONE

VILLAGE OF THE DAMNED

★ ★ ★

Late July 2006
Afghan-Pakistani border

THE BOY COULD NOT HAVE BEEN MORE THAN A COUPLE OF feet tall. Dressed in rags, he limped in circles, head to the afternoon sky. I sat in the right seat of my Humvee, staring through the dirt-encrusted windshield as he spun and staggered in the road ahead.

What now? Did somebody get this kid high?

I ordered the platoon to halt a safe distance away from him. We were deep in bad-guy territory, behind Rakhah Ridge again and only a few clicks from the Pakistani border. After what had happened to us all spring, my men stayed alert, ready for any ruse the enemy might spring on us.

Was the kid their bait? I wasn't going to put it past them. When we had first arrived in country, we had expected an enemy that had no tactical prowess or creativity. Farmers with guns and maybe a few RPGs and mortars, nothing more. Instead, they had schooled us on the fine art of light infantry warfare for the past five months. Now, at the midpoint of our tour, we took nothing for granted.

Tires ground to a halt in the parched dust of the mountain trail. Most of the roads here would not qualify as cattle runs in the United States.

Campbell dismounted from our lead truck. Since Baldwin had gone down, Campbell had been our point man and had done a great job. He stepped cautiously toward the boy. With our vehicles idling, I could hear the child now, keening in a high-pitched whine. Was he crying? It didn't seem like it, but that voice was soaked in fear.

He made another half turn and wobbled on rubber legs along the road, chin on chest. To his right was a steep slope that ran up several hundred meters. A tiny Afghan village stood on its peak, overlooking the trail. It was one of the few left in the area that had not been destroyed or abandoned in five years of fighting. I supposed that its sheer remoteness had protected it from the ravages of war. Though we'd been all over the area, we had not yet visited it.

Campbell suddenly slowed, and my alertness level ratcheted up a notch. He'd clearly seen something. I suppressed an urge to call out to him. Campbell would tell me in his good time, and as leader I had to trust that.

Another step closer, then he paused. The boy stopped his looping circles and stood, shoulders sagging, in the middle of the trail.

"Um, sir," Campbell called over his shoulder to me. "I think you need to see this." His voice had an odd quality of weakness that I'd never heard before. It spurred me out of my rig.

Greeson dismounted and appeared alongside me. In one hand, he carried a can of nonalcoholic beer. During World War I, British officers charged German machine guns carrying swagger sticks and whistles. My platoon sergeant never failed to wield his can of faux brew.

I was glad to have him back from leave. Greeson and I had bonded in a way I had never experienced before. In combat, our sixth senses worked on the same frequency. It allowed us to intuit what the other needed. That proved an invaluable asset in the heat of a fight and made sure we could function smoothly even when we faced annihilation, as we had on June 10.

"Somethin' ain't right, sir," Greeson said in that sleepy Sam Elliott voice of his. The years of smoking and drinking had given it a gravely, rugged quality. Indomitable, really.

"Nope," I said, shaking my head under my helmet.

Campbell was kneeling in front of the boy now, talking in a low, comforting voice. The boy whined, his head waving from side to side. He seemed disengaged, lost in his own tormented world.

Who the hell would give dope to a little kid? Would the ANA do something like this?

Fifteen feet from the boy, we both gasped and stopped in our tracks. Under a shock of dirt-encrusted black hair, we saw a disfigured face about six years old. His eyes had been gouged out, the sockets burned black by whatever heated implement had been used to do the deed.

Next to me, Greeson exhaled sharply. "Jesus Christ, what is this?"

The boy opened his mouth again. Another whine spilled out between cracked lips. Behind them, we saw ruptured gums and no teeth.

"You're fuckin' kidding me?" Greeson said.

"Get Yusef and Doc Pantoja," I said to my platoon sergeant.

Yusef reached us first and looked down at the boy. Either he'd seen this sort of thing before, or a half decade of war had steeled him to such sights. The boy's condition evoked no visible emotions

in my 'terp. He stood quietly next to me, his used-car-salesman affection stowed for the moment.

A moment later, Doc Pantoja came forward. He knelt next to
Campbell, talking in a reassuring voice to the boy. The compassion
in his words touched me.

Without prompting, Yusef spoke to the boy, translating for Pantoja. In stark contrast to my medic, Yusef's tone was clipped and
devoid of sympathy. For a second I wondered what he was actually
saying to the boy. Once again, I wished Abdul were here. Trusting
a 'terp to translate accurately without injecting his own agenda or
machinations into a conversation requires trust. With Abdul, such
a leap of faith was easy. With Yusef, not so much.

The boy calmed but said nothing in reply.

I looked up the slope and saw the village's mud-walled dwellings in the flat morning sunlight. Could he have stumbled down
the hill and gotten lost? He was a good six hundred meters from
home, a considerable distance given his age and condition. Perhaps
his family was up there, searching for him.

Next to me, Greeson swore softly. His eyes, always hard and
capable, looked totally vulnerable now, as if this child had opened
up something in him that he had worked hard to conceal from us
these past months. Underneath that steel-belted exterior, Greeson
had a huge heart. All great infantrymen do.

I didn't want the rest of the men to see the boy. They'd been
through enough already, and the platoon's morale had not recovered from the day our dogs had been tossed into the burn pit. I
was starting to worry about the state of mind of even the most
hard-core members of the platoon. Leaving them behind would
be a risk. What if we climbed the slope and walked into an enemy
stronghold? Our little group would be in serious trouble, and help
would be more than half a kilometer below us.

But then I thought of Cowan's crushed expression as he had

come to tell me about Zeus. The Mail Bitch, the FOB politics. I thought of the many little injustices they'd faced, the Alamo rockets, June 10. Brown venting at the ANA.

Protecting them from this sight was worth the risk.

"Let's take him up to the village." I said.

Doc Pantoja scooped the little boy into his arms. The boy offered no resistance. As Pantoja held him, the boy curled his tiny hands around my medic's neck and lay the side of his ruined face against his armored chest.

"Ready, sir," Campbell said in a reedy tone. This was getting to all of us.

We started up the slope, the jagged peaks of the Hindu Kush the backdrop of our half-kilometer hike.

This was the land that time had forgotten. Civilization, progress—those things had never taken root here. It was not a stretch to imagine the first cave dwellers gazing upon the exact same view thousands of years ago.

The village was a frightful sight. A clean bed would have been a priceless luxury in this place. The mud-walled huts were barren of even the most basic essentials. Little food, no clean water. The ground between the dwellings was riddled with human feces, animal dung, and filth. The smell of such a place is one that none of us will ever forget. It lingered like a tangible presence in the air. I could feel it seeping into my clothing, and for a second I flashed back to my first day in country. After the girl had died in my arms, I had burned my blood-soaked ACUs.

No amount of cleaning would ever get this stench out.

A boy perhaps six years old limped out of a nearby hut and took station near one corner, watching us with burnished black eyes. There was a wary worldliness in them that I'd never seen back home. Welts and bruises ran the length of his face, neck, and arms. He'd been badly beaten.

Movement inside a nearby shed caught our attention. In its gloom, we glimpsed a hint of a shape, a shadow of a bent knee kicking weakly at the darkness. Campbell went to investigate. He stopped at the entrance, and the color vanished from his face. He looked away.

"Doc. Get over here," he said.

Doc put the boy down. Greeson knelt next to him, and I heard him quietly soothing the boy with words softly spoken. Gone were Sling Blade and Sam Elliott from that voice, replaced by a soft Arkansas tone that rang of fatherly devotion.

A little girl peered out from one of the huts. The girl's face, once beautiful, was striped with purple and yellow bruises. I smiled at her, wondering how old she was. It was impossible to tell.

She smiled back at me, her lips raw and torn.

Pantoja reached the shed. "Oh shit." I turned to look at him, his bronze face ashen.

"Sir?" he managed. I walked over to him.

Lying on the shed's dirt floor was another boy, perhaps a year old. He was partially naked, and flies had infested his body. They crawled in his eyes, through his nose, ears, and mouth. His breathing was labored and came in short, spastic gasps. One impossibly fragile hand waved listlessly at the insects.

His legs, covered in slicks of drying diarrhea, kicked and twitched, as if he were trying to get out from under covers in a bed. The effort was exhausting him.

"Doc, do whatever you can for him."

"I don't think there's much hope, sir. They're eating him alive."

I looked over at Campbell. "Go back to the trucks. Get all our medical gear, food, and whatever water we can spare."

"Roger, sir." Campbell seemed relieved to get away from the place. I watched him disappear over the crest of the mountaintop on his way back to the rigs.

An ancient man, clad in dirt-marred clothes, emerged from one mud hut. His beard was dyed red, something that all village elders do to show their status as community leaders. When he saw us, he paused and offered a guarded greeting.

Then he saw the eyeless boy. His composure cracked, and a look of pure love and relief crossed his face. He hurried over and wrapped the boy in his arms. The two shared words, and the elder held the boy in a fierce, protective embrace.

He looked at me, the boy's head tucked under his jaw and pressed against his neck, and I could see that the old man's eyes had grown wet. He began to speak to me.

Yusef listened, then said in his clipped and professional tone, "The village elder thanks you. This boy is his grandson."

Greeson, his voice barely a whisper, said, "Yusef, find out what happened to this kid."

Yusef nodded and engaged the village elder in a long discussion. We listened as the two conversed in their native language, anxiously awaiting the answer. At last Yusef turned his attention to us, his face a mask, and matter-of-factly told us the elder's story. The enemy had swept into the village a few weeks ago, bent on punishing its inhabitants for supporting the coalition. I doubted that any Americans had ever visited this place.

The enemy had kidnapped the elder's oldest grandson. He was the future of the family, the boy most cherished and revered in Afghan culture. Taking him was a blow that nobody in the village would forget.

They had taken the elder's grandson back to one of their mountain hideouts, where they gouged his eyes out. They had turned him into a sexual plaything, knocking out his teeth to increase their pleasure with him. They had raped this six-year-old boy for weeks.

The village had formed a posse of its most capable men. They had tracked the enemy gang back to their lair and somehow liberated the elder's grandson. But by then it was too late. The enemy had inflicted so much torture and trauma on the boy that he had ceased to function. After he'd been carried back to the village, his family had cared for him as best they could. On this morning, he had somehow simply wandered off and could not figure out how to get home.

Doc Pantoja appeared. "Sir, the boy in the shed is in the final stages of what is probably malaria. There's nothing I can do for him."

He looked down at the elder, crouched on his knees now, embracing his grandson.

"What happened to him?" our medic asked.

Greeson seethed. He dropped his cigarette and crushed it out with a boot. "Believe me, Doc, you don't wanna fucking know that."

More members of the elder's family ventured out. They came to the boy to hug and reassure him. He whimpered softly, and I wondered if he was crying. Then I realized he couldn't cry. His tear ducts had been burned away.

"Ask the elder what happened to the other children," I said to Yusef. That stirred another long discussion. When it ended, Yusef reported, "The enemy came back to the village and beat the other children as punishment."

Why would they do this to their own people? This village was no threat to anyone.

Greeson had taken a knee. He was trying to coax the little girl I'd seen out from her mud-hut home. Eventually she ventured to him. Greeson produced a piece of candy and gave it to her. She took it with delicate, dirt-stained fingers and placed it in her mouth.

"Yusef," I said, "tell the elder we're bringing him medical supplies, food, and water. Anyone who needs help, we will treat."

Yusef did as he was told. The elder's emotions swamped his self-control. He thanked us profusely.

Campbell returned with some of the men and bags of supplies. We went to work treating the battered children.

Greeson chitchatted with a little girl. It didn't matter that neither understood each other's words. Their body language broke through that communication barrier. Every time he smiled, she lit up, her dark eyes bright and full of mirth. How that could even be possible in this awful place just underscored how the human spirit adapts to hardship.

In other villages, when we'd enter and visit with the people, we'd discovered a grim reality of the Afghan social structure. We'd first noticed it in one particular village when the boys and girls had come to us wanting candy. We'd passed out what we had, taking note that the girls hung back behind the boys. Not wanting to leave them out, my men had made a point of getting candy into their young hands. When we had run out of things to give them, we'd loaded up into our rigs and rolled out of town. That's when our trailing vehicle's gunner had seen the village boys descend on the girls. They'd beaten them senseless right in front of their parents and stolen the candy we had just given to them. After that, we always made sure the girls had ample time to escape before we left.

In this village, there was none of that. The community had been too traumatized by the enemy's assaults to inflict violence on one another. The boys who came to us stood side by side with the girls, all sharing the same purple-yellow bruises across their vulnerable bodies.

Doc Pantoja went from child to child, treating each one with his typical gentle manner. I marveled at his ability to connect with his patients. His face had not quite healed from his June 10 wound, and as I looked at the jagged scar, I remembered how he had shielded Sergeant Garvin with his own body even after taking the bullet to his face. He was a gift to our platoon, the resident keeper of empathy and tenderness. Until now, the rest of us had been forced to wall off such emotions in order to maintain our ability to kill without remorse.

Nearby, Yusef had started to play with several battered boys. They joked and laughed together, and I saw the 'terp's professional demeanor vanish, if but for a moment. I wondered how he could be so jovial now amid all this suffering. Maybe he'd just seen so much of it that he too had become desensitized to such things. Or maybe he was just a better actor than Greeson.

I tried to stay focused on the tasks at hand. I oversaw the distribution of the food and medical supplies. We gave the elder's people all our medicine, and Doc Pantoja carefully explained their use and function. The villagers had gathered around us now, their wind-lashed faces full of smiles as they shared words of gratitude with my men. On his return, Campbell put on his best game face. He smiled and laughed as he helped pass out the supplies. The Afghans around him reacted with delight at the things he pushed into their eager hands. But when he glanced at me, I knew him well enough to see past the facade. He was swimming in two rivers simultaneously, his outward demeanor driven by the necessity of the mission to be cheerful. But in that other river, the one that flowed deep within him, I sensed that the sights here had left his soul wounded. Just like Greeson's.

Part of me wondered why I didn't feel that way. This place would have had a huge effect on me four months ago. Now I recognized the horrors, but there seemed to be a cushion between them and the recesses of my spirit. No doubt keeping busy and focusing on the mission had a lot to do with that. But when that little girl had died my first day at Bermel, I'd felt something collapse within me. After the other things we'd experienced, I'd grown weary and numb. Now that numbness served as a shield. I relied on it, used it to stay functional.

Had it turned me cold? I wondered what kind of person was

emerging inside me. I wasn't sure who I was anymore. For a moment I dwelled on where my heart was headed. And I grieved for the loss of the Sean Parnell I once had been.

Unconsciously, I reached for my St. Christopher medal. Touching it, I felt my grandfather's spirit close. The medal served as our anchor now that death had separated us.

The gesture attracted a child's attention, so I bent and showed it to him. He looked it over, feeling the inscription on its flip side with a doll-sized finger.

All my love, Virginia. 12-25-49.

It will keep you safe.

But will it protect my soul?

I stood up. The child smiled. I tucked the medal back under my IBA, the feel of silver between my fingers suffusing me with a sense of peace.

I was going to return home a different Sean, one my grandfather might not have recognized. How that would play out was still ahead, and I could not ponder that right then. Those were thoughts for lonely, darkened rooms far from this miserable country. In the meantime, there was work to be done.

The village elder thanked me again with an earnestness that almost embarrassed me. His grandson clung to his leg, listening to us as his sightless face tracked the sound of our voices. Yusef conveyed my sentiments. We were here to help. This was why we had joined the army in the first place. We hadn't done it because we lusted to kill. We had joined because with our flag on our shoulders and the power of the army at our backs, we thought we could help change the world.

Today, we had changed a tiny piece of it. But as we said our farewells, I noticed Greeson's face and wondered about the price we'd be paying for it.

Greeson was my rock. He stood calm in every fight, rarely

taking cover as he radiated confidence. Now he walked with a weight on him. Greeson could take more than any other man I knew. If he was at breaking point now, that was a bad sign for the entire platoon.

We walked back down the slope together, our horror and grief spinning together into a ball of molten rage at the men who could inflict such torture on innocent people. When we encountered them again, there would be a reckoning. And mercy would not be a factor.

We loaded up into our Humvees. Weary engines coughed to life. We rolled forward to continue our patrol. Behind us, on a hilltop half a kilometer above this trail, a village existed on the edge of nowhere, its brutalized children sustained by love alone.

TWENTY-TWO

SHAKE AND BAKE

★ ★ ★

Late July 2006

PINHOLT AND I SAT TOGETHER WATCHING AN EPISODE OF THE TV series *The Office*. We howled with laughter and thought about how foreign the world of cubicle land was to us.

"This is the greatest show ever," I told Pinholt.

"I knew you'd like it, sir."

For a rare change of pace, we were inside the wire with the day off. We had desperately needed the break, and the men were relaxing, sleeping, or lifting weights.

The episode ended. "Got any more?" I asked.

"Whole first season, sir."

"You're awesome."

We started another episode. Midway through, Pinholt wrinkled his nose and looked at me.

"Uh, sir, that's pretty nasty."

"What?"

"That shit coming out of your ear."

I reached up and felt something like Jell-O on my neck. It was pink and red and streaked with yellow.

"It smells like bananas, sir," he added.

I got up and wiped it off, thoroughly embarrassed.

"Sir, you need to go get checked."

I nodded as I sat back down. "I know. I'll get a scan at Bagram in a few days when I head home on leave."

"Thank you. Everyone's worried about you."

I was worried too. But I knew that if a real doc examined me, he'd never let me return to the men. I was having bouts of double vision and frequent migraines, and at times I was having trouble remembering things. As a result, I made an obsessive effort to write everything down before missions.

We finished the second episode, and I said good-bye to Pinholt and headed back to my room.

"Lieutenant?" a deep and booming voice called.

A staff sergeant was walking down the hallway in our hooch, a cigarette dangling from tight lips. About my age, with receding brown-black hair, he walked with gravitas, as if he were made of chiseled granite. He had a rounded face with sharp cheeks, eyes partially concealed by a squint, a Ranger tab on his shoulder.

"What can I do for you, sergeant?"

Who the hell is this fucking guy?

"Jeff Hall. I'm your new squad leader, sir." He stuck out his hand. I shook it and nearly had my fingers squashed like sausages.

"Glad to meet you, Hall," I said. "Welcome to Outlaw Platoon."

"Thank you, sir."

I'd been a little nervous about this development. The platoon's chemistry was working great with Wheat, Cowan, Sabo, and

Campbell as my squad leaders. When battalion told me we were getting a staff sergeant to permanently replace Waites, I hated to have to shuffle the platoon's leadership. With no other choice, Greeson and I had decided to move Wheat to Cowan's squad, where he'd go back to being a team leader. Pinholt would be promoted and take a team under the new guy. That seemed like the best way to handle the situation.

An outsider made for an unknown quantity. Would we get a Burley or a Baldwin? An R. Kelly or a Bennett Garvin?

"Lieutenant, I've heard about what y'all been doin' here," Hall said, a slight smirk on his face.

"You have?" I asked, taken off guard.

"Yeah. Here's the thing, you've been too fuckin' soft on the enemy."

"Excuse me?"

He punched his palm with a fist. "We gotta get after 'em. Come on, sir. Yer a Ranger too. Ya'll know this!"

I raised an eyebrow and suppressed a burst of anger. Who was this guy to say this shit? Then I saw that his squint had opened up, revealing mirth in his hazel eyes.

I couldn't help but laugh. He stood rigid, regarding me until I stopped.

I spent a little time getting to know Jeff in that hallway moment. Jeff had served in 3rd Ranger Battalion and later completed a tour as a Ranger instructor in the mountains of Georgia. He'd only recently joined the 10th Mountain Division.

He was from Huntsville, Alabama, but somehow had escaped from the Deep South without Wheat and Colt Wallace's accent. He worshipped at the altar of Crimson Tide football. He loved the outdoors and extreme sports such as skydiving. "There ain't nothin' like jumpin' outta a perfectly good airplane to make yer day."

But there was a flip side to Hall as well. I discovered that he loved to read, both fiction and nonfiction. As the conversation turned to good books we'd recently finished, he mentioned how much he loved the Harry Potter series.

Finally.

I couldn't get Pinholt to read Rowling's books, and the platoon's NCOs hassled me mercilessly over my Potter obsession. At last I had somebody to talk with about Dementors and Diagon Alley and whether or not Snape was in Voldemort's pocket.

I made a mental note to get Hall to work on Cowan with me. Of any of the other NCOs, I sensed that Chris might actually cave and start reading the series too.

As we chatted, time passed without effort; whatever I had to do was forgotten for the moment. I had no doubt that Jeff Hall would fit right in with us.

"You married, Hall?"

For the first time, he cracked a smile. "Not yet, sir, but I sure as hell plan on it when I get home. Her name is Allison, and ya know somethin'? She is way too hot for me." He paused, considering whether to go on, then he added, "I'm her Southern Stubborn Baby."

Badass, without a doubt, but Jeff Hall was a man who was comfortable with that designation without taking himself too seriously.

Hall's arrival could not have come at a better moment for the platoon. His innate tenacity gave the whole platoon a much-needed boost. On his first patrols with us, he seemed to be everywhere at once, fearing nothing and wanting nothing more than a chance to kill the enemy. He seethed with impatience, and I knew he would not have long to wait.

Rumors abounded that a coalition of Taliban-led insurgents from Waziristan had entered into negotiations with Pakistan's president, Pervez Musharraf. Exactly what they were negotiating was unclear, but none of us had any illusions that such talks would benefit Afghanistan or us.

Meanwhile, the battle rhythm continued without letup. We spent most of our days out beyond the wire, stopping into Bermel only to grab water, MREs, and hot chow. Once again, the enemy proved elusive. From the chatter our Prophet spooks detected, they were avoiding the Green Skull platoon again. But they were out there, watching us all the time.

On the afternoon of July 26, we checked in at Bermel for a half-day refit. We were filthy, coated in layers of dirt and dried sweat, and giving off such a stench from our ACUs that we elicited gags from the Fobbits.

As I walked to the operations center to discuss the night's mission with Captain Dye, it dawned on me that I'd missed my birthday. It had been the week before. That was the first time in my life that it had passed unnoticed. I'd been so busy that it had never even entered my head.

Captain Dye waited with an interesting night mission for us. We were to roll out with Delta Platoon and slip behind Rakhah Ridge at dusk to establish snap traffic-control points and observation posts along the main routes to Pakistan. If the enemy decided to engage us, we'd have the advantage, thanks to our night-vision equipment.

After meeting with Captain Dye, I found a mountain of paperwork awaiting our attention. I told Greeson to hang back and work on it; I'd lead the night's patrol. He didn't like that. "Sir, lemme take the patrol," he argued. "You're due to go on leave. Stay here."

"I got it. Besides, I need you here to catch up on all this shit so that when I am gone, you can be completely devoted to the men."

Grudgingly, he accepted that.

He locked himself away with a computer, a carton of smokes, and a six-pack of near beer. Greeson and computers never quite got along, so before I even left his frustration level was already spiking.

"Fucking machine!" I heard him growl as I headed out to grab chow.

Late that afternoon, Captain Herrera, Sergeant R. Kelly, and I sat down to plan the mission. Big Red was on leave, and though Herrera was a fine officer, he had very little experience with the infantry. Captain Dye wanted Delta on point, a fact that rankled me a little. We'd taken point on every mission to date; bringing up the rear seemed out of place.

We selected our route. Same as always—down to Malakshay, push east around Gangikheyl Hill until we reached Route Excel and the wadi system behind Rakhah Ridge. We noted departure times and rally points and preplanned our indirect fire support. When we finished, I returned to my hooch to take a quick nap. As I lay down on my bunk, I glanced over at the wall where Freddie's picture used to hang. I had replaced it with a map of our battle space that I had carefully marked with every ambush we'd experienced since arriving in theater. The red dots were clustered around the road leading from Malakshay.

A lightbulb flicked on in my head. We'd all been trained to be unpredictable, and had there been more roads leading to the backside of Rakhah Ridge, we would have used them. There weren't, so we'd been forced to rely on the same road mission after mission.

I studied the map, remembering all the things wrong with it that we had discovered during our early patrols around the area. Just north of our June 10 fight sat the abandoned village that Captain Dye and Delta Platoon had burned that day. I recalled that a goat track ran east from the village of Malakshay. It intersected our main infil route just outside our destination.

The village was labeled Kamid Ghul, and it sat on a hill overlooking Route Excel. The little dirt track that ran through it continued east toward Pakistan, then dipped into the wadi system that became part of Route Excel. If we could use that track, we'd be able to take a shortcut around most of the earlier ambush points and get in behind Rakhah Ridge, moving from east to west. It would be risky. Since we'd never used the track, we wouldn't know if Humvees would fit on it until we were actually out there. It would be dark, and we could get stuck, forcing us to double back and use our old route east of Malakshay. We might even be forced to back up in the dark for kilometers until we found a spot wide enough to turn the rigs around.

I left my hooch and ran the change of routes past Captain Herrera. He agreed it was worth a try. An hour before sunset, our two platoons hit the road, Herrera's rig on point. We found our detour and cautiously took it, looping south of our destination. A few minutes later, we rolled into Kamid Ghul from the east as planned.

"Hold up. What was that?" Herrera asked over the radio.

The column stopped in the middle of the burned, roofless dwellings.

"I thought I saw an RPG team running on Hill 2522," Herrera reported.

I glanced at my map. That was a ridge about half a click east of the village, across the wadi system that served as part of Route Excel.

The sunset had bathed Bermel Valley in a crimson glow, making Kamid Ghul's ruins look sinister and imposing. It was a weird hour to be starting a mission.

A puff of white smoke rose from Hill 2522, stark against the hellish sky. A split second later, a rocket-propelled grenade exploded next to our column. Before we could react, the hills to the southeast flared with muzzle flashes. Red tracer rounds zipped like laser bolts between our trucks. Others struck home, ricocheting crazily upward into the red sky.

Our gunners traversed right and returned fire. But then another enemy force opened up on us from the northeast. I scanned the ridges in that direction and guessed we were facing another forty or fifty men from those positions.

By taking a different route, we'd bisected an ambush they'd established for us. How they'd known we were coming was anyone's guess, but they had intended to turn Route Excel into a kilometer-long kill zone. The team atop Hill 2522 was probably just scouts with an RPG whose job it had been to alert the rest of the ambush force to our approach.

We'd triggered the ambush early and from a different direction than they had expected. As we pulled into a perimeter around the village, their fire was disjointed and not nearly as accurate as usual. We'd thrown them off guard, and they had reflexively opened fire. Had they waited until we'd turned onto Excel, the northern part of the ambush force would have been able to hit us as they'd originally designed.

The sun fell behind the ridges to the west, casting darkness over our raging battle. The enemy seemed content to spray us from a distance. We hammered back at them with our crew-served weapons, our Mark 19s chugging out grenades in steady bursts.

Our dismounts got out of the trucks and turned the village's dwellings into fighting positions. When the squad and team leaders finished their work, they huddled up in the middle of the perimeter. Captain Herrera had taken our 60mm mortar team and was busy directing its employment. For a moment, I wished Captain Dye were here. Having two platoons to manage was awkward since I couldn't really give orders to Delta, I could only give the platoon's squad leaders guidance.

Each man in the leaders' circle gave me a quick status report. They had everything well in hand. Given the darkness and the amount of fire, we'd been through this enough to know that trying to stay in communication with one another via radio would be difficult. In past fights, I'd moved around the perimeter. In the darkness, that didn't make much sense since it would be hard to find our NCOs, even with night-vision goggles.

"Meet back here in fifteen minutes," I said. The huddle broke. The firing rose in volume and intensity. The enemy was getting their legs under them after our surprise appearance from the west. We swapped lead and high explosives from long range, the long, flaming streaks of tracer rounds gave the scene an almost sci-fi appearance. I flicked my night vision down over my eye, and the battlefield was transformed into shades of green.

JUST AS OUR LEADERS RETURNED TO THE MIDDLE OF THE PERIMeter, the enemy commander made his move. Hall, whose rig was on the eastern side of the perimeter, said calmly, "Sir, they're rushin' us. Comin' at our hill now."

I looked around our huddle. Delta's squad leaders were solid. Big Red had mentored them, set the example, and they'd long since come into their own. Mine were ready for some payback.

"Okay, we've been through this before," I told them. "We're gonna have to hold them off. I'll work the indirect. You do whatever you gotta do. Meet back in twenty for a sit rep."

The huddle broke. I went to call for artillery with our forward observer.

The two enemy forces struck the northeast and southeast parts of our perimeter in one pell-mell charge. This time, they did not bound as on June 10; instead they ran straight for us. Wheat picked out a leader and sniped him in midstride. He went down with a wound to the shoulder. In a flash, two insurgents grabbed their fallen comrade and whisked him to the rear. Their casualty evacuation was stunningly fast.

They reached the base of the hill now, and our gunners discovered that they couldn't depress their weapons enough to track them. They pulled out rifles and started blazing away.

Below us, the enemy's undulating war cry rose in the darkness. Through our night vision, we saw them charge, triggering their AKs from the hip. None of them had our technology advantage, and the night was so black now that they stumbled over roots and rocks, making a headlong rush into the teeth of our firepower.

Right then, the first 105 shells exploded in their midst. We'd called for fire dangerously close. Captain Dye, who was at the operations center at Bermel, had made sure we had ample support again. The gunners back on base had poured it on, mixing high-explosive shells with white phosphorus, the dreaded "Wiley Pete." The gunners called this deadly mixture "Shake and Bake." The high explosives shook the ground, while the Wiley Pete cooked anything it touched.

A curtain of fire and steel, streaked with tendrils of phosphorus, erupted behind the enemy's main line of advance. We'd pinned them against us. If they tried to break contact, they would be massacred by the artillery fire. If they stayed in place, they'd be mowed down by our men. If they tried to close, we'd mow them down faster.

Desperate now, the trapped insurgents bolted for us, their wounded and dying carpeting the hillside in their wake.

There was a confidence in the men that we'd lacked on June 10. We'd seen this drill before with a more talented enemy force, and the men reacted with ruthless violence. No shouting this time. No euphoric moments or episodes of near despair. Our emotions remained even-keeled, cold but laced with controlled rage that had been bottled up inside us for weeks. We unleashed it all in a merciless torrent.

The enemy closed to twenty-five meters. We could see those wicked eight-inch knives dangling from their belts. The sight infuriated us. The men fired and reloaded with accomplished speed. The artillery rain grew ever more intense.

Over the radio, Captain Dye reported that he'd dispatched Second Platoon as our quick reaction force. They were bringing out more ammunition and supplies. I was grateful to have it, but part of me did not want to deal with Sergeant Burley. Lieutenant Taylor had left a few weeks before to tend to a family emergency back home. Second was all Burley's platoon now, and his posing had become even more grandiose without Taylor there. Silently, I wished again Captain Dye was out here with us. I'd have to coordinate all three of the company's platoons now.

Twenty minutes later, the NCOs returned to the middle of the perimeter. A lull had descended on the battlefield as the enemy's lead waves had been killed almost to the last man. One at a time, our squad leaders reported the situation to be well in hand.

Hall triumphantly announced, "We're fuckin' wasting 'em, sir!"

"Yeah," Campbell echoed, "the men are slaughtering 'em."

Behind us, the moon rose over the endless ridges of the Hindu Kush, brightening the battlefield with a silvery glow.

"They're coming again, sir."

"You know what to do." The huddle broke, and back into action they went.

The slaughter continued unabated for almost three hours. Again and again, the insurgents threw themselves blindly at our perimeter. Their tracers flew around us wildly as they shot into the darkness that only our technology could penetrate. They had no support-by-fire positions on the ridges to suppress us, and only one of our soldiers was slightly wounded.

Even without our heavy weapons in the fight, we cut them down with cold fury. As they started up the hill one final time, ignoring their screaming wounded lying helpless in the dirt, our men lobbed hand grenades down the slope into their armorless ranks. Through our night vision, we could see the fading heat signatures from their dismembered remains.

We killed so many of them that their casualty evacuation plan collapsed. They simply didn't have the manpower left to pull their men out. The torn bodies lay uncollected on the hillside, bits of white phosphorous embedded within them. Their fat sizzled and popped for hours, until the metallic stench of the Wiley Pete blended with the sickly odor of burned flesh. Hell's barbecue.

The squad leaders joined me in one more leaders' huddle at the end of the fight. Campbell reported that his rig had been heavily damaged. One soldier had taken a minor shrapnel wound from an enemy hand grenade. The rest of both platoons were good to go.

Sergeant R. Kelly walked up to us. We looked up at him through our night-vision goggles. This was the first time I'd seen him all night.

"This ain't so bad!" he exclaimed, his smile shining white-green in our goggles, "Whatcha all been bitchin' about?"

He unleashed a peal of laughter. Nobody responded. The other NCOs turned back to one another and continued with the status update. Kelly stood looking down at us for a moment, then wandered away. As he left, I heard somebody mutter, "Save your shit and get away from me."

Second Platoon arrived, Burley all over-the-top energy. His voice echoed over the hilltop as he bellowed orders at his men. Greeson jumped out of one of Second Platoon's trucks and on bow-legs sauntered over to us.

"Hey, sir," he said, sounding like Sling Blade, "lookitcha, acting all John Wayne out here without me."

"WHERE THE HELL HAVE YOU BEEN?" I ASKED. IT HAD TAKEN US forty-five minutes to get to this abandoned village after leaving

Bermel. It had taken Burley and our quick reaction force three and half hours to cover the same distance.

Greeson leaned forward and whispered, "Goddamned Second Platoon draggin' their asses."

Greeson later told me that Burley had called up a possible roadside bomb a few kilometers away from our fight. He had ordered the platoon to stop. As they sat parked on the road out of the fight, Greeson grew increasingly frustrated. He saw no evidence of a roadside bomb, and nothing was being done to investigate or clear anything in the road ahead. But since he was only a passenger, he could not do anything about it. As soon the assaults against us had ended, Burley declared the road ahead clear and the platoon had continued on its way to us.

At least we had most of the company inside our perimeter now, which would give us a lot more firepower in case the enemy stormed our positions again. Though they probed us a couple of times, and a few tracers shot up through the night as they randomly strafed our hilltop, they made no further attacks. We took nothing for granted, not after what we'd been through. We spent the night in readiness, awake and alert, watching the mountains through our night-vision goggles.

Early the next morning, we remained on the battlefield until the ANA swept the hillside to search the burned bodies scattered around us. We took no contact; the enemy had withdrawn. Moral victory achieved, we pulled out and returned to Bermel to trade out Campbell's truck. After a quick bite, we went out searching for trouble, but the enemy was nowhere to be found. We later estimated that we had killed between forty-five and sixty of the enemy on July 26, so it was no wonder we didn't see them the next day. Even they were starting to run low on bodies. Or at least, so we thought.

The next day, our once overweight forward observer, Cole, came to see me. He'd been working out nonstop since arriving at

Bermel several months before. He'd dropped more than twenty pounds, looked lean and mean, and was all set to go out on patrol with us. The first sergeant had cleared him to roll beyond the wire, and he was eager to rejoin us and be part of our band again. A few more days in the gym, a couple more after that for final preparations, and he'd transition back to us. In the meantime, he was still working with the aviation guys to schedule seats on available helicopters.

"Sir, we have a bird coming in an hour. Aren't you supposed to go on leave? Do you want a slot?"

Cole was wearing ridiculous yellow sneakers. Through my exhaustion, I gaped at them. "Uh, yeah, Cole. That'd be great. But what the hell?" I said, pointing at his shoes.

He grinned. "They're cool!"

"Cole, they look like Big Bird shoes."

"They make me run like the wind, sir. Run like the wind."

I had no time to shower, barely time to pack. I threw a few things into a bag. I'd change my uniform later.

Cole checked back with me about a half hour later. "Sir, the flight's full. But I'm going to get you on it, don't you worry!"

He told me to get out to the landing zone and wait for the helicopter.

I said a hasty good-bye to the platoon—I had no time to do anything else—and made my way to the pad. The abrupt farewell, even if it was temporary, felt jagged and raw. Truth was, as much as I wanted to see my family back home, I didn't want to leave the one I had here.

A pair of Chinooks appeared on the western horizon. I'd once heard a Black Hawk pilot quip, "Those Chinooks look as ugly as two palm trees fuckin' a Dumpster."

Regarding them now, I could see the resemblance.

Cole dashed up to me a moment after they'd touched down. "Got ya a spot, sir! You know I'll always take care of ya!"

I was profoundly grateful. "Yeah, Cole, you sure do. I'll see you when I get back."

He smiled and waved. "Can't wait to be out there with ya, sir!"

I shook his hand and thanked him for all he'd done for me. He seemed embarrassed. He hated to have attention drawn to himself and felt most comfortable working in the background, taking care of the platoon any way he could.

I climbed aboard the Chinook with Brian Bray, who was also going home on his midtour leave. Cole had scored two seats for us on a full bird.

When we landed at Bagram, Bray and I headed to the fixed-wing terminal together. Bagram looked like a stateside base compared to where we'd been. Signs advertised salsa dance nights, jewelry shops, a café called Green Bean Coffee. The main drag, Disney Drive, was cluttered with vehicles, the sidewalks full of military personnel from all over the world. Koreans, Jordanians, Poles, Czechs, sour-looking French aviators, all shouldered past us as we carried our bags to the terminal entrance. We passed one reader board that said, SAFETY FIRST. DO NOT WEAR EAR BUDS WHILE JOGGING.

We were swimming upstream in an ocean of Fobbits on that main road, Bray and I looking utterly out of place in our filthy, battleworn ACUs. My IBA still had bloodstains on it from June 10.

Inevitably, our condition attracted unwanted attention.

"Lieutenant?" A U.S. Army major demanded. He stood staring at me, hands on hips, a look of disgust on his face. His ACUs were so clean and well fitting that I assumed they had been tailored and pressed. He wore no combat badges, no sign that he was a Ranger or even infantry. I had never noticed that sort of thing until that moment. I wondered if he was going to be salsa dancing tonight.

"Yes, sir?" I asked wearily.

"Clean yourself up. Your uniform's a disgrace."

His war and mine were so different that there would be no way for our worlds to meet. I didn't even have the energy to try.

TWENTY-THREE

THE FAR SIDE OF THE SKY

★ ★ ★

August 16, 2006
Ocean City, Maryland

They're charging up the hill!"

Like shades, the enemy slides around trees and rocks, slithering ever closer. Masked faces, chest rigs bulging with extra ammunition, their pulsing voices howl their alien war cry.

"Lilililililililililililililili . . ."

Our men fire their last rifle rounds. Campbell's fifty falls silent. Pilon's SAW spits flame no more. Sabo, bloody-faced and saucer-eyed, turns to me and shouts something I cannot understand. Greeson drains his last mag. I check my rifle. I have no bullets left. Not even a last round for myself.

This is the end.

The enemy pours over the ridge, firing into my men. I fall to a knee. There's nothing left but to fight with rifle butt and fists.

My men lie facedown in heaps around our smoking trucks. Those wicked knives are unsheathed. A blade shines in the morning's sunlight, held high for me to see. They straddle my men, pull their heads up by their hair to expose their Adam's apples. A few gurgle with fear, and with yawning horror I realize that some are still alive.

I watch from my knees, raging at my impotence. I cannot act. I cannot move. I am an observer of the beheadings of those I love the most.

And then the men with masks come for me.

With a shudder, I awoke with racing heart and sheets soaked with sweat, the stillness of the bedroom a stark contrast to the battlefield painted in my mind.

I lay and listened to my breathing, almost missing the background noises that accompanied nighttime at FOB Bermel. The quiet of this rented condo seemed unnerving.

Where's the roar of the diesel generators? The rumble of Humvees returning from patrol? The echo of distant gunfire?

I rose from the bed and went to the open window. My family had rented a place on the Maryland shore in honor of my temporary homecoming. We'd be here for a week; then I would return to the war.

The salt air smelled divine. I closed my eyes and filled my lungs. With each exhale, I tried to purge my mind of the foul odors I had stowed away with every Afghan breath: burned flesh, white phosphorous, and steaming bodies rent asunder. Filth, sewage, mold, and decay.

I pulled a chair to the window. In the distance, a dog barked. My watch read three in the morning. The tourists of Ocean City had long since retired to tranquil sleep.

My heart rate slowly returned to normal. It didn't help. The nightmare had left me unsettled. My mind raced. There'd be no return to slumber for me.

Something's wrong.

Maybe it was the dream. Maybe it was something more profound and less explicable. Whatever it was, I felt disquiet rippling across my psyche. I sat in the dark, probing my mind in the hope of finding its source.

In their most naked moments, veterans tell stories of the unseen bond, founded on love, that unites us psychologically to those who matter most to us. In times of hardship or disaster, wives have risen from half-empty beds, *knowing* that their warrior husbands have suffered harm. The morning arrival of the contact teams on their doorsteps is no surprise but rather a confirmation of what their hearts already understand.

Those were the wires humming inside me that morning.

I felt disconnected, unplugged from my hive at Bermel. Now all my instincts telegraphed that something had gone terribly wrong, and I wasn't there to help out.

We'd been lucky so far.

Lucky?

How ridiculous would that sound if I said it out loud back here within the insulated confines of my former life?

Mom, Dad? We've been lucky. Only about half my men have been wounded. Only three seriously. Hey, Baldwin's home with his family! So is Garvin. And my machine gunners—they've only taken six head shots among them.

The very framework of my thinking had been recast.

The scary thing was, it was true. We *had* been lucky. How many times could we have lost someone? Luck, the hand of God, fate— whatever it was had kept us all alive. But every gambler knows when you roll the bones, the winning streaks never last.

Fuck it. I was probably just being paranoid. Distance and lack of communication had created a void in which the darkest elements of my imagination flourished. When you're in the relative safety of the United States and know the evils that lurk beyond our borders, how can you be anything but paranoid?

I tried to shut it off, but the wires kept humming.

I sat by the window, watching dawn break over the serenity of home.

Would Brown be dancing on the back of his Humvee? Who would Cowan have in a headlock? Was Greeson already knocking back near beers as he trooped the line to ensure that all our rigs were squared away and ready to roll?

Then I remembered that they were eleven hours ahead. They'd be done for the day before mine had even begun.

Somewhere on the far side of the planet, I imagined the platoon cleaning weapons and getting ready for chow.

Had Pinholt finally finished *Atlas Shrugged*?

I loved being home.

I hated being home.

At seven thirty, I wandered downstairs and over to my parents' rented condo next door. From the kitchen, my grandmother welcomed me. "Sean, would you like some French toast?"

"Thank you," I replied. She'd gotten up early just to do this for me, knowing that I hadn't been able to sleep in all during my leave. I was touched by her gesture.

A moment later, I balanced a plate and a glass of milk in my hands and sat down in front of the television. My grandmother had turned on Fox News. I took a bite and said, "Grandma, this tastes great!"

"Glad you like it, Sean. There's plenty more if you want it."

I turned away from the television to see her regarding me with a look of pure love. I wanted to tell her about the St. Christopher medal, of how Grandpap had roused me from unconsciousness on the hilltop during the June 10 fight. I wanted to tell her that the spiritual connection she'd assured me I'd have with him had saved my life more than once.

But all I could do was smile back. The words remained unformed, burdened with regret that I could not find a way to let them out.

My folks appeared in the kitchen, and my grandmother wished them good morning. I went back to watching Fox News, savoring every bite of my home-cooked breakfast. The little things matter most after combat.

The news anchor began talking about two Fox reporters who had been kidnapped at gunpoint the day before in Gaza.

Then the news ticker at the bottom of the screen caught my attention.

AMERICAN SOLDIER KILLED BY ENEMY MINE STRIKE IN EASTERN AFGHANISTAN . . .

My fork hovered midway between plate and mouth.

I need Net access.

My laptop was over in my condo, but we had no Internet hookup here.

Stay calm. Don't alarm your family.

The wires inside my head were screaming now. I stared at the screen and listed all the reasons why this couldn't have happened to anyone I knew. The Outlaws were a tiny unit, just a platoon. There were thousands of U.S. troops fighting in eastern Afghanistan. The chances that it was one of my men were astronomically small.

I tried to find comfort in the math, but my heart rejected it as a false hope. I couldn't eat. The sweet smell of maple syrup drizzled over the French toast, so appealing a moment ago, made my stomach churn.

I stood up and left the condo. Up the street was a coffee shop that probably had Internet access, so I grabbed my laptop and hurried over to it.

The place was deserted when I walked in. Quickly, I sat down and started my laptop. As soon as I logged into Yahoo! Instant Messenger, a conversation box popped up. It was Rowley.

Hey Sir.
Rowley, everything okay?
Actually, no.
What's wrong?

I received no immediate reply. I waited in dreadful suspense.

Cole is dead.

TWENTY-FOUR

WE STUMBLE THROUGH

★ ★ ★

August 16, 2006
Ocean City, Maryland

MY FINGERS HOVERED OVER THE KEYBOARD, NOT KNOWING what letters to press. A few tourists, dressed in T-shirts, shorts, and sneakers, wandered inside to order their morning lattes. They gave only passing attention to the platoon leader at his laptop, twelve thousand miles from his men, whose composure was on the verge of collapsing at the thought of an infant boy who'd never know his father, Big Bird shoes, broad smiles, and those final words so casually spoken as the Chinook waited to take him home: "I'll see you when I get back."

Rowley sent a file. The download took forever. When it finally finished, I opened it and saw a photograph of one of our Humvees blown to broken junk.

With me back home on midtour leave, Greeson was taking the platoon out on our assigned patrols. For the past two days, while I'd been lounging around the Maryland coast, the Outlaws had been under mortar and sniper fire southeast of FOB Bermel. The platoon had spent the previous night on a hilltop overlooking a village. Come morning, Greeson had decided to head back to Bermel for chow and a quick refit. Through thick fog, they had driven home, where Greeson had met with Captain Dye to discuss the plan for the rest of the day.

They'd decided to return to the hilltop, establish an observation post, and see if the platoon could root out any of the mortar or sniper teams.

The platoon had gotten back into position later that day. The villagers had come outside to observe the platoon as the men held their hilltop perimeter. Nothing like that had ever happened before. Being gawked at had made the platoon nervous. Hours later, with no sign of the enemy, Greeson had called it a day and ordered the platoon home.

While driving off the hill, the third Humvee in the column rolled over an Italian-made antitank mine. The explosion ejected Doc Pantoja from the rear of the truck and flung him seventy feet down the side of the hill. Greeson was knocked unconscious, as was Colt Wallace, who was driving. Echavez in the turret, manning the Mark 19, was also wounded.

Doc somehow found the strength to get to his feet and run back up the hill, where he found Cole grievously wounded, still inside the mangled Humvee. Greeson regained consciousness and pulled him clear. Doc flung himself behind Cole's limp body and began to treat him. Cole's heart stopped. Doc started CPR, and the men heard him begging Cole to stay alive. Meanwhile, Wallace regained consciousness as the rest of the platoon dismounted to protect the shattered rig.

Five minutes later, Cole slipped away. Doc refused to give up. Frantically, he kept working, praying that he could restart Cole's heart. But the blast had done too much damage. Even if he'd been in the best trauma center on the planet, his life would not have been saved.

FINALLY, GREESON TOUCHED PANTOJA'S SHOULDER AND TOLD him to stop. Even then, it took a direct order for him to give up. Doc stood up, walked a short distance away, and let out a primal scream. Rage, despair, and helplessness poured out of him.

The villagers watched the entire event. In his turret, Chris Brown saw Cole die and unleashed a barrage of obscenities at the villagers. They knew the bomb had been planted; that's why they'd come outside. They'd wanted to see what would happen. Nobody had warned our platoon, despite the fact that we'd been bringing aid supplies to the village all summer long.

Brown racked the bolt on his 240 and swung it around, wailing with grief. It would have been easy to touch the trigger and walk that machine gun back and forth until those Afghans were nothing but bloody chunks. A less disciplined man in a less disciplined unit would have done it. The same sort of thing had triggered the My Lai massacre of Vietnam infamy.

Those villagers who had viewed our men die and suffer wounds as though it were a soccer spectacle owed their lives to Chris Brown's sense of duty. Instead of killing them all, he tipped the barrel up and strafed an empty hillside as he vented his anguish.

Doc Pantoja returned to the demolished Humvee, where he treated Greeson, Colt Wallace, and Echavez. He ignored his own wounds again.

The quick reaction force, Delta Platoon, arrived on scene. A short time later, so did Second Platoon. Both platoons faced the same dilemma: should they proceed to the battered Humvee to help my platoon and risk triggering another bomb or mine? Was risking the lives of more men worth coming to the aid of Third Platoon?

Big Red never hesitated. He drove straight up to the Outlaws and his men went right to work. That gesture, though it might not have been the militarily correct one, fostered the bond between the platoons.

Burley made the opposite decision. Considering it too risky to take his rigs up the hill, he parked about a kilometer away. His medic, Doc Campbell, erupted at the decision. Burley would not budge. Ignoring his superior rank, Campbell unleashed on Burley and told him to get his ass on the hill to help out. When he refused, Campbell dismounted, said, "To hell with this shit," and ran the kilometer to the blast site to treat the Outlaws' wounded.

It was a tough call to make. There are moments in combat where our moral obligation to our comrades conflicts with the tactically correct decision on the ground. While Burley protected his men—with the exception of Campbell—Burley lost an opportunity to heal the divide between our platoons. Had he driven up the hill to assist, all that had passed between us would have been water under the bridge. Instead, the rift between the platoons became almost open warfare later that day when the Outlaws returned to Bermel. Their morale broken and Greeson at the aid station awaiting evacuation, Cowan's squad filed into the chow hall. If nothing else, a bite of warm food couldn't hurt. They found Second Platoon inside. They'd come home before Delta and had taken every seat in the place. Cowan's men stood to one side, waiting for them to finish eating so they could have a turn. Second Platoon ignored or didn't notice them. Their men seemed oblivious to the effect the day had on my stricken soldiers. After about ten minutes, the Outlaws couldn't endure it any longer and left the chow hall. As they left, Chris Cowan stalked over to Burley's men and said, "I hope you are fucking proud of yourselves."

All that had gone down without me there to fight for them. At the moment they needed me the most, I was on the other side of the planet, spending a leisurely day on a family beach vacation.

Through circumstance, I had failed them. Now, in the café, as Rowley signed off with me on IM, I realized that I would not be able to get back in time for the memorial service. They'd have to go through that without me as well.

I returned to the condo and tucked my laptop away.

Thank God Lieutenant Colonel Toner let Cole stay back for the birth of his son.

Somewhere a woman's world had just come apart. Was Andrea holding baby Nicholas in her arms when she answered the knock on her door?

You cannot think about that.

Over the Atlantic, air force F-15 fighter jets engaged in practice maneuvers. A pair thundered across the horizon, their sonic boom rattling the condo like rocket fire.

Pinned against the Hesco-bag wall at the Alamo, we lay helpless in the enemy's sights as they fired at us from our ally's trenches.

"Are you fucking kidding me?" I whispered, feeling ready to explode.

Hey, sir, don't I always take care of ya?

Leave is not optional. I'd had no choice but to take it.

Tell that to my heart.

The inner circle was the only place where such a wound could be shared. I was an outsider to this moment, sifted by time and space, and I would have to grieve alone. At least until I was able to get home.

And by home I meant Bermel.

I thought about telling my family. The elation they'd felt at my return had triggered an outpouring of love and affection. It had drawn us closer than we'd been in years. Here at the beach, we'd been riding that high and living in the moment, trying to forget that in a week it would come to an end.

I could not wreck this for them.

I considered pulling my dad aside and sharing it with him. One night, my mom had told me how my e-mails were affecting him. Though he stood strong for me—had been my rock in the crisis moments of my deployment—my mom explained the consequences. He bore the burden of knowledge. He knew the enemy we faced. He knew how close to death I'd come. Every patrol left him a slave to his computer, counting the seconds as he waited for news that I was home safe. He kept Yahoo! Instant Messenger running from the second he set foot in the door to the point exhaustion overtook him and he fell asleep in a chair beside the computer. The IM's chime became his angel's bell, and when its ring awoke him, his fears melted away in a flood of relief. It was the sound of my safety.

Until the next patrol began. Our cycle outside the wire became his prison; the unknown his affliction. To get through it, he leaned on my mother, completing the circle of hardship that combat wreaks on families back home.

I could not do that to my father anymore. I resolved to keep Cole's death to myself. But I was a bad actor, and before the day was out, everyone sensed that something was wrong. We all pretended to have fun, to share light and bonding moments, but beneath the facade, my anguish sucked the vibrancy out of our reunion.

That night, we went to play miniature golf. I piled into a car with my sister and brothers and rolled through Ocean City with country music blasting on the radio.

In the backseat, I existed in two worlds. I had to be tough for my men, always. Now I had to do it for my family.

Brad Paisley's song "When I Get Where I'm Going" flowed through the car's speakers. Around me, my siblings laughed and teased each other.

When I get where I'm going
on the far side of the sky.

Cole, always so gentle-hearted. He was a good man whose devotion to Andrea had shone through in every conversation we'd had about her and Nicholas. He loved Outlaw Platoon almost as much as he loved her and his little boy. It had killed him to not patrol with us, and he had virtually lived in the gym during his off-duty hours as he worked to drop the weight First Sergeant Christopher had demanded he lose.

We drove through the streets of Ocean City. Carefree vacationers crowded the sidewalks, window shopping and eating ice cream in the summer heat. The sight of their insulated happiness made my burden seem stark. I was not one of them anymore, and I could never be that person again.

Cole had dropped twenty pounds. He'd been cleared to patrol only a few weeks before. After working so hard to rejoin the platoon, he had been killed on one of his first missions. If he hadn't cared and had kept the weight, he'd still be alive.

My composure slipped. I turned my head to the window so my siblings did not see.

PART IV

INDOMITABLE MOMENTS

★ ★ ★

TWENTY-FIVE

CROSSES TO BEAR

★ ★ ★

Late August 2006
Bermel

H EY, SIR, I NEED TO TALK TO YOU," GREESON SAID TO ME AS
I entered our hooch. His room was across the hall from
mine. He was supposed to get evacuated back to Bagram so his
head wound could be treated. Instead, he refused to leave the men
and continued to lead them after the aid station at FOB Salerno
had patched him up as best they could.

We'd just come back from my first patrol since I had returned
from leave. I'd felt jumpy and insecure, so I had asked Greeson to
come along to keep an eye on me. I didn't want to make any decisions that would endanger the men because I was off my game.

The taste of my stateside life had again reminded me of what was
at stake here. Holding on to that had reinforced my sense of mortal-
ity and made me fearful and overly focused on my own safety, to

the detriment of my leadership. That could not continue, and it was a relief to have Greeson out there making sure I didn't mess up.

Now, as we returned for the night, I knew that I needed some time within my head to reset my emotions and recover my resolve.

Greeson waved me into his room. Closed-door session? Something was up. I waited for him to tell me the mistakes I'd made out there today.

"Sir, what I am about to tell you cannot be mentioned to anyone."

His preface caught me off guard.

"Okay," I said cautiously.

"It's about one of our interpreters."

He had my complete attention now. Quietly, he began to talk.

Unbeknown to us, some top secret national-level assets had been tracking unusual communications coming from our area. Over the past several months, they had narrowed those transmissions down to FOB Bermel.

Somebody on post had been using our sat phones to contact an Iranian bomb-making cell operating out of a madrassa just over the Pakistani border. We had an enemy mole in our midst.

On August 16, the mole had made contact with the Iranian team. In coded references, he had revealed the exact location at which Outlaw Platoon planned to establish an observation post that day. Somehow, between the time the platoon had come in from the hilltop in the morning and the time the men had returned to it, the mole had penetrated our operational security and learned exactly what we were going to do. Then he had tipped off the Iranians, who had contacted Galang's old force. The insurgents had beat us to the hilltop and seeded it with mines. No doubt, the nearby villagers had seen them emplace the devices. When our platoon had arrived a few hours later, they wanted to see what would happen.

When that information reached Captain Dye and First Sergeant

Christopher, Yusef fell under immediate suspicion. He'd been observed asking questions he shouldn't have been asking. He had often wanted to know where we were going before we left the wire, something that had annoyed us throughout the deployment. A quiet investigation had revealed that he was the only local national on base who could have had foreknowledge of the platoon's destination. Plus, Greeson had caught him talking on a phone, introducing himself with a different name to whoever was on the other end of the connection. When Greeson had said, "Hey, I thought your name is Yusef." Our head 'terp had offered a wide, suspicious grin and replied, "That's just my stage name."

Greeson finished his story, "Captain Dye is going to take him to Orgun-E later today to arrest him. Nobody can know about this; we can't risk spooking Yusef and causing him to bolt."

"I want to go to Orgun-E," I said in a furious voice.

Greeson growled, "Fuck no, sir. You're way too close to this. So am I. Let Captain Dye handle it."

He was right. As the news sank in, my own responsibility in this disaster became apparent. I had become complacent with the cozy nature of Yusef's relationship with the men. He'd been too close to them for months, and every time I'd seen him around the barracks, hanging out with them, it had rankled me. Greeson had noted it too, urging me to put a stop to it, and though I'd mentioned it to the platoon in passing, I'd not done so with any conviction. When it had continued, I should have put my foot down hard and ended it. Fraternizing with a local national, no matter how much he was trusted, was an operational security breach, plain and simple.

Even more damning was his use of the satellite phones. That never should have happened. Though we had told him he couldn't use them, he still had access to the soldiers who worked in the operations center and could get his hands on the phones whenever he wanted.

It had always seemed like a minor problem, and my plate had been so full that dealing with Yusef's behavior had ended up on the bottom of my priority list. I had never gotten around to dealing with it. And now what Greeson had just told me revealed the consequences of that failure. It had gotten Cole killed.

No, I had gotten Cole killed.

This was not on the men. This wasn't on Greeson. This was my cross to bear. In similar situations, I'd seen other leaders flay themselves and twist themselves into guilt over decisions they'd made that, in hindsight, had led to a soldier being in the exact wrong place at the exact wrong time to be killed by our enemy. The logical side of our brains could recognize that there was no way to know that an order would lead to that moment and ultimately snuff out an American life. But in such situations, the heart refuses to accept such logic. In that conflict, the heart almost always wins. It was a struggle that had destroyed countless leaders like me.

My brain connected the dots between my failure to act and Cole's death. Logically, it made sense. My heart joined my head, and the unity demanded that I accept responsibility. There was no escape. I hadn't place the mine, but I had set the conditions that got Cole killed.

How could I ever look Andrea in the eyes?

I don't remember much of the morning after that. I know I went to my room to change out of my filthy uniform. I know I felt my strength failing me as I faced the totality of my guilt. Another part of me slipped away and died; I didn't even have the will to fight for it this time.

The war had sucked me dry.

How much time passed? I had no idea. Finally I roused myself from my hooch and forced myself to go eat. For as long as Captain Dye and Lieutenant Colonel Toner wanted me, I was still Outlaw Platoon's leader, and the men needed me. And that required overcoming the self-loathing I felt and staying focused on the job I had to do.

I would stay atop everything; I would give everything I had in the months we had left to ensure that I didn't screw up again and get somebody else killed.

In the chow hall, I did not feel worthy to sit with any of my soldiers. I picked an empty table and sat down alone.

"Hey, Commander Sean, welcome back!"

Yusef smiled down at me with his used-car-salesman affectation. He held a tray full of food and sat down across from me without asking if I wanted his company.

"Thank you," I managed. I could not screw this up and tip off Yusef that we were on to him. Getting up would have been suspicious. My plate was full of food. Not engaging would have been equally suspicious. I had no option. I was forced to break bread with our betrayer.

He took a bite of our American chow. As he chewed, he asked, "You drink beer back home?"

"A little," I said. For an instant, we made eye contact. He looked like a puppy eager to please.

"You get wasted? Have good time?"

"Sure, I guess."

"What about . . . you know . . ." His smile became even broader, revealing yellowed teeth. He looked like a ferret.

"What?" I asked.

"You know." He cupped his hand to his lips, leaned forward, and whispered, "The pussy. What about the pussy? Didya get any?"

His smile grew lascivious. My stomach burned with hate. I fantasized about pulling out my pistol, racking the slide, seeing his eyes widen in fear.

When I didn't reply, he frowned. "Come on, Commander Sean, you musta gotten some of that, no?"

Cold barrel pressed to his dark-skinned forehead. I would atone for the unforgivable sin of allowing this human filth to kill Cole.

"No?"

"No," I said.

"That is shame, you handsome guy, Commander Sean. You shoulda gotten some of that. So where we going today?"

I could murder you, Yusef. I would pull that trigger and feel less remorse than if I'd just crushed a cockroach.

I had never considered myself capable of murder. Afghanistan had opened that door, and now I knew the full extent of what I'd become. I could kill without so much as a ripple on my conscience.

We locked eyes. Oblivious to my hatred, he spewed the vile patter that had succeeded in disarming us for so long: the Bermel clown, always dirty and irreverent. Now it was a threadbare costume that no longer concealed the scum beneath it.

"Sir? You're wanted in the operations center," said Greeson. He'd entered the chow hall and seen Yusef sitting with me. He'd come to my rescue.

I got up from the table. Yusef cheerily waved good-bye. When we got outside, my voice broke. "Thanks, man."

"No worries, sir."

Later that day, Captain Dye assembled a patrol drawn from part of my platoon and part of our headquarters element. Yusef was assigned to be the 'terp. He suspected nothing and climbed aboard one of the Humvees.

At Orgun-E, he was confronted with the evidence against him. At first he denied everything. But when the sat phone was mentioned, he laughingly confessed, "Yes, yes. You got me. I did it."

His attitude earned him a face plant on the hood of a Humvee. Our men zip-cuffed him and pulled him to the battalion detention center. Later that night, he was flown to Bagram.

In any other time, in the hands of any other army, Yusef's body would never have been found. He'd have been dispatched and dumped, his corpse left for scavengers. Nobody would have known or cared that an enemy spy had vanished.

Discipline was the only thing that saved his life. Instead of a bullet to the brain, he faced due process and a prison cell. In the days ahead, I wondered if that was a weakness or a strength. There's a certain elegance to outlaw justice. Besides, the enemy would have afforded us no mercy if the roles had been reversed.

Americans of a different generation might not have been so disposed either. I recalled hearing stories of the original soldiers of the 10th Mountain Division killing German captives in the final stages of World War II's Italian campaign. In Stephen Ambrose's *Band of Brothers*, men from Easy Company massacre German prisoners in the wake of the casualties they'd taken during the D-Day campaign.

The army of the War on Terror holds itself to a higher standard. Our discipline and ability to choose the hard right in times like these are what make us the best army the world has ever known. And so Yusef lived.

We later discovered that Cole's death was not the extent of Yusef's treachery. The investigation revealed that he had arranged Abdul's death as well. He had tipped the enemy off to Abdul's nocturnal departure. Knowing where Abdul had been going and the road he had to use to get there, Yusef's tip had allowed the insurgents to establish an ambush in time to catch Abdul on his way back to Bermel from his family's house.

With Abdul dead, Yusef knew he would be promoted to head interpreter. That position gave him greater freedom of movement around the base. It also granted him access to a higher level of mission planning since he often patrolled with our company commander. Assassinating Abdul was a move of Machiavellian genius. We were so naive and trusting that we never even considered who in our midst would benefit most from Abdul's death. Those two nested elements of our culture are what made men like Yusef so foreign to us. It is what made Major Ghul's behavior at Bandar so inexplicable. We'd gone through our year in country, judging these Afghans through the prism of our own value systems, never fully grasping what we were up against. Well, now we knew. And we would never trust like that again.

TWENTY-SIX

THE PLACE WHERE
METTLE GROWS

★ ★ ★

IN EARLY SEPTEMBER, THE TALIBAN CONCLUDED A CEASE-FIRE with Pakistan's president. The terms of the deal were almost farcical: Musharraf agreed to suspend attacks on Taliban hideouts in Waziristan. In return, the Taliban promised not to launch any more operations in Pakistan or cross the border to attack targets in Afghanistan.

Without PakMil operations against their safe havens, the insurgents we faced now had both hands free against us. Almost the moment the cease-fire went into effect, the enemy swarmed over the border after us. They brought with them 122mm rockets—far heavier and more destructive than the usual 107s—which they fired on Bermel to great effect. By the end of the month, we'd taken so many rocket strikes that some of the men slept in the bunkers. Others, fearing they'd be killed while going to the latrines at night, urinated into empty bottles so they didn't have to leave the relative safety of their rooms.

While we were out on patrol, the enemy skirmished with us constantly. Those running battles had long since lost their mystique. The adrenaline rushes no longer gave us the euphoric high we had experienced in the spring. Our bodies suffered under its constant injection, the stress, and the physical demands of our daily lives.

We defeated the enemy every time they challenged us. We took to rounding up their dead after each firefight and delivering them to the local mosques. We masked this move as a gesture honoring Muslim burial rituals that required the deceased to be laid to rest within twenty-four hours of expiring, but the truth is that we were tired of the killing and were making a point: fuck with us, and your sons, brothers, and husbands will die. Their mangled bodies will be dumped like bloody trash at your houses of worship.

Our morale never recovered from Cole's death and the Fourth of July. Chris Brown stopped dancing on my Humvee's back deck. The joking and lighthearted banter were drained away by the daily grind. Our lives narrowed to two elemental aspects: survival and devotion. We put our heads down and simply endured.

It is easy to be a virtuous man in good times. It is easy to be judged a success when luck runs with the fortunate son. But when adversity strikes, the true measure of a man percolates to the surface. That is why combat became the great sifter—it tested our mettle. Not once but again and again until those who could not hack it were simply written out of the script.

Combat deployments make men incredibly vulnerable. Back in the States, it is all too easy to hide behind facades and defenses, pretensions and rank. But on the field of battle, the threat of death boils all of those things away. What remains is the true measure of a man's character. Some conduct themselves with honor. Some do not. But everyone who serves knows who is who, and that establishes dividing lines that lifetimes of effort can never bridge.

Though some around us failed and would have to live with that failure for the rest of their lives, a curious dynamic developed within Outlaw Platoon. Beaten down, weary, full of unfocused anger and lasting sadness, the men grew more selfless and devoted to one another. To a man, we would have given almost anything to be stateside, but the one thing we would not give up on was each other. We would not make excuses, and we would not leave our brothers behind.

Our Vietnamese day trader, Khanh, exemplified that spirit. After he was shot in the head in a firefight in Helmand Province, we heard that he was medically evacuated to Germany, where doctors discovered blood clots in his brain. He should have gone home for treatment. His condition could have killed him. Instead, he demanded to be sent back to Bermel. It took him months to get the hospital to release him, but he finally made his way back to us.

Khanh's dad had been captured by the North Vietnamese in the 1970s and had spent time as a prisoner of war. Somehow he'd survived and after his release had escaped to the Land of the Free. Like father, like son. Khanh's toughness and utter devotion to the platoon inspired the rest of us to stay in the game. I know that was the case for me. My headaches had grown worse. The stuff leaching from my ears and nose continued to grow more foul. I was told it was cerebrospinal fluid. Neurological symptoms had begun to manifest themselves while we were on patrol. My vision blurred at random intervals. My temper lay just below the surface, and my control over it slipped too many times. I'd get dizzy, and my memory loss grew worse. I knew there would be a reckoning at some point for not getting my injuries treated, but how could I leave when men like Khanh fought so hard to return?

We leaned on one another and refused to let the rain of adversity destroy our bond. The more hardship we faced, the more ennobled I saw my men become as they stood in the storm, indomitable spirits with no ability to quit. Those despairing days became the platoon's finest hour.

Back home, the leaves turned brown; Halloween came and went. Thanksgiving approached. We were scheduled to go home in January, and it became harder not to count the days.

The first snow fell in the mountains around Bermel. Quietly, I think we all prayed that the enemy would pack it in for the winter and return to their Pakistani havens. It didn't happen that way. Through October and early November, the rocket attacks against our base grew intolerable. Day after day, the enemy hammered us with indirect whose accuracy only increased.

Enough was enough. Lieutenant Colonel Toner coordinated a battalion-sized mission to clear the area behind Rakhah Ridge once and for all. From all over the area, reinforcements poured into Bermel, including combat engineers and more Afghan troops.

We would jump off from Bermel, move behind Rakhah Ridge, then use Route Trans Am to penetrate all the way to the Pakistan border. We rarely went down Trans Am; it was too dangerous. Prior to our arrival in country, a small unit of Special Forces soldiers had tried to do just that. They lost three men during the effort. None of us had any illusions: the enemy would fight to the last man.

We would be out for five days, covered by A-10s, Apaches, Predator drones, and an AC-130 Spectre gunship. We'd have 105mm artillery support, mortars, and three companies of Afghan infantry.

Lieutenant Colonel Toner selected Outlaw Platoon to spearhead the battalion's main assault. Second Platoon would follow behind us. A company of Afghan troops would dismount and support us from the ridges on either side of Route Trans Am. Delta would function as our quick reaction force. Another company from the battalion would support our right flank with a secondary thrust along a track south of Route Trans Am in concert with our own.

Forty-eight hours before we began our offensive, Lieutenant Colonel Toner notified the Pakistani military that we would be operating on the border. All of us assumed that information would be passed to the Haqqani Network. There would be no element of surprise for us to exploit.

During our final briefings, Sergeant Burley made one of his characteristic bombastic comments. It rang of false bravado, and our battalion sergeant major would not let it pass. "Oh, come on, Burley," he said derisively, "doesn't everyone call your platoon the 'Running Birds'?"

Stung, Burley went silent. That didn't bode well for us. If this operation was going to work, Second and Third Platoons would need to work closely together. I feared that the animosity between us could derail the mission.

The next morning, we poured out of Bermel more than four hundred strong. Our part of the assault included fifteen Humvees among our two platoons, Dye's company section, and Lieutenant Colonel Toner's command element. We moved unopposed to the gaping maw of Route Trans Am. It would be our jump-off point.

As we waited for the other units to get into position, I dismounted and checked on my men. I sensed an eagerness in their mood that had been dormant since early summer. We had the power, the men, and the support to deliver a knockout blow to an enemy that had tormented us for almost a year. This would be their reckoning. Get it over with, and we could go home on a high note.

The Afghan troops filed by on both shoulders of the road, their marine embedded trainers walking alongside them. The ANA moved with a different vibe that day. Straight-backed, uniforms squared away, eyes brimming with self-assurance—these Afghans were ready to fight.

One of the marines saw me watching his men and said, "This is gonna be a fun one, eh?"

"We'll see," I offered.

"Don't worry, we'll be good."

The ANA peeled off the road and scaled the ridges on either side of us. Route Trans Am lies in the middle of a valley that runs east–west to the Pakistani border. The ridgelines dominate the valley all the way to the frontier. With the ANA advancing along them, we'd keep the enemy from hammering us from the high ground, and our force of Humvees could serve as mobile support-by-fire positions for both companies.

Lieutenant Colonel Toner walked up alongside me. "You ready to do this, Sean?"

Through the deployment, he'd rarely talked to me. His tone conveyed confidence. Just seeing him with us inspired me. His command presence was amazing.

"Yes, sir," I replied, trying to mimic his calm.

"Good." He smiled and slapped my shoulder, then turned to go chat with Captain Dye. They talked in private farther down the column while I stared out at the forbidden landscape ahead.

You have to be perfect on this one, Sean. No mistakes.

A few hundred meters up Route Trans Am, a dirt track ran off to the north through some low ground that bisected the ridgeline. Three figures emerged from that little side trail, all toting AK-47s.

Chris Brown spotted them right away. So did Rowley, who was my driver that day. Nobody could handle a Humvee like Rowley, so I usually made sure he rolled with me.

"Hey, are those ANA?" Chris asked.

As if in answer, one of the figures exposed himself fully. For twenty seconds or more, we stared at each other, neither side making a move. Then, in sight of hundreds of coalition troops, the man raised his AK-47, grasping it one-handed by its pistol grip, as he defiantly shook it over his head.

"What the fuck is he doing?" Rowley asked, half in awe.

His two buddies moved to join him. They wore black headdresses, black man jams, and the typical green chest rigs full of AK mags.

Behind me, I heard Lieutenant Colonel Toner say, "Those are not ANA."

He and Captain Dye started walking forward.

The enemy taunted us. An RPG exploded among the Afghan troops on the north-side ridge. The three enemy fighters uttered a war cry, then dashed up the trail and disappeared. The ANA went berserk. The entire company spontaneously charged after the insurgents, shooting wildly as they sprinted along the ridge.

Lieutenant Colonel Toner saw this and intuited the situation at once. He grabbed his radio. "Cat three, this is Cat six, stop the ANA. Repeat, stop the ANA."

But it was too late. Their bloodlust stoked, the Afghan troops veered north and disappeared over the ridge, their marines chasing after them. A sudden eruption of gunfire broke out on the far side of the ridge. Rocket-propelled grenades exploded. AKs barked. Machine guns chattered and boomed.

Disorganized and strung out from the pursuit, the Afghan company ran headlong into a cunningly placed ambush. Those three men had been bait to lure our men over the ridge after them. Hit from three sides, the ANA started taking casualties. With our Afghans pinned down in the kill zone, the enemy counterattacked and cut them off from us.

The marine radio operator came over our frequency, his voice panicky. "Lieutenant Burthonette is down! Bleeding bad . . . ANA is going down too."

"Sean?" Lieutenant Colonel Toner asked.

He didn't need to say a thing. "I'm on it, sir."

Chris Cowen was on point that day, the very tip of the battalion's spear. I ran to him and said, "Chris, take us in."

"Roger that."

A moment later, Outlaw Platoon rolled into the fight.

On the far side of the ridge, the ANA had six men seriously wounded. The marine radioman called back to us and tried to describe his position. The company was trapped in a depression and being raked from elevated positions. "Lieutenant B's hurt bad. Shot in pelvis. Arterial bleeding."

"Give us your GPS coordinates," I ordered him. The radioman couldn't give me clear directions.

"Don't have a GPS, sir."

Fuck. I keyed the mike and said, "Okay, give me your grid."

"Don't have a map," the radioman's voice cracked.

"We'll find you, hang in there." Switching radios, I told Cowan, "Take us onto that trail running north."

We made the left turn. The trail ran between two sets of cliffs that towered more than a thousand feet above our heads. As soon as our last truck got on line, the enemy struck from concealed positions along the cliffs. Machine guns lashed our trucks, and I watched Cowan's take an unrivaled beating. We pushed through, our gunners unable to raise their weapons high enough to shoot back.

"Keep going, we'll get through the kill zone and find the marines," I told the platoon.

We came out from between the cliffs into more open country. Somewhere to our left, a marine lay bleeding out, but we could not see him or the men with him. On the slope to our right, muzzle flashes winked and glowed. My gunners could bring their weapons to bear now, and they went to work suppressing and killing the enemy.

John Saint Jean, our Haitian national, manned the fifty mounted on Hall's truck. As he traversed, looking for targets, he spotted an enemy fighter in a tree partway up the eastern slope. The insurgent saw Saint Jean's barrel swing toward him and brought his own rifle to bear. They opened fire simultaneously.

Saint Jean's burst knocked the enemy fighter out of the tree.

He tumbled down the slope and flopped onto his back beside the road next to my truck's right-front fender. His AK came to rest between his legs. His arms lay limp at his side. At first I thought he was dead, but then his head slowly fell to his left shoulder and his flat-brimmed Afghan hat fell to the ground, revealing long, well-groomed black hair. He was not dark-skinned, so he could not be an Afghan. Dimly, I wondered if he could be Chechen.

His reedy mustache twitched as he grimaced in pain, revealing pearl white teeth. Then his face went slack. His chin moved upward, and he speared me with dark, hate-filled eyes.

His chest moved up and down as he took ragged gasps. His clothes were soaked in blood, some of which was spilling into the dirt by his side. I noticed he wore Merrell combat boots, which were better footwear than what we had been issued. His AK appeared brand new.

Saint Jean had hit him in the stomach. How the fifty hadn't torn him in half is anyone's guess. Now, in his final earthly moments, his eyes betrayed nothing but loathing. No fear, no love; whatever indoctrination he'd experienced had burned away the compassion in his soul. As he died, all he had to hang on to was hate.

"Let me finish him, sir!" Chris Brown shouted from the turret. He was too close to kill with the 240, so my gunner had shouldered a Mossberg 500 shotgun, which he had trained on the dying man.

To hell with this guy. Look at him. He's filth. Some men just need killing.

The enemy fighter awaited his fate, no prayer moving on his lips, his eyes his only weapon now. They bored into me. I felt poisoned by his gaze.

"Come on, sir. Let me kill him!"

How I wanted to give that order, to see him die.

"No."

"What? Whaddya mean, no?"

His eyes never moved from mine. I've never felt a more malign and sinister presence. This dying man was corrupted by his hate. As he lay helpless, that was all he had left.

"Sir! Let me fucking kill him!"

"Don't do it, Brown."

"Why not?" His voice sounded almost anguished. Chris Brown wanted vengeance. I didn't blame him. Nor did I blame him for arguing with me, which under normal circumstances he never would have done.

Blood began pooling between the man's legs. His hands twitched. His eyes never broke contact with mine.

"Please!"

"No, Brown. You will not shoot this man."

"Why the FUCK not, sir?"

Why not? It had nothing to do with the rules of land warfare or compassion or mercy or my Christian faith.

In college, I had written a paper on the My Lai massacre. In the course of the research, I had met and interviewed some of the soldiers who had taken part in the killing. At the moment, they'd been swollen with rage and had slaughtered old men, women, and children. Though they had survived their time in Vietnam, they had come home lost souls, destroyed by the realization of what they had done. The guilt they'd felt ever since had ruined their lives.

I loved Chris Brown too much to let him burden his conscience with this man's foul soul. Twenty-five years from now, I needed Chris to be living a happy, fulfilled life. Cole would never have that chance. But Chris could. And I would not let him squander it with a trigger pull I know he'd never forget.

"No. Rowley, drive."

Rowley edged us past the dying man. His eyes tracked mine until we left him in our dust.

★ ★ ★

"THREE-SIX, THIS IS THREE-THREE," SAID JEFF HALL.

"Go ahead,"

"We have a casualty."

"Who?"

"Saint Jean, three-six. Shot in the head."

The man we'd just abandoned to fate had hit our Haitian national at the same time he'd been shot in the stomach.

"What's his status, three-three?"

"He'll make it. I'll take care of him."

I called the marine radioman and told him to pop smoke so we could get a fix on his position.

"Have no smoke," he said.

"Can you see us?" I asked.

"Negative, can't see you. So much blood. Hurry!"

"We'll pop smoke. Once you fix our position, talk us onto yours. Got it?"

"Roger."

Colt Wallace opened his armored door in the middle of the firestorm striking our rigs and tossed a purple smoke canister into the road. Greeson did the same.

"I can see yellow smoke! I can see yellow smoke!" the marine shouted.

Shit. We don't have yellow smoke. This guy's losing it.

"Tell us how to get to you!" My patience wore thin. We had not escaped the enemy kill zone. In fact, the volume of fire had increased. My trucks were getting shellacked, and every second wasted was one more my gunners had to endure.

"You've gone too far! Turn around and come back!"

Oh, fuck. Are you kidding?

The trail was so narrow, we'd have to change direction with individual three-point turns.

In the middle of a firefight, this would be no easy task. We'd be virtually stationary for several seconds, making us prime targets for RPG teams. I gave the order. The drivers nosed to the edge of the road, then backed up with the gunners guiding from the turrets.

Back and forth, back and forth, we eased around even as the enemy hammered away at us.

Cowan reported in, "We're taking a shitload of machine-gun fire." As he spoke, I heard three *thunk*s in quick succession. "They've just about shot my window out. We can't sit here any longer."

We completed the turn, then slowly started back down the trail. Greeson's rig now led the way, while Cowan's held the rear. In violation of our own established tactics, we had doubled back in the middle of a kill zone.

Swept with fire, windows spiderwebbed with cracks, tires shredded by repeated hits, we searched for the wounded marine officer. The marine was getting hysterical and becoming incoherent. We stopped on the trail as I asked him to give cardinal directions. I did not want to overshoot and have to double back again.

Greeson came over the radio and said, "We're up front. We'll handle it." His rig inched forward through the sea of tracers and lead sparking like fireflies off his Humvee.

No luck. We couldn't find the marine.

An RPG hammered Hall's rig. Gardea had climbed into the turret after Saint Jean had gone down. Shrapnel from the rocket had sprayed across his turret. One splinter had flown up under his helmet and ricocheted into his forehead directly between his eyes.

Enough of this. We needed to get Saint Jean and Gardea out. I made the decision to fall back. We would evacuate our two wounded men, reorganize, and figure out another way to get to the wounded marine. Clearly, sitting here or wandering around in the kill zone was only going to get more of my men wounded.

We pushed between the cliffs, raked by gunfire the entire way.

A pair of Apache gunships swung over the ridgeline, cannons blazing. Their strafing run caused the enemy fire to slacken long enough for us to finally escape.

Back at Trans Am, we turned right and rolled back to Second Platoon, our Humvees riddled with bullet marks. Greeson dismounted and went to work evacuating our casualties. Captain Dye and I huddled up to discuss our next play. He ordered us to counterattack on foot over the ridge and down into the ANA's position, link up with the marines, and call in a medevac chopper.

Second Platoon would form the main part of the assault; Third Platoon would support with another thrust through the kill zone until we could link up on the north slope of the ridge.

Jeff Hall came up to us and said, "There's no way you're leaving me out of this. I'm going up there like it or not." On top of being a Ranger, he was Pathfinder- and Jumpmaster-qualified. There'd be nobody better to work with the chopper crew to get the marine out of the fight and to a surgical unit.

"Okay, do what you need."

Second Platoon had recently received a replacement officer, Lieutenant Carnegie, who had taken over command after Lieutenant Taylor had gone home to deal with a family emergency. Burley had finally returned to being the platoon sergeant, not its leader. Carnegie had endured a tough learning curve that fall, but he was coming into his own. He took fifteen men from his platoon, plus Jeff Hall and part of his squad, and led the way up the ridge.

The joint platoon attack slammed into the enemy and broke through the growing cordon around the trapped Afghan troops. As Carnegie and Hall fought their way forward, we took our Humvees back down the narrow trail. As we battled our way through the enemy kill zone, Hall found Lieutenant Burthonette and treated his wounds as best he could. He called in the medevac helicopter, but since there was no flat ground, the bird was unable to land. The only way to get Burthonette out would be with a jungle penetrator lowered from the Black Hawk. This would require the bird to hover over the fight as the crew unwound the device. Then the wounded marine would be placed inside and reeled up to the aircraft.

Earlier in the deployment, such an evacuation had been tried, only to have the penetrator's cable snap. The mishap had killed four men. Knowing this, Hall had to talk the Black Hawk crew into giving it a chance. That they'd be hovering over a raging firefight made it doubly dangerous.

With the Black Hawk inbound, our Apache gunships made repeated gunnery runs. In the past, the presence of those deadly helicopters had usually caused the enemy to break contact and slip away. Not this time. From hilltop bunkers and rocky trenches, the insurgents poured accurate fire at the two birds, striking one in a fuel tank. Badly damaged, the Apache crew pulled up and out of the fight. With his wingman as his shepherd, he limped back to FOB Orgun-E.

Ignoring the danger, the Black Hawk crew flew through a hail of enemy bullets and roared into a hover over the battlefield. Hall guided them to his position, then secured the penetrator and loaded Lieutenant Burthonette into it.

The ANA fought in place, delivering volleys into the dug-in enemy with resolve and grit we'd never seen before. The marines had rubbed off on them at last.

Their wounded, who were not as critically injured as the marine lieutenant, were later extracted via their Toyota pickups and taken back to Bermel.

Meanwhile, my column reached the far side of the ridge, my gunners concentrating on the slopes to our east. The time was ripe for another countermove. My men and I quickly dismounted from our trucks and assaulted the eastern slope of the enemy ambush line. As the men bailed out of our trucks and formed up, the enemy picked that moment to break contact. Our blow struck empty trenches and abandoned machine-gun nests.

Once again, Galang's old command had proven themselves to be formidable warriors. Deftly, their survivors slipped away to fight again. Little did they know that we'd be coming after them like a steamroller in the days ahead.

Thirty minutes after Lieutenant Burthonette had been flown to safety, stillness descended on the battlefield. The two platoons met back at the original jump-off point. We shared mutual hardships. Lieutenant Carnegie had been a tiger in the fight, and Second Platoon's men had fought with tenacity and skill. Their counterassault had broken the insurgents' grip on the ANA at a vital moment and probably saved our allies from being overrun. Though we would never be close—too much water had passed between us—a new-found respect bloomed.

I climbed out of my truck and found Jeff Hall.

"Goddamn, Sergeant Hall! What you did—that was fucking amazing!"

Laconically, he replied, "Sir, don't even think about putting me in for an award. Getting that marine out is the only award I need."

We later found out that Lieutenant Burthonette had survived, but just barely. Another few minutes on the battlefield, and he would have bled out and died. Jeff had not needed to join Second Platoon's attack. He had waded into the fray even after losing two of his men earlier during our run-and-gun through the kill zone. I never put him in for an award, a lasting and profound regret. But in my book, Jeff Hall's selfless devotion to a fellow American, a man he didn't even know, exemplified the best of what had held Outlaw Platoon together against all the forces that threatened to tear us apart.

TWENTY-SEVEN

THE LAST LAST STAND

★ ★ ★

FOR FIVE DAYS, WE PUSHED THE ENEMY EAST TOWARD THE Pakistani border. They fought us ridge by ridge with the ferocity of a caged animal. We couldn't understand why this was the case. After every other engagement, they had retreated to their safe havens to resupply and absorb new, fresh-eyed jihadists to fill in for all the ones we'd killed. This time, they didn't quit. They stood toe-to-toe, displaying all the grit that we had demonstrated throughout the year.

They were slaughtered by the firepower Lieutenant Colonel Toner brought to the fight. During the day, we pounded them with artillery, A-10s, Apaches, and our own heavy weapons. We dismounted and assaulted hilltops and ridgelines and cleared long-abandoned qalats. We found their dead. We found their weapons caches and casualty clearance stations. Once again, most of their medical supplies came straight from Pakistani hospitals.

At night, we'd halt to establish a perimeter and await the arrival of our AC-130. Ten thousand feet overhead, it orbited for hours, zapping bad guys with miniguns, forty millimeters, and a 105mm cannon. It was a scourge in the sky, equipped with technology so significant the enemy simply could not hide. They moved, they died. Darkness gave them no respite.

Lieutenant Colonel Toner decided to mess with our enemy's minds. He brought forward a psychological operations truck, whose crew insulted the insurgents in multiple languages through a loudspeaker system.

"Women! Come out and fight!"

Such insults would inevitably trigger a response to us via radio: "American pigs! You will die like dogs!"

That would be enough for us to smother the foolish insurgent with artillery fire after we triangulated his position.

We kept up the pressure. As the enemy's men fell wounded, they would send trucks to carry them across the border to Pakistani hospitals. We wanted to target them. The A-10s' drivers would have loved to blow them to pieces with their 30mm Avengers. But we could not absolutely confirm that they were hostile, so by the rules of engagement we had to let them be.

On the final day, we seized the high ground overlooking the frontier. The remaining enemy holdouts chose to make their last stand here, between us and a Pakistan Army border checkpoint. They marshaled their remaining weapons and had emplaced their machine guns with their usual tactical cunning.

We'd been under fire for almost a week. Filthy, reeking of gunpowder and body odor, constipated by the MREs, we'd spent Operation Catamount Blitz sleeping in our rigs between skirmishes. Now came the climactic moment. We'd spent all year making last stands against their furious assaults. Here the roles were reversed, and they would die in place.

They went out hard. Machine guns laced our battered Humvees. They had a few RPGs left and sent those our way as well. I dismounted onto the ridge and lay prone, watching their muzzle flashes dancing across the valley floor.

Chris Cowan suddenly dismounted from his truck. Casually, he strolled toward me. Tracers zipped like lasers just over his head. The bullets snipped branches from the nearby conifer trees. He walked on as limbs and needles fell around him. Once he stopped and carefully brushed some needles off his ACUs.

He reached my door and looked down at me. "Hey, sir."

"Chris, are you fucking crazy?" I shouted over the battle's din. "At least take a knee!"

He acted unconcerned. "Oh, yeah. We're being shot at."

He dropped down as I sat up. We met halfway.

"Sir, just wanna make sure you see those machine-gun nests over there." He pointed at a couple of muzzle flashes.

"You walked all the way over here to tell me that?"

"Well, yeah," he said, almost embarrassed.

Together we lay down in the Afghan moondust and watched the battle unfold. The enemy was down to about fifty men dug in around an abandoned village that, according to our intel, had served as a training area for them.

At length Chris grew angry. "You know, sir, I don't get why those PakMil bastards don't just unload into their backs. They're supposed to be on our side, right?"

"Not after their peace summit."

"Fuckers."

Our forward air controllers called in a final series of air strikes. The A-10 pilots were unleashed to do what they do best. With JDAMs and 30mm strafing runs, the Warthogs pulverized the enemy. When it was over, there was no need to assault their last stand. Not an insurgent remained upright.

Captain Dye and Lieutenant Colonel Toner walked to our ridge.

They'd been working the radios with the forward air controllers and now gazed down into the smoke-shrouded valley. The last A-10 swept past, its chain gun throwing lead in one final act of overkill.

As it pulled up and raced skyward, Dye and Toner erupted in cheers. Soon, all along our line the men joined in. Victory cures all pain.

When Catamount Blitz ended, the battalion had killed a hundred and sixty men, including the leader who had replaced Galang. This branch of the Haqqani Network had been totally destroyed.

Or so we thought. Not a week after Catamount Blitz, the enemy crept back across the border to rocket FOB Bermel again. We had to sweep the frontier a second time. Not able to use the Humvees for this, Outlaw Platoon climbed over countless ridges on foot, our bodies aching under the weight of our gear and armor.

I was up front with a fire team from Third Squad and had Khanh Nguyen on one shoulder and Sergeant Keith Lewis (no relation to PFC Lewis, who had been wounded on June 10) on the other. Khanh was telling me about how his father had survived his years as a prisoner of war in North Vietnam when I spotted something yellowish lying in the dirt halfway up a small rise. I bent down and examined my find. It was a footlong length of rubber-sheathed wiring. This was out of place, and I immediately held my fist up as a signal to halt the entire platoon.

Khanh dropped to a knee beside me, his M4 and its M203 grenade launcher pointed toward the top of the rise.

"Whatzit, sir?" he asked in a whisper. Khanh spoke broken English at best. He mixed up his tenses and never got plural forms right, but we'd long since come to understand him perfectly, though men from outside the unit usually could not.

"Hold on. I'll be right back," I said.

I moved quietly to each squad and explained what I'd found. We'd move forward, expecting contact now.

Lewis and Khanh led the way when I gave the order to advance. The trail had just gone hot.

We reached the top of the rise and ran straight into the enemy. A complete Soviet 107mm rocket-launching system sat tucked away in a firing pit at the bottom of the reverse slope, shielded by another ridgeline opposite us.

We appeared just as three insurgents were trying to carry a dead comrade away from the pit. When they saw us, they dropped the body and reached for their weapons. Both sides opened fire simultaneously, but the shock at this sudden close encounter caused everyone to shoot wildly. Both sides sprayed bullets in one spasmodic moment. Despite the fact that we were less than twenty meters away from each other, nobody was hit.

Khanh went wild, screaming Vietnamese epithets like a berserker as he pumped rounds at the enemy. They broke and ran, firing over their shoulders as they sought cover over the next ridge. Khanh triggered a 203 round after them, but it went wide.

Suddenly Khanh rushed forward after the rocket team. It was as if all our hatred for these psychologically devastating weapons vested our Vietnamese warrior with maniacal fury and singular purpose: kill these men who had tormented us for months. Firing 203 rounds as he ran, reloading on the fly, he reached the rocket pit and banzai-charged up the far slope.

Before I could stop him, Sergeant Lewis burst forward after Khanh. Soon the entire platoon was energized, and the men poured over the rise. But Khanh and Lewis sprinted far ahead, trying to gain ground on the fleeing enemy.

They went over the far ridge and disappeared. When I got to the top, I saw them halfway down, blasting away at the enemy. Finally Khanh winged one of the insurgents with a well-placed 203 round. It exploded next to him and blew him off his feet. As he struggled to stand back up, still hefting his AK, Lewis drilled him. He flopped into the dirt. Before we could reach him, his comrade dragged him over the crest of his hill, where both disappeared.

The other two got away, but that didn't stop the platoon from celebrating. Khanh bellowed an outsized victory cry. Lewis yelled obscenities. The rest of the platoon high-fived each other. We needed this moment. After all the frustration, it felt glorious to watch the enemy flee or die.

The chase and the kill had been cathartic, payback for months of helpless moments on our base as rockets exploded around us. After that mission, the attacks diminished. We had succeeded at last in securing our base from attack. It had taken ten months too long.

After Thanksgiving, a lull descended on the border. With the snow piling up in the mountains, we began to think the enemy had packed it in for the winter. Fine with us. We had less than sixty days before we were supposed to head home, and as far as we were concerned, Cat Blitz had put us over the top. We were ready for a boring stretch, then a flight home to our families. They had never seemed closer or farther away from us than that Christmas season.

Lieutenant Colonel Toner had other plans for us. Instead of coasting through the final weeks of the deployment, he kept the battalion operating at full speed. Our entire strategy in Afghanistan was in the process of a significant transformation, based on the counterinsurgency model developed in Iraq. We started constructing remote combat outposts all across the frontier that were designed to collocate U.S. troops with the local populace. Each outpost would be defended by a platoon or two.

The new strategy spread us thin. Our ability to patrol diminished as each platoon had to take a turn manning our new outpost at Margah, about forty miles north of FOB Bermel. In early December, our engineers drove down there to start work on the place. Captain Dye ordered them to build it across from the Margah bazaar, in keeping with the intent of our new strategy. I protested to him that the location was too vulnerable. It sat between two gigantic mountains, one called Tur Gundy and the other Khowt Gundy. Two wadi systems wound their way along the north and south ends of the proposed perimeter, less than fifty meters from where the walls would be constructed. An enemy force could mask its approach on the outpost by closing on it from behind the mountains, then slip into the wadis to close undetected to point-blank range. They'd be at our walls before we could really even fight.

Captain Dye understood where I was coming from but overruled me. The engineers went to work. In late December, while the outpost was only half completed, the enemy attacked the engineers and Second Platoon with a station wagon loaded with four hundred pounds of ammonium nitrate. Second Platoon smelled the attack coming and lit the vehicle up, and it exploded prematurely. Had Second Platoon not reacted so quickly, the suicide bomber might have inflicted catastrophic casualties. As it was, the effects were bad enough. Lieutenant Carnegie's radioman was seriously wounded, as was his gunner. Carnegie himself was blown clear of his Humvee.

As Second Platoon evacuated its wounded, Captain Dye sent us down to take over the outpost's defense. We joined up with Lieutenant Carnegie, whose men had done a phenomenal job. They handed the Margah outpost over to us and returned to Bermel to refit. The next morning, without telling Lieutenant Colonel Toner, the engineers left unexpectedly. They had not even finished constructing the walls yet, and as they loaded up to bug out, we tried to stop them to no avail. They abandoned us in a poorly sited outpost without even the basics of force protection completed.

Five Humvees, less than thirty men—that's what we had to hold the Margah Combat Outpost. We had two weeks left before we were scheduled to go home. This was our last cycle out beyond the wire, and, given the tactical circumstances, all of us were jittery.

Wheat and Wallace did their best to lighten the tension we felt.

They built a wooden bull from pieces of scrap lumber they found lying around, then spent hours trying to lasso it from different angles. The men watched and cheered them on. But the levity was forced.

Small wonder. Looking around at the half-filled Hesco bags that formed what walls we did have, I could not help but think of Rorke's Drift, the tiny British outpost struck by thousands of Zulus in 1879. We were hung out on a limb, and I knew that if the enemy came at us from across the border, it would be our last last stand.

That's exactly what they planned to do. Since Cat Blitz, the Haqqani Network had rebuilt its local forces from the safety of its Pakistan bases. Bringing in Al Qaida–supported foreign fighters and others, they put together a force of more than two hundred and fifty men. Shortly after we reached Margah, they passed through the PakMil checkpoint at the border and infiltrated to staging bases east and northeast of our outpost.

In doing so, they passed through the Village of the Damned. The elder held his blind and traumatized grandson until the Haqqani fighters left the area. Then he packed some meager provisions and limped on aged legs down his hilltop to the road where we had first discovered his grandson, lost and keening with fear.

The elder walked for days, his feet blistering, his old man's bones protesting every step. Finally, long after dark on January 10, 2007, he reached his destination: FOB Bermel's front gate. Taken inside, he was brought to Captain Dye. The elder told him that he had at least two hundred insurgents pass his village, bound on attacking the new base at Margah.

We had saved his grandson in July and given his people all of our medical supplies. Those gestures had formed a bond between us and this old man. It had compelled him to cross more than forty miles of mountainous countryside to try to save us.

He was not a moment too soon.

At 0230 that morning, I was sitting in my Humvee next to Rowley, bored to tears and strongly considering taking a nap. We had spread our five rigs around the outpost's perimeter. Mine was on the west side.

The radio crackled. "Three-six, this is six."

"Go ahead, six."

"There are two hundred plus men coming to attack you."

The news failed to register.

"Uhh." I looked at Rowley, who was driving, "Roger?"

Greeson appeared at my door. "Did you hear this shit?"

"Yeah."

Greeson shook his head. "Son of a bitch."

I thought of the open walls on the east and west sides. I thought of the wadis to the north and south. One rush, and they'd soon be climbing over the half-filled Hesco bags.

Two hundred men or more? We had twenty-five.

Our tactical position could not have been worse.

Second Platoon was hours away. So was Delta. We'd get no reinforcements anytime soon.

In anticipation of my homecoming, my father had found me an apartment in Watertown, New York. My family had been driving up from Pittsburgh to get all my stuff moved in so that I would have a place of my own as soon as my boots touched American soil.

I wondered if I'd ever see that beautiful gesture.

Greeson said, "Sir, I'll work on improving the perimeter. You work the radio."

I nodded dully.

Two weeks left. Two weeks.

Captain Dye checked in. "Three-six, we're working to get you indirect, and I'm sending Delta platoon your way now."

"Roger, six." Dye always had our back. Tonight we'd need everything he could dredge up for us. Delta Platoon and a battery of 105s would not be enough.

I radioed the platoon and gave them the news. Nobody had any illusions of our chances.

"Three-six, we've got a drone overhead. We're uploading the enemy's location to the Blue Force Tracker now."

"Roger."

Each platoon leader's Humvee came equipped with a computer system connected via satellite to a military network. Every friendly vehicle in theater was displayed on a monitor. Click on an icon, and the unit's identity would pop up. Scroll around the map, and even a junior lieutenant could see what every U.S. unit was doing at that moment.

We could also track enemy movements with the system. Now, as the information was uploaded from our battalion operations center, two red blips popped up about four kilometers away from our outpost. One force, about a hundred and fifty strong, was closing in to the east behind Tur Gundy. Another hundred men lurked to the north, using Khowt Gundy to conceal their movement.

Without the village elder's warning, we would never have seen them coming until it was too late.

"Three-six, this is six."

"Go ahead, six."

"We've got 105s ready. Cat six is working air."

"Roger."

Greeson and the men worked to do what little we could to improve our defensive perimeter. He used two of our Humvees to plug the gaps in the east and west walls. That would at least slow them down for a little while. Two of our other trucks were stationed atop dirt ramps behind the north and south walls constructed by the engineers so that our gunners could fire over the Hesco-bag wall. Since we had no guard towers yet, the Humvees served in their place.

I checked the Blue Force Tracker. The two enemy forces were closing fast now and were less than three kilometers out.

"Three-six, this is six."

"Go ahead."

"We're gonna bring in A-10s for you. Working on more."

"Roger."

Greeson positioned our mortar team. Garrett and Bear made sure they had plenty of ammunition at hand, including illumination rounds. When the enemy got to the wadi system, we would dump everything we had on them to slow their advance.

The Blue Force Tracker updated itself automatically every few minutes. When the screen refreshed, the enemy force was only two kilometers out.

"Three-six, this is six."

Please give me more good news.

"Okay, we've got two Apaches on standby for you at Orgun-E. A Predator's on its way."

"Roger."

"You'll have an AC-130 overhead any minute."

"This is sounding good, six."

"And a B-1."

Lieutenant Colonel Toner has scored us a strategic bomber?

I radioed my trucks. "Okay, they're two clicks out, about a click from getting to the wadi systems. Battalion's stacking up air for us. We won't be alone. You know what to do. Lay the hurt on 'em, guys."

Around our makeshift perimeter, my gunners charged their guns and dropped their night-vision goggles down over their eyes. Our dismounts spread out along the walls, weapons leveled over the Hesco bags.

At battalion headquarters, Lieutenant Colonel Toner and the staff worked feverishly to pull assets from all over Afghanistan for us. As the aerial armada raced the enemy to Margah, the staff rehearsed exactly how Lieutenant Colonel Toner wanted this to go down. Three times they talked through the plan. The aircraft reached our area as they finished the third run-through. Battalion put them in orbit overhead, where they waited for the call to strike.

Our Prophet spooks reported the enemy's radio chatter. Their northern force leader checked in: "We're here."

They must have reached their objective rally point. This was their last stop before launching their attack on us.

Their new enemy commander replied, "Hold there, and tell your men to take a knee."

I checked the Blue Force Tracker. The enemy pincers had stopped about a kilometer and a half away.

GALANG'S REPLACEMENT GAVE HIS MEN FINAL INSTRUCTIONS: "When you overrun the Americans, cut their heads off and mount them on stakes. Good luck, and I'll see you on the objective."

Lieutenant Colonel Toner ordered, "Hit them now."

The satellite-guided bombs, dropped from the strategic bomber, struck first. Before the smoke had even cleared, the A-10s rolled in and unleashed all their fearsome firepower. The Predator launched its Hellfires, and the Apache batted clean up.

Around us, the night sky was rent asunder. We watched in awe as bombs burst, tracers flared, and rockets sizzled. When the AC-130 opened up, its battery of weapons only rearranged the bodies.

The strafing runs continued. Nothing that moved survived. Not a single enemy fighter got within a mile of Combat Outpost Margah that night. We stood on our makeshift ramparts and cheered wildly with every blast. Perhaps some of the men were celebrating the destruction of our enemy. I screamed for joy at our survival.

At dawn, we ventured out to conduct a "sensitive site exploitation." This was army-speak for policing up weapons, documents, and any other intelligence we could glean from the night's holocaust of fire, lead, and steel.

To the east, we found the blackened ground carpeted with human remains. We dismounted and picked our way through hundreds of meters of arms and legs, ragged half torsos, severed heads with flat-brimmed hats still covering blood-encrusted hair. The stench of death hung in the air. In places, patches of snow that had somehow survived the night had been stained red. In others, small fires still burned and sent palls of grayish smoke wisping across the battlefield.

Broken trees littered the landscape, their barren limbs decorated with ghastly pieces of human beings. From one, a web of intestines dangled from the branches, dripping gore onto the snow below.

We'd seen death's many faces before this morning. We'd grown hard carrying the dead enemy to our Humvees and dumping them at the local mosques. But even for the most cynical and steeled among us, this charnel house had an effect. Nobody who walks among such things is ever the same again.

We focused on our job. The AKs and machine guns we gathered looked brand new. We stacked them in our rigs alongside RPG launchers that looked factory fresh. The boots scattered about were of better quality than ours. The enemy carried sophisticated radios and military-issue compasses. On dismembered legs we saw kneepads. Torn clothing—the remains of desert camouflage uniforms—fluttered in the morning breeze.

Farther east, we began to encounter more intact corpses. To our astonishment, they wore body armor. Some even had World War I–style helmets still strapped to their heads.

Suppressing our horror was no easy task that morning. But we had to do the job right. At each corpse, the men cleared it for booby traps or unexploded ordnance. They found hand grenades and hundreds of AK magazines. In the pockets of the dead were documents—visas, passports, and notebooks that we knew would be of value. And then we made a startling discovery. Some of these enemy fighters were not Haqqani or Al Qaida at all.

They were Pakistan Army Frontier Corps soldiers, Pakistan's ragtag border militia. We found their identity cards.

In the spring, we had discovered how Pakistan was allowing our enemy to use its sovereign territory as a rest and refit area. The Haqqani Network trained in Pakistan and received logistical and medical support from our ally's hospitals.

In the summer, at the Alamo, we had watched helplessly as our enemy used the Pakistan Army troops stationed along the border as willing human shields to prevent us from launching counterbattery fires.

In September, the president of Pakistan had made peace with Taliban representatives, freeing our enemy to throw their full weight against us.

In December, we had been sent out north of the Alamo to escort an Afghan infantry company as it conducted a site survey for a proposed border fence. The Pakistani troops on the slopes overlooking Angoor Ada opened fire on the ANA and pinned them down with those ZSU-4 quad machine guns. Afraid we would fire back and create an even more serious international incident, my platoon was ordered to fall back to FOB Shkin while a Special Forces unit sortied out to rescue the ANA. Greeson and I thought that for sure the episode would become headline news around the globe. We feared that it would spark an open war between the United States and Pakistan. But the incident was never reported.

Now, in January, miles inside Afghanistan, we had discovered that Pakistani Frontier Corps troops had launched a joint offensive with Al Qaida and Haqqani Network fighters against a U.S. combat outpost.

We bundled up the evidence and stowed it in our rigs. Later, it was rumored that the documents found their way out of theater to the secretary of defense, who dropped them on President Musharraf's desk in Islamabad. We never found out if that was true or not, but I'd like to think it was. Somebody needed to call the Pakistanis on what they were doing to us.

The weapons we collected were later examined by a civilian intelligence team, who matched their serial numbers to recent production runs from Iranian factories.

The Sony DVD Handycam was one of the last things we found while rifling through the pockets of the enemy dead. We carried it back to FOB Bermel that day and watched its disc on a laptop computer in the company's operations center.

I stood behind Greeson, Cowan, Sabo, and the rest of our platoon, watching the footage we'd captured.

It started with a rousing recruitment speech delivered in a Pakistani border town. Jihadist orators urged the crowd of hundreds of men to join the fight against America. By the time they finished, the enraptured crowd began to dance and sing.

The next scene showed a training range, also in Pakistan. The Haqqani fighters were practicing short-range marksmanship, a necessary skill for urban fighting. In other scenes, teams of jihadists practiced evading simulated gunfire.

When the training scenes ended, the screen went black for a moment. At first I thought that was the end of the DVD, and I almost turned away. I wish I had.

The next scene showed an Afghan Border Police checkpoint in the aftermath of a night assault. The enemy had overrun the ABP. Bodies lay in heaps, illuminated by flashlights.

Then the cameraman stepped in front of a screaming captive. Somebody shone a spear of light on him as he lay on his stomach, facedown, his arms and legs held by masked men. Somebody else straddled his back, reached around and lifted his head by his chin.

The terrified face was that of a teenager. He wore a 1990 Chicago Bulls Championship cap.

Pinholt exhaled sharply. "That's the ABP who met us at the gate at Bandar last February," he said softly.

The man on the boy's back drew a knife from a sheath on his belt. He showed the eight-inch blade to the camera, then slid it under the boy's chin. The teenage boy screamed hysterically as the knife sank into his flesh.

It wasn't sharp. It wasn't quick. I could not watch the end. I'd seen too much already.

Without us there to protect them, the Afghan police of Bandar checkpoint had been overrun. I wondered how the enemy had done it. Had the garrison been betrayed from within? Or had the men been so demoralized and poorly equipped that even their remarkable hilltop redoubt could not save them from defeat?

Was Major Ghul out in that darkness, dead among his men? I doubted it. A man like him who played both sides was a survivor. Our shortage of troops had forced us to put Bandar at the bottom of our priority list as we faced the enemy's spring offensive. That teenage kid in his Bulls cap had paid the ultimate price for our weakness.

The sounds of his dying moments lingered in my ears as I left the operations center. Without Lieutenant Colonel Toner and an honor-bound old man, that would have been our fate.

TWENTY-EIGHT

HOMEWARD BOUND

★ ★ ★

FOB Bermel
January 20, 2007

OUTLAW PLATOON'S FINAL MOMENTS TOGETHER TICKED down as we waited for the Chinooks to come and start our journey home. The men sat on the Hesco-bag wall skirting the helicopter landing zone, smoking and joking again at last. The pressure was off. We were going home. Finally it was okay to have hope. Excitedly, we spoke of beer and steaks, of sex and taverns and leaves planned with eager families. Photos of children and wives and girlfriends appeared and were passed around. The men took photos and hammed it up for rolling video cameras.

Greeson and I watched the scene, light of heart yet sensing an underlying sadness. Despite all that we had endured—or perhaps because of it—we had become a family. Greeson was our father figure, Pantoja our selfless nurturer. Sabo was the crazy uncle who made every family event an adventure. Wheat and Wallace were our cowboy twins. Cowan was the hardass who kept things running, Hall the favored son whom everyone admired. Rowley was our smart-ass prankster; Brown was the platoon comedian. And of course there was Pinholt, the family's rising star, whose future would be limited only by the goals he established for himself.

Our strength lay in our diversity. In that regard, Outlaw Platoon was a mirror image of the society we had sworn to protect. Harnessing the power of our differences and talents kept us alive. It made me understand my country a little bit more. With men like these, no wonder we'd become the greatest nation of our age.

The absent faces weighed on me in that moment. Cole had been inspirational to us. Instead of remaining content in his noncombat role, he pushed himself to the limit to make his way back into our ranks. When he hadn't been able to roll with us, he did everything he could to lighten our load and contribute—on top of his duties at Bermel. That work ethic, that determination to stay part of the family evoked admiration and love from the rest of us. In death, his loss welded us even closer together through our shared grief.

And Baldwin—where was he? We'd heard nothing from him since he'd been flown out of theater. He was the big brother everyone missed. His loss had left a void in our group that had never been filled.

Then there was me. I was the ultimate authority within the platoon. I just tried not to use it. I'd learned that the strongest thing a leader can do once his men entrust power to him is put it back into their hands. I'd spent the year watching them run with that authority and do amazing things with the freedom it gave them. We were creative, flexible, and light on our feet out there. Serving the men of Outlaw Platoon was the greatest honor of my life.

Greeson sensed the pride I was feeling. He leaned into my ear and whispered in his deepest Sling Blade voice, "You're a good dude, sir. Helluva job."

I couldn't turn to look at him just then. I knew if I had, I would have lost my composure.

Who was I that day? I was a man who bore witness to greatness. A leader and servant of heroes. Being a part of the platoon validated my life.

Looking around, I could see the physical scars of the deployment on our men. Pantoja's face still bore the white-and-red weal from the bullet he'd taken on June 10 while saving Bennett Garvin's life. Saint Jean had refused to be evacuated from Bagram after he'd been shot in the head. He'd come back to us two days later, his head bandaged like a mummy's. He'd patrolled that way with us for weeks. Chris Brown, Bray, McCleod, Campbell, and Howard—and how many others carried shrapnel souvenirs within their bodies? In the years to come, how many times would their bodies set off airport metal detectors? My men had been cut and torn; six of them had been shot in the head. A handful of us had suffered traumatic brain injuries whose insidious symptoms had plagued us through the rest of the deployment. How many would feel the effects of this time in their lives through those wounds? Almost all of us.

The thunder of incoming Chinooks swelled in the distance.

The sound of our freedom.

The men grew silent, realizing that soon our union would be broken apart. The bond would always exist, nested permanently within us, but the lives that awaited us on the other side of the globe would take us ever farther from this brotherhood.

The hugging began. Promises to stay in touch were made. E-mail addresses were scrawled on slips of paper.

The birds landed.

One by one, the men filed past Greeson and me to say their good-byes. Perhaps more words would have been shared among men less acquainted with one another. Not so with us. We knew one another so intimately that words were superfluous. We hugged and shook hands and locked eyes one final time. Never before and never since have I shared so much in near-total silence.

We had done it. Survival was our destiny, home our destination. After a year of stripping ourselves of hope, we could now relax into the anticipation of our loved ones' arms.

The men threw their arms around one another's shoulders and walked to the waiting Chinook. Pinholt paused on the ramp and waved to Greeson and me one last time. We leaned on the Hesco bags and waved back, knowing that the defining period of our lives had come to a blessed end.

When the Chinooks lifted off and bathed us in dirt, I felt more alone than at any other moment in my life.

Greeson and I didn't board the bird with the men that afternoon because we'd been ordered to stay behind for a bit to help acclimate our replacement unit, an element of the 82nd Airborne Division, to the Bermel area. We were to take them out on patrols and show them the ropes, teach them about the villagers and the enemy. Then, after a couple of weeks, we would be stateside too.

Five days later, at 0300, Greeson and I were roused from restless sleep and told to report to the operations center. We rushed over to find Lieutenant Colonel Toner waiting for us on our computerized conference system.

When Captain Dye joined us, Lieutenant Colonel Toner said, "Men, I'm going to read you a quote from the former Marine Corps commandant, General Charles C. Krulak: 'When the hard times come . . . and they will . . . people will cling to leaders they know and trust . . . To those who are not detached, but involved . . . and to those who have consciences. They will seek out leaders who stand for something bigger than themselves and who have the moral courage and strength of character to do what they know in their hearts to be the right thing.'"

What the hell?

"Men, we have been extended for a hundred and twenty days."

He let that sink in. Thoughts of home vanished as I did the math. June. We would be here until June. We would have to survive another spring offensive. What were the odds of that?

The room spun. The men around me looked ashen. After Lieutenant Colonel Toner signed off, Greeson let out one of his classic Sling Blade laughs, as if he didn't have a care in the world. "I need a cigarette," he growled and stepped out into the night.

I followed, furious at his reaction. "What the hell is wrong with you?" I yelled. "How can you not be pissed off at this?"

Greeson just shook his head. "Sir, every deployment I've ever been on has been extended. It don't mean nothin'. Just means we get to play army for four more months."

I stalked off to be alone with my thoughts. Here and there, the remaining men from the company suffered in the dark. A door opened, I saw our armorer stagger outside and vomit. Others wept.

I called my father. He'd been my lifeline through the entire year. He had planned a huge party for my return. After all I'd burdened him with, after all the nights he'd spent sitting next to his computer waiting for that angel's chime, he would at last have his son back.

The news of the extension broke him. I heard it over the phone, felt my words slay his spirit. He would have to bear this, and he'd given all he had and then some.

Over the next forty-eight hours, my platoon reassembled at FOB Bermel. Most of the men had learned the news at Bagram as they were waiting for their flights home. They were reissued their body armor, helmets, and gear and thrown back onto a Chinook.

Others had already made it back to the United States. Military police knocked on their doors or met them at the airport and told them the news. They were told to pack and escorted onto the first available flights out.

They came back sullen, fearful, and devoid of hope. Everyone knew the odds. We had all had our close encounters with death. A few inches one way, a failure to duck, a left turn instead of a right—and death would have had us. We'd cheated it so many times that it seemed inconceivable that luck would have our backs now.

When we all had gathered back at Bermel, Captain Dye addressed us. "Men," he announced brusquely, "we will begin continuous combat operations tonight. We're back on it. Suck it up."

We became a platoon of the condemned.

As darkness fell, our bullet-scarred Humvees awaited us. In ones and twos, the platoon gathered around them. Drivers slipped behind the wheels. Gunners climbed into the turrets and loaded their weapons. My dismounts stacked extra ammunition into their rigs. Greeson smoked and stalked around with his near beer, unflappable as ever. Sabo blew a fuse and yelled at one of his men. I watched the familiar scene and felt nothing but abiding love for these incredible human beings. Did America know the mettle of her warrior sons?

Not a man refused his duty. Despite everything, we had not lost the one thing that mattered most: faith in one another.

Chris Brown stood in my turret, shoulders sagging. As I opened my door, I asked him, "How you doing, brother?"

He looked down at me with young man's eyes a thousand years old. "We got this, sir. No worries."

I slid into the truck commander's seat and settled down to wait. My fingers grew restless. I reached for my grandpap's St. Christopher medal and pulled it out over my IBA. The last time I'd looked at it, its silver surface had been dulled by Afghan grime. Now, to my surprise, it was shiny and spotless.

Stay with me, Grandpap. This isn't over yet.

I checked my watch. Time to put on my game face. I leaned forward and grabbed the radio's handset. "You guys ready to rock?"

One by one, my leaders checked in.

"Roger that, we roll in five minutes."

We counted the seconds and tried in vain not to think of home.

EPILOGUE

★ ★ ★

Summer 2009

GREESON AND I WALKED SIDE BY SIDE THROUGH THE ROWS of white crosses, so many of which were marked "Unknown Soldier" or "Unknown Marine." The summer heat beat down on us, and our dress blue uniforms were soon soaked with sweat. Arlington National Cemetery in August is distinctly unpleasant. We itched and stank, and it made me feel a little as though I was back overseas.

"You ready for this?" I asked Greeson.

"No. Are you?"

"No."

In silence we headed for the mausoleum to say good-bye to a fallen Catamount. A group of mourners was clustered in the area, and my heart leapt to my throat as we approached them.

"I am so fucking sick of this," Greeson growled.

How many funerals had we attended this summer?

Too many.

Outlaw Platoon had deployed to Afghanistan again, but this time Greeson and I had been left behind. The wounds I had sustained on June 10 had resulted in a traumatic brain injury. I suffered migraine headaches, memory loss, and blurred vision. All of those things grew worse until my cognitive ability began to degrade. I had trouble driving. My motor coordination suffered. I finally got help and was going through intensive neurocognitive rehabilitation. But I knew that I'd never be the same again and my time left in the army was coming to a close. I would soon be medically retired from the career I loved.

While Greeson and I were riding desks back at Drum, Outlaw Platoon ran into a Taliban hornet's nest. As our men died or suffered harm, it was our job to notify the families. In several firefights, five were killed and several more were wounded. After a while, the task left both of us feeling gutted.

June had been the worst. Greeson and I had driven to Huntsville, Alabama, to say good-bye to Staff Sergeant Jeff Hall. He had been killed by a roadside bomb in Afghanistan. At the time he had been the senior NCO from our deployment left in the platoon. The men revered him. He was larger than life, and stories of how he had bolted through enemy lines to save the wounded marine were whispered among the platoon's new members with reverence. Before he'd left, he had married Allison. She'd mourned his death at the funeral with their little girl, Audrey, in her arms.

Back at Arlington, we reached the mausoleum. We stayed close to each other, brothers in a crowd of strangers, bound together by a common sense of loss. We'd grown accustomed to the protocol of these military funerals. The folded flag, the final salute, white gloves and roses for the widows.

But we could never grow accustomed to the emotional toll each death took on us. Here we were, once again, grieving for a fallen member of our platoon.

★ ★ ★

TWO YEARS EARLIER, A YOUNG MAN HAD WALKED INTO MY OFFICE at Fort Drum. Fresh-faced and all smiles, the kid had saluted me and told me that his uncle had told him to seek me out.

"Who's your uncle?" I had asked.

"Phillip Baldwin, sir. I want to serve with you, in his old platoon. I'm Baldwin."

Stunned, I had said to him, "Do you know your uncle was a hero?"

He shook his head. I told him the story of what Baldwin had done on June 10. When I finished, I said to him, "You have some really big shoes to fill. If I put you in the platoon, you need to measure up."

Resolute, steady eyes greeted those words. I could see he'd been cut from the same mold as his uncle.

Not only did he join Third Platoon, his brother-in-law, Private Matthew Wilson, did as well. Third Platoon had become more than a brotherhood, it had become a family.

Private Wilson was killed in action during the same attack that claimed Sergeant Hall. Baldwin's family had paid a terrible price for their love of country.

Now Wilson's coffin lay before us, sealed, with his body inside. We stood in the back of the crowd, alone with our thoughts.

That's when we noticed him, a tall man wearing a black suit. He had a goatee now, and he leaned heavily on a cane.

"Is that Baldwin?" I asked.

He saw us and hobbled over. Before words were exchanged, our arms wrapped around each other in a fierce embrace. Long into that desperate and sad moment, I could only think of how I'd last seen him. *"I can't feel my legs, sir! I can't feel my legs!"*

As we talked among the crosses, Baldwin's mother and grandmother walked up to us. Phillip turned to them and said, "Mom, Grandma, I want you to meet the man who pulled me off the battlefield and saved my life."

They drew me into their arms and told me I was family. I held them close, total strangers but still connected in ways most people will never fathom.

"Thank you, thank you, for what you did for Phil," they said through streaming tears.

"He is my brother" was all I could manage.

I held on and never wanted to let go.

Though it was impossible to include all members of the Outlaws in the narrative, here posted for all to see are the heroes who made this book possible.

Sergeant First Class Gregory Greeson
Sergeant First Class Marty Belanger

Staff Sergeant Phillip Baldwin
Staff Sergeant Charles Byerly
Staff Sergeant Gordon Campbell
Staff Sergeant Jeffrey Hall
Staff Sergeant Jason Sabatke

Sergeant Christopher Cowan
Sergeant Michael Emerick
Sergeant Michael Marshall
Sergeant Bennett Garvin
Sergeant Keith Lewis
Sergeant Jose Pantoja
Sergeant Tim Stalter
Sergeant Ryan Wheat

Corporal Jeremiah Cole
Corporal Robert Pinholt
Corporal Colten Wallace

Specialist Mitchell Ayers
Specialist Brian Bray

Specialist Chris Brown
Specialist Erwin Echavez
Specialist Richard Haggerty
Specialist Mark Howard
Specialist Anthony Kienlen
Specialist David McLeod
Specialist James Murray
Specialist Khanh Nguyen
Specialist Aleksandr Nosov
Specialist Bobby Pilon
Specialist Josiah Reuter
Specialist Travis Roberts
Specialist Marcel Rowley
Specialist John Saint Jean

Private First Class Joseph Connor
Private First Class Joseph D'Ambrosia
Private First Class Jonathan Dugin
Private First Class Matthew Gallagher
Private First Class Juan Garcia
Private First Class Brandon Knight
Private First Class Dennis Leiphart
Private First Class Kyle Lewis
Private First Class Luis Perez
Private First Class Jose Vega
Private Daniel Schmid
Private Russell Warren

ATTACHMENTS:
Sergeant Dustin Dixon
Sergeant Paul "Bear" Ferguson
Sergeant David Kolk
Specialist Robert Abbott
Specialist Tony Garrett

POSTSCRIPT

★ ★ ★

HOME

SPRING 2007

ALL I WANTED WAS A NIGHT ON THE TOWN WITH MY PRE-ARMY buddies back in Pittsburgh. Instead, as we hit the South Side bars, I ended up staring right into the eyes of the son of a bitch who tormented me all those years ago. Memories of public humiliations flooded through me. He'd gained seventy pounds and had that waxy, pale look of a druggie glutton. The best he could do was bouncing at a South Side dive bar.

He took my ID and sneered as he recognized me from our mutual past. As my friends and I went inside, I could see him tracking us with his eyes. The hackles on my neck went up.

There's going to be trouble if we stay.

Less than a month ago, I'd been at FOB Bermel. All my combat instincts were still honed and right there under the surface. I did my best to ignore them. I was home now. Safe and sharing drinks with friends who had never seen a rocket or heard the sound of a Dragunov echoing off mountain slopes. They'd never seen a child die either.

We drank, and I listened as they joked and made small talk. I didn't say much. What could I contribute? It was like stepping back into time and climbing into my old self when I was still insulated from the world's harsh realities.

My old self and new self weren't compatible. I felt awkward. We ordered more drinks and I downed more than my share. What was the connection between us? Where was the bond? College? Fun times, but how do you skate the surface of human interaction after the level of intimacy I'd known in battle?

I missed my men. Badly.

We drank more, talked about women and sports and mutual friends. They talked about Big Ben Roethlisberger's fifty-nine percent completion rate. I thought of the village elder who saved my platoon. They talked of the Penguins and the year they were having. I thought of Baldwin shouting, "I can't feel my legs, sir!" and the terror that filled his voice. I'd never seen him show fear until that moment.

Was I really like this once? Was this all I was? I felt a sense of loss at the same time I felt guilt and shame. It shouldn't have taken the Army to wake me up to the shallow life I had.

Right then, I knew coming home was going to be much harder on me than I had ever expected. I wanted to run. Find a place just for me and figure this all out in beautiful solitude. My old life was gone. Dead. Burned away by mortar fire and the sonic crack of AK rounds passing overhead. I began to wonder if any of it could be saved. Could I take pieces with me into the future? Or was I going to have to build from scratch?

Sometime after midnight, I slid out of my seat and walked for the bathroom. I'd had too much to drink, and the forced merriment I felt compelled to project was actually making me feel worse.

On the other side of the bar, the bully saw his chance.

I went through the bathroom door and stood before the urinal. Behind me, I heard the door swing open. My combat instincts went crazy. Alarm bells rang in my head. Danger was imminent.

The bully stepped behind me and I could tell it was him. Taller, heavier—as he always was—he saw his chance to pick up where we left off in high school. . . .

He swung one meaty fist at the back of my head. I ducked, spun, and struck. Shock registered on his face.

I drilled him square in the jaw. He recoiled and stumbled backwards. I gave no letup. He'd crossed a line, and I switched into survival mode as we all learned to do in Afghanistan. Pure hate fueled me. This guy had done so much damage to my life; he would get no mercy now that he'd flipped my combat switch.

He didn't stand a chance. Far from the underweight kid he once tormented, I'd become a warrior. He'd devolved into an obese, self-indulgent failure.

I choked him out and left him unconscious on the bathroom floor. A trickle of blood striped the tile by his bruised face.

I went back upstairs, told my friends we had to leave. Later, long after I'd said goodnight, I wondered if I'd killed him. I went back to the bar the next morning and learned he'd survived, but was pretty banged up.

I drove back to my folks' home and realized I was going to need to get a handle on the fire raging inside of me before it torched my life. Equally as important, I needed a goal, something to strive for lest I get lost and drift now that I was home. I wanted to stay in the Army. I wanted to go back into combat, return to Afghanistan and be with my men. I couldn't do that. The wounds the enemy inflicted on me on June 10, 2006 were insurmountable. I'd waited too long to be treated.

The signs were there almost from the outset. I'd be driving someplace and suddenly forget where I was going. It was like waking up from a dream and realizing I'd been sleep walking. How did I get there? Where was I supposed to be? It was terrifying. Other times, I'd get dizzy. I'd drive on, growing increasingly unsteady on my feet as the day wore on. At times, I'd run into things. I'd misjudge turns, clip walls and corners with my shoulder. Motion would sometimes make me nauseous.

I couldn't lead men in battle anymore. It was the one thing I most wanted to do. When the company went back over and served in the hell of Wardak, Afghanistan, I remained behind as the Rear Detachment Commander. When the enemy killed my men, I was the one who notified their families. Each trip to those front doors cut another piece of my heart away.

Through all this, my folks remained steadfast. But my circle of friends grew smaller and smaller, until only a few stayed close to me. The dirty little secret about combat deployments is you learn more about your home front than you'll ever want to know. The hangers-ons drop away first. Casual friends, acquaintances from school or elsewhere in the Army just sort of fade away. Your old crowd, the ones you think of with fondness—they drift away as well as the differences between the veteran and the college kid you used to be. Then, there are the close relationships, the ones you hold most dear. Some reveal themselves to be imbalanced. Others are not what you thought they were. The stress of homecoming and adjusting to life away from rockets and mortars becomes too much. Those connections fray. Some break in spectacularly ugly ways.

I didn't realize it in the moment, but looking back, the entire fabric of my life was being torn apart one thread at a time. I watched it all come unraveled and clung to a vision of a better future, even if I didn't know exactly what that was.

Then I met Laurie, and the direction of my life changed. She was a television anchor on one of the local stations in New York. Brilliant, incisive, funny, athletic—she was everything I'd ever hoped for in a companion. Even more important, she had a soft soul and a giving heart. She poured love and energy my way, and I felt much of the blackness inside me recede. She reached out, listened, and wanted to understand. That was ultimately what started the healing process for me.

She became the star I navigated toward. We married and started a family. In time, I felt a shift inside my own heart. Since 2005, the Outlaws had been the center of my life. Every decision, every thought and action I had made was for them. When we came home and were blown to the winds, I felt severed and lost without them in my daily life.

Laurie and our children flowed into that damaged part of me. I felt rejuvenated. The old Sean was gone. The innocent and insulated college student I couldn't relate to anymore was someone I came to mourn. When the little girl died in my arms, that part of me was lost forever. It set me apart from everyone else at home, especially after I left the Army. I saw families and people I once knew going about their daily affairs, wrapped in their routines—and I couldn't relate. I envied them. I hated them. I'd become the odd sheep in our suburb of blissful insularity.

To my surprise, our children Ethan and Emma, healed this part of me. In their eyes, I saw what I had lost. In them, that spirited innocence shines like it once did in me. Being with them, feeling it flow from them as they explore the world with unabashed wonder—that has made me whole again. It feels like a circle has been completed.

As I left the Army and transitioned to life as a civilian again, I stayed cloistered from my fellow Americans. Veterans have learned that interaction with strangers can be a double-edged sword. Some thank you for your service, some make cutting remarks. You never know what you'll encounter, so it is best to maneuver through each day with caution. As tough as we are in combat, the bad encounters back here can be as painful as battle wounds.

Through this whole process, I kept the Outlaws close. We

talked, we e-mailed. We took care of each other. I saw my own troubles mirrored in their daily lives. Some of the platoon stayed in the Army; most are out now. Sergeant Wheat is a police officer in Louisiana. Baldwin's going to law school. Colt Wallace breaks horses for a living. Pinholt is going to college. He's going to be a millionaire someday; that kid is freaking brilliant. Nosov is a pilot these days, and Rowley's an off-road truck racer. I'd like to think that his driving us through firefights sparked that calling.

In one way or another, Afghanistan became the dividing line in our lives. I saw evidence of it in every man in our platoon. Their lives are works in progress—we're all rebuilding. We started over. Some of us have done okay. Some of us have really struggled. There've been those moments, chance encounters with Americans who simply don't understand, or don't care to. They've done much damage, and I watched the fallout with a sense of helpless frustration.

One of our most beloved Outlaws went back to school after he came home. He had a professor who hated his political views, hated the war, and hated the troops. My soldier threw his heart into every endeavor, and school was no exception. Every paper he turned in was savaged by this professor and graded down for no other reason than the professor hated his viewpoints. It became personal, and it crushed my soldier's spirit. He dropped out of school and fled to Canada.

I wanted to help. I wanted to make their experience mean something. I wanted the country to know what they had given, who they were, and what inspiring men they are.

Here are your sons, America. These are the men you've thrown into the fire. This is their story, and it is one of achievement and love, triumph and victory.

As I found with Laurie, the only true path back to a new life here at home is through understanding us. It is the bridge across the divide we feel once we lay down our rifles and return to our own. That is why I wrote *Outlaw Platoon*. For warriors to truly assimilate, people at home need to know what we experienced and achieved. I wanted to contribute to that effort.

The response to the book has been overwhelming, and I have been so gratified and humbled by how my men have been embraced by their communities and countrymen since the book hit the shelves. Every year, we get together for a reunion at my house in Pennsylvania. This past spring, the men told me stories of celebration and acceptance. More than anything else, hearing them tell me these things brought meaning to my own life in ways I never could have hoped. The book is part of our bond now.

There is a dark side to its publication, though. Families read the book and rallied to their sons and husbands. I'd hoped for that. But elsewhere, as some of my men struggled to find their way, the book extended the black emptiness that comes with recasting our lives. One Outlaw told me that his parents refused to the read the book. They did not want to know what he experienced. He took it that they didn't care, that in avoiding the pages of their son's past they were not being supportive.

I took it a different way. If you love deeply enough, it takes real courage to learn the truth. Not everyone can carry a rifle. Not everyone has the emotional strength to read what happened to their son, or husband, or father.

Whatever the reason, the copy of *Outlaw* he gave them still sits, unopened on the shelf of his childhood home. It has become part of the divide. I grieve over that, and wish I could find a way to help. But all I can do is stand with my brother and let him know the Outlaws will never leave a man behind. Not in Afghanistan, not back home.

The book also generated a lot of emotion from support personnel—the FOBBITs. The divide between combat infantryman and those who support him is as old as the profession of arms. I think in *Outlaw* I made it worse by overemphasizing the bad elements back on base. Plenty of times we were given tremendous support by dedicated and loyal troops at Bermel, and their contribution was obscured by the ones who did not measure up. Specialist Corey Brass reminded me of this. Corey owned his own business before 9-11. Overweight, working seventeen-hour days to put food on the table, he left everything behind to serve his country after we invaded Iraq. He devoted himself as passionately to the mission in Afghanistan as the Outlaws did while at FOB Bermel as a supply specialist. His letter was a wakeup call for me, and I've included part of it at the end of this post script to illustrate how all of us sacrificed to be out there on the edge of the Hindu Kush. I hope it helps set right a wrong I made as well.

The Outlaws are your neighbors, your postmen, your police officers, and your airline pilots. On the outside, they are no different from any other American. Perhaps in time the divide will narrow. We'll grow and let time wear away at the rawness of our experience. I pray that to be true. But I suspect that we will never be like our fellow Americans again. Those days were lost a long time ago.

In the years ahead, I'll keep navigating for the horizon. My family will be my guide. For the Outlaws, all I can do is hope that each one finds their path. We will be there in moments of support and in moments of great success. That's how the brotherhood works. We will always be family.

SPECIALIST BRASS'S LETTER:

SEAN,

If it is okay, I would like to share a little bit of my story with you.

I was 25 and about 320 lbs. I'm sure you thought I was a fat ass in the Army but that is nothing compared to where I was before. I started to lose weight. Everyone thought I was nuts. My friends and family told me not to do it. If the Army didn't work out, I had nothing to come back to. But my plan was to make a career out of the Army. I joined March 3, 2004.

I found a low density job called Unit Supply Specialist. I knew that at the age of 27, with shitty knees and ankles, it was a mistake to assume that I could keep up with a 20 year old kid, and a bigger mistake to have their lives in my hands. I thought that I could earn the respect of my 11B peers by carrying the weight, humping the miles and being cold in the field with them. After about nine months I learned that was not going to happen.

While in FT Drum I fell in love with a woman named Belen. We really hit it off and before I left we got engaged. I was 3 days from flying home from Bermel when we got our orders to stay. I called Belen. That was it. She had had enough of this life before it even started. She told me it was off.

I had no job to go home to. I had no wife to go home to. It was clear to me that the Army and I couldn't make a go of it. I passed every PT test up to that point and was an awesome supply specialist but the fact that I was fat trumped all.

Right now I am sure you are asking yourself "so what, what's this got to do with me?" Here it is. People gave up a lot to serve their country. The "fobbits" gave up something too. For some it cost them their marriage and for some it cost them their life. For you to show them so little respect shocks me. Those men work HARD to keep those trucks running and to keep those 105s firing.

This is not about me, I know what I did and didn't do there. I am proud to have served with all of you. I just wish that that respect was reciprocated to all of us who gave up 1.5 years of our lives to the United States, the Army, 10th MTN Div, 2–87 INF and to Bravo Company.

Corey

Corey, thank you. Thank you for reminding me that we as soldiers share a common bond, no matter where our workplace took us. Thank you for reminding me that infantrymen don't have a monopoly on heart, and that men like you can inspire and elevate just as equally as those of us who rolled out beyond the wire.

Most of all, thanks for setting the record straight. No matter who you are or where you served, if you gave your full measure to your country, you'll always be a hero.

Sean Parnell, November 2012

ACKNOWLEDGMENTS

★ ★ ★

SEAN PARNELL:

This book would not have been possible without the cumulative efforts of several amazing, talented, and supportive people.

First and foremost, I would like to thank my loving wife, Laurie. A year after redeploying home from Afghanistan, my life was in shambles. Depressed and lost, I had strayed from the warrior path. You saved me and gave me purpose. This book was your idea from the start and was ultimately born out of your loving devotion to me and my men. You are the glue that holds our family together and the most wonderfully compassionate person I've ever known. Ethan and Emma, watching you grow under the loving eye of your mother has been the greatest joy of my life. The happiness you've given me while writing this book cannot be expressed with words. I love you all.

I am blessed to have parents who love and care about me. Mom and Dad, you are responsible for all of my successes and none of my mistakes. My only hope is that I can continue to make you proud all the days of your lives. Thank you for always having my back through all the tough times. To my siblings, Shannon, Scott, and Andy, you're the best a brother could ask for.

Nate and Kathy, first and foremost thank you for shattering the negative stereotype of the crazy in-laws. You are incredibly kind, compassionate, and giving people. Thank you for the support you gave me while I was writing this book. You're the best in-laws anyone could ask for.

A special and heartfelt thank you to Mother of Sorrows Church, whose care packages and Christmas gifts boosted the morale of my men in ways I never could have imagined. Your dedication to the men of Outlaw Platoon was absolutely incredible. Thank you.

To my agent, first editor, and friend, Jim Hornfischer, I am eternally grateful for your dedication to this project. In a rough-and-tumble business, you are a man of impeccable integrity and character. I was truly blessed to have your guidance and support every step of the way on this project. Thank you for taking a chance on my men.

I wish to express profound thanks to my editors at William Morrow, David Highfill and Gabe Robinson. I knew from the first moment we spoke on the phone that you and your team were meant to publish this book. Your patience, vision, and positive attitude were rocket fuel for someone new to this business. Thank you so very much.

I also owe David Bellavia—writer, warrior, and cofounder of Vets for Freedom—a warm and heartfelt thank you. When this project was in its infancy, you gave me the support and advice I needed to help get it off the ground. You're an American hero for gallantry in battle but, more important, you're an honorable man. Thank you.

I have so many people to thank from my time in the military. Thank you, Lieutenant Colonel Chris Toner, for giving me the opportunity to lead men in your battalion; Captain Jason Dye, for the trust and support you gave me during combat operations; First Sergeant David Christopher, for teaching me the ropes of being a new officer in the infantry; Captain David Brown and Billy Mariani, for your steadfast friendship.

To my soldiers, the Outlaws, you are the finest group of warriors and men I have ever had the privilege to serve. Working for you was the single greatest professional honor my life will ever know.

To my noncommissioned officers, thank you for taking the time to train and mentor me as a young leader. The life lessons you taught me extend far beyond the scope of my experience in the military. You were the heart of this platoon and the reason for our overwhelming success. There isn't a day that goes by when I don't think about each and every one of you. Thank you.

To Master Sergeant Greg Greeson, you were the best platoon sergeant a young officer could ever have. Down and out, outmanned and outgunned, you managed to inspire confidence in a group of men who had no business even whispering the word. Yet your ability to do so saved us all. Thank you for always being there for me.

Last but certainly not least, I'd like to thank John Bruning. John is the most passionate and powerful military writer I've ever read. I can't put into words how blessed I have been to work with him on this project. For over a year John was wholeheartedly invested in our story. He made it his business to figuratively climb rugged mountains, man every foxhole, and engage the enemy ferociously with my men. Then, inspired by the story of the Outlaws, he went and did it all for real in the mountains of Afghanistan. John, you are a man of the finest quality and have the heart of a warrior. I'm proud to call you one of my closest friends. Perhaps fitting for a moment such as this one are words once uttered to me: John, you are a member of this platoon now. Don't mess it up.

John Bruning:

In a career where I have been fortunate to have worked with fine people on meaningful projects, *Outlaw Platoon* represents one of those once-in-a-lifetime moments that change everything for a writer. I remember writing *The Devil's Sandbox* after I came home from post-Katrina New Orleans and hating to write the book's final words. I felt that again as Sean and I finished *Outlaw Platoon*. I knew one of the most profound episodes of my life was coming to its inevitable conclusion. When we turned in the manuscript, I grieved its passing.

When Sean first contacted me via e-mail through my sister, Sherry, I was in a dark place. I'd withdrawn from a collaboration, and two of my proposals had failed to sell, ruining my perfect track record on that front. I was also still wrestling with the loss of a young man who was like a son to me. Specialist Taylor Marks had been killed the previous August in Iraq; I had been the one who set him on his course to join the military, and he had turned down a scholarship at the University of Oregon to serve his country. He was in Baghdad for six weeks before he was killed by an IED. After his death, I didn't want to write military history anymore. I felt lost and unsure of the way forward.

Then Sean and I talked on the phone. It was easy to see that Sean was a man of great character, a human with compassion, unique insight, and a determination to serve his men even years after the platoon had come home from Afghanistan. He didn't want to write a book for himself. This was not an ego trip. This wasn't about money. He wanted the country to know what his men experienced and how selflessly they gave of themselves to one other.

I knew taking the project on would force me to face elements of my own grief and sense of loss over Taylor's death. I wasn't sure how I would handle it, but I knew there was value in Sean's story. This was a special group of men who deserved to be immortalized on paper.

I also knew Sean and the rest of the platoon needed my absolute best. In the spring of 2010, I made the decision to go to Afghanistan to experience a little of what they experienced so that I could write with a deeper understanding of combat. I set to work dropping weight and lost a hundred pounds in seven months of training. Thanks to my friends in the Oregon National Guard, I was able to go out with B Co. 1-168 Aviation, a Chinook unit. Later, I embedded with TF Brawler and the 162 Engineers. Both units gave me the opportunity to go out on ground patrols with them, and I gained insight into the daily lives of our soldiers on the ground and in the air. It was a harrowing experience.

I came home late that fall to discover more about my home front than I ever expected to learn. My decision to go overseas created an upheaval in my life that destroyed almost all my relationships here at home.

Sean had already experienced that phenomenon, and as I struggled to get through it, he was a rock of support and friendship. We became far more than collaborating authors. Through the writing of *Outlaw Platoon,* we became brothers.

Writing the book did not come easily at first, but when we hit our stride in the spring of 2011, it bloomed. All of the experiences I gained in Afghanistan gave me a greater appreciation and understanding of what Sean's platoon had endured. I witnessed the interpersonal dynamics fostered by combat. Thanks to Dan Lauer, Hunter Lescoe, and a Czech mechanized battalion, I fired most of the weapons described in the book including an RPG-7 and a Dragunov sniper rifle. When that experience meshed with Sean's incredible memory and perspectives, I knew we had something truly special. The words that flowed between us and onto the page are the best of my career, and I will always be most proud of this book.

Writing *Outlaw Platoon* became the cornerstone of my new life back home after my brief time in Afghanistan. Without Sean and Baldwin, Pinholt and Greeson, and their examples, I never would have made it. Ultimately, *Outlaw Platoon* saved my life.

Sean, thank you for seeing this through and putting your faith in me. I know I tested that more than once, but I hope you know that I gave you and your men everything I had. It was the only thing I could do for you, and yet after all you have given me, it still seems inadequate. Your friendship, and our partnership, will always have a profoundly special place in my heart. I am honored to have been entrusted with your platoon's story. I cannot wait to work with you again.

Our editors, David Highfill and Gabe Robinson, gave us the opportunity to write *Outlaw Platoon*. When we finished the first draft, your passion and enthusiasm took the book to a new level. It is rare in this business to find two editors so in sync with their authors. David and Gabe, it was a true joy to work with you. In a business that Stephen King once described as "the tiger pit," working with you both has been energizing and rewarding. Whatever success the book has in the years to come will be largely the result of your unwavering support.

Ed and Renee, those months apart were difficult on all three of us. I missed you dearly. Coming home to your waiting arms, then feeling your love through the writing of *Outlaw Platoon* gave me the push I needed to sustain two and a half months of twenty-hour days.

Ed, I will never forget sitting at my desk at FOB Shank, reading the local paper's article about your achievement on the track at school. Your embrace at McChord when I returned—nothing like that in the world.

Renee, over the years I have watched you grow from my little girl to a young woman of tremendous substance. Your sense of humor and your cheerful and wacky disposition leave me in stitches. You have been inspirational to me. This book could not have been written without you, Renee. This work is your achievement too.

Jenn, you weathered every possible storm while Sean and I wrote *Outlaw Platoon*. Running the household, taking care of Vol, supporting the children as their dad was on the other side of the planet—these were challenges enough. A myriad of other issues made things exponentially more difficult after I returned home. Through it all, you gave me the space and support to write, and never pushed when I struggled. Thank you for everything you did for me and the family. Whatever success we have with *Outlaw Platoon* will be our triumph over every possible curveball life could throw at us. If anything, I've learned that there is no obstacle that cannot be overcome.

To Larry and Mary Ann Beggs, your support and love for my family has been pivotal. *Outlaw Platoon* would not have been finished without you, and I cannot express enough gratitude for your devotion and steadfast support.

To Lis Shapiro, my dear friend from Saratoga days, you carried your own burden as well. The packages you sent while I was in Afghanistan were manna from heaven, and I'll never forget that first taste of your daughter's homemade brownies. Thank you for all your help and love.

Brenda, Ox, and Julie, thank you for the mail, the notes, and the support. They were key for me while I was overseas. Thank you for keeping in touch and reminding me that I was cared for by good and devoted friends.

To everyone in TF Brawler and the 162 Engineers, I cannot thank y'all enough for allowing me to spend time with you and experience a little bit of the war from your perspectives. Rob Ault, Scott Tant, Eric West, Kyle Evarts, Craig Talarico, Anson Smith, Joe Speal, Kyle Stimson, Bob Bacca, Andrew Carlstrom, Bill Sickendick, Craig Marston, Bradley Stanley, Daryl Jones, Andrew Alvord, Felix G., Evan Mace, Joe Pruitt, and SFC Middleton were just a few of the great folks who made me feel so welcome and at home during such a disorienting time. This book is better for your trust in me and support of my writing projects while in Afghanistan. The Thomas Jefferson Award is as much yours as mine. That is especially true of Steve Bomar and Nick Choy. Your belief and faith in me made *Outlaw Platoon* so much better. I cannot express how grateful I am for the opportunity you gave me.

To Captain Cassie Moore, thank you for your friendship. It has made a tremendous difference in my life. You are a role model for Renee, and a great inspiration to me.

Through this entire project, I've had one constant source of support and strength. Allison Serventi Morgan, your faith in me at times surpasses the faith I have had in myself. When Taylor was killed, your warmth and passionate heart helped balm the guilt and grief. Your fitness training made my trip overseas possible. In Afghanistan, you made sure I always came home to find notes and messages waiting for me. When you found out I was getting cold on missions, you fired off a package full of the best winter gear available. As I embarked on *Outlaw Platoon,* you read every chapter, sometimes waiting up until ridiculously late hours to see the day's effort and give me suggestions or comments. When I searched to find the words that would do Sean's story justice, you helped me discover the path to them. You are an invaluable part of my life. *Outlaw Platoon* would not have been finished without you. You are a gift.

Finally, I would like to thank Jim Hornfischer. Jim has been my agent since 2006, and we've been through some incredible projects together. We've also had some rugged moments in between. Jim, you constantly push me to be my best, to grow and develop as a writer. You challenge me in ways nobody else has. You've changed my life with your belief that I could play in this league, even when I was so full of doubt that I wasn't sure I'd ever write again. Thank you for hanging in there with me. It says legions about your character and your loyalty. I am honored to be your client, and am deeply grateful for your loyalty.

And for Taylor: Your spirit of adventure will guide me down the road ahead. Live out loud. Always, for you.

GLOSSARY

★ ★ ★

105mm Howitzer A large cannon that combines the velocity of a gun with the high-trajectory firing capability of a mortar.

107mm rocket An artillery shell used by the enemy in Afghanistan for attacks against U.S. bases and, on occasion, for improvised explosive devices (IEDs).

122mm rocket A larger, more devastating shell than the 107mm.

A-10 Thunderbolt II An American single-seat, twin-engine jet aircraft, nicknamed "the Warthog." Its primary mission is to provide close air support for ground troops against tanks, armored vehicles, and enemy infantry.

ABP Afghan Border Police. Often underequipped and undermanned, they are responsible for Afghanistan's border security.

ACU Army Combat Uniform.

AH-64 Apache A four-blade, twin-engine attack helicopter armed with a 30mm chain gun, Hellfire missiles, and Hydra rockets.

AK-47 A Soviet-made, gas-operated 7.62mm assault rifle. Inexpensive and easily maintained, it's the weapon of choice for most insurgents and foreign fighters in Afghanistan.

Allahu Akbar A common Arabic Islamic expression that universally translates to "God is great."

ANA Afghan National Army.

AO Area of Operations.

AWOL Absent Without Leave.

B-1 Lancer A supersonic long-range bomber that when loaded to max capacity, is capable of dropping over 125,000 pounds of ordnance in one flight.

BFT Blue Force Tracker. A computer that mounts on the dash of a Humvee and tracks the location of all friendly forces in the area, displaying them on a digital map.

blue-on-blue Military terminology for friendly-fire mishaps.

breaking contact Military terminology that is synonymous with retreating on the battlefield.

call sign A nickname used over the radio to identify units and people in combat.

CCP Casualty Collection Point. The place where casualties are brought during battle.

chest rig Military slang referring to a soldier's chest-mounted ammunition holder.

choke point A geographical feature that forces an armed group to narrow its front, reducing both its numbers that directly face the enemy and its combat power.

CIB Combat Infantryman's Badge. An award given to U.S. Army Infantry soldiers for engaging in combat against an enemy of the United States.

Cipro Short for Ciprofloxacin. A strong antibiotic given to U.S. Army soldiers to protect them from the bacteria in local Afghan food.

double tap Military slang for shooting two quick, back-to-back shots at an enemy.

Dragunov A Soviet-developed 7.62mm sniper rifle used by foreign fighters and insurgents in Afghanistan.

exfil route Short for exfiltration route. Preplanned exit strategies used for a quick and easy escape.

fields of fire Military terminology that describes a weapon's ability to cover a given area.

FOB Forward Operating Base.

gunnery pass Military slang for an aircraft's gun run on the enemy.

hooch Military slang for personal living quarters.

IBA Interceptor Body Army. A protective vest worn by all U.S. Army soldiers.

indirect assets Any type of weapon system, such as a mortar or artillery, that does not rely on a direct line of sight between the gun and the target. Aiming is done by calculating an azimuth and elevation angles, and the soldier adjusts the weapon based on his observation of the rounds as they land.

intel Military slang for Intelligence.

JDAM Joint Direct-Attack Munition. A bolt-on guidance package that turns unguided bombs into precision weapons. JDAM-equipped bombs range from 500 pounds to 2,000 pounds.

jihad A Islamic term that comes from the Arabic word for "struggle." The word describes three types of struggle: to maintain the faith, to improve Muslim society, or to defend Islam.

jungle penetrator A cable and stretcher lowered by a helicopter capable of medically evacuating wounded ground troops.

Kuchi A nomadic Afghan tribe that times its moves with the changing of the seasons.

M14 A U.S 7.62mm semiautomatic rifle typically issued to designated marksmen in light infantry platoons.

M18 Claymore Mines A command-detonated, antipersonnel mine used by the U.S. military, which is capable of throwing a shower of shrapnel at an enemy force.

M2 Browning .50 caliber machine gun A heavy machine gun used extensively by the United States from the 1920s to the present. The M2 is often referred to as the "fifty" or the "Ma Deuce."

M203 A single-shot 40mm grenade launcher designed to attach to the M4 Carbine.

M240B A gas-operated, open-bolt-firing 7.62mm general purpose machine gun that is highly regarded for its accuracy and reliability.

M249 SAW The Squad Automatic Weapon is a U.S. 5.56mm, belt-fed light machine gun. This weapon system was designed to give light infantry squads maximum fire power and accuracy.

M4 Carbine A gas-operated 5.56mm rifle used heavily by the U.S. Army. It's a shorter, lighter version of the M16 and the weapon of choice for close-quarters combat.

M9 or 9mm pistol A semiautomatic pistol and the official sidearm of conventional U.S. Army troops.

M998 A pickup truck version of the standard military Humvee. Because the M998 was not manufactured with armor and is largely intended for logistical use, deployed soldiers are forced to attach makeshift armor to protect themselves in combat.

madrassas An Arabic word for "educational institution." Usually it refers to a school, but on the Afghan border many were used as training grounds for new enemy fighters.

man jams Military slang for loose-fitting traditional Afghan clothes.

MK 19 The Mark 19 is a belt-fed, fully automatic 40mm grenade launcher capable of firing 325 to 375 rounds per minute.

MRE Meals Ready to Eat. The standard issue meal of choice for all U.S. military units in the field.

NCO Noncommissioned Officers. The enlisted leaders who directly supervise day-to-day operations. The NCO Corps is often referred to as the backbone of the U.S. military.

near beer Nonalcoholic beer available to U.S. soldiers while they are deployed in combat.

night letters Death threats from insurgents. Typically written on paper and stapled to the front doors of Afghan citizens who are being targeted by the enemy.

ordnance Military provisions of weapons, ammunitions, and explosives.

Pashto, Farsi, Dari, Waziri, Arabic Five of the local dialects that dominate the border region.

Predator drone An unmanned aerial vehicle used by the U.S. military or CIA, primarily for reconnaissance purposes. They can also fire Hellfire missiles if needed.

qalat An Afghan dwelling.

QRF Quick Reaction Force. A unit held in reserve whose primary mission is to respond as fast as possible to a call for help.

radio chatter A phrase used to describe both friendly and enemy groups communicating via radio.

ranger An elite infantry soldier recognized by the coveted Ranger Tab worn on the left shoulder.

redoubt A defensive perimeter, typically on the top of a hill.

rig Military slang for Humvee.

RPG Rocket-Propelled Grenade. A shoulder-fired portable, anti-tank weapon system. Designed by the Soviets, this rugged and inexpensive weapon is a perfect fit for insurgents in Afghanistan.

RPK A Soviet-made, gas-operated 7.62mm light machine gun.

ROTC Reserve Officer Training Corps. A Department of Defense program that offers college scholarships in exchange for a military commitment after graduation.

RTO Radio Telephone Operator.

scut work Unpopular but often essential premission or postmission dirty work.

SF Special Forces. An elite unit of highly specialized U.S. Army soldiers whose primary mission is to train indigenous forces in military tactics.

SITREP Situation Report.

sortie A synonym for the deployment of a military unit or units.

stacking air A term used to define the echeloning of air firepower.

UH-60 Blackhawk A U.S. helicopter designed for the tactical transportation of troops to and from battle.

wadi An Arabic term that refers to a dry riverbed used for vehicular traffic.

walk/troop the line A task that leaders of small units perform in order to check on their soldiers pulling guard duty.

Wiccan A nature-based religion, also known as pagan witchcraft.

the wire Military slang for the outer perimeter of a friendly base